FROMMER'S

W9-AXZ-612

COMPREHENSIVE TRAVEL GUIDE

BUDAPEST
1ST EDITION

by Joseph S. Lieber
Assisted by Christina Shea

PRENTICE HALL TRAVEL

NEW YORK • LONDON • TORONTO • SYDNEY • TOKYO • SINGAPORE

FROMMER BOOKS

Published by Prentice Hall General Reference
15 Columbus Circle
New York, NY 10023

ISBN 0-671-86979-5
ISSN 1072-3692

Design by Robert Bull Design
Maps by Geografix Inc.

FROMMER'S EDITORIAL STAFF
Vice President/Editorial Director: Marilyn Wood
Senior Editor/Editorial Manager: Alice Fellows
Senior Editors: Sara Hinsey Raveret, Lisa Renaud
Editors: Charlotte Allstrom, Thomas F. Hirsch, Peter Katucki, Theodore
    Stavrou
Assistant Editors: Margaret Bowen, Christopher Hollander, Alice
    Thompson, Ian Wilker
Editorial Assistants: Gretchen Henderson, Douglas Stallings
Managing Editor: Leanne Coupe

Special Sales
Bulk purchases (10+ copies) of Frommer's Travel Guides are available to
corporations at special discounts. The Special Sales Department can produce
custom editions to be used as premiums and/or for sales promotion to suit
individual needs. Existing editions can be produced with custom cover
imprints such as a corporate logo. For more information write to: Special
Sales, Prentice Hall Travel, 15 Columbus Circle, New York, NY 10023.

Manufactured in the United States of America

CONTENTS

LIST OF MAPS

FOREWORD

by Arthur Frommer

At least a dozen years-and-more before the collapse of the Eastern Bloc, Hungary had already embarked on a free-market economy—and it showed. On my own several trips to Budapest in the late '70s and early '80s, I was at first astonished and then almost awed by the growing resemblance of that historic city to the prosperous capitals of Western Europe. It had everything the other Eastern cities lacked: Western newspapers and magazines on sale everywhere, foodstuffs in amazing variety, privately owned shops and stores by the many hundreds, people who spoke to you candidly and without fear.

From such a lengthy head start, Budapest has today become even more dynamic—and impressive; it displays none of the shabbiness of an East Berlin or a Bucharest; it is picturesque, comfortable, wonderfully endowed with good-quality hotels, shops, and restaurants in every price category; and it is a top touristic destination.

For those reasons, Budapest now becomes the first of the former Eastern Bloc capitals to become the exclusive subject of one of our Frommer's city guides. Will Moscow, Kiev, and Vilnius follow? I have no doubt they will. Just as mapmakers are today working around-the-clock to reflect new political realities, so we guidebook writers are now faced with an immense expansion of the places to which we can direct our readers—and that's the happiest of recent developments.

May I propose my own suggestions for a stay in Budapest? They include at least the following visits:

- To one of the many bath establishments, where you sweat in steam or soak in mineral waters at the lowest costs in travel today. In the giant, tiled halls of the Hotel Gellért along the Danube, admission is all of $3.50 to both an indoor and outdoor pool and several ornate and gilded saunas, and a 30-minute massage costs about the same.

- To one of Budapest's mammoth indoor food markets; they are shrines to good eating, and awesome sights.

- To the city's resplendent Museum of Fine Arts, with its half-dozen Goyas and El Grecos, alongside other priceless works of every age; and then to the equally grand National Museum not far away, with its strangely affecting collection of the ornate armor and uniforms of those dashing Hungarian hussars of old (it's here, too, that you find Beethoven's piano, presented on his death to Ferenc Liszt).

- To the vast Dohány Synagogue (second largest in the world) in central Budapest, still constantly active because of the fact that a sizable number of Hungarian Jews survived World War II; 75,000 of them currently live in Budapest, a community of such size found nowhere else in the Eastern states apart from Russia. When you witness a joyous wedding or other ceremony here, as I recently did, you reflect with anguish on what might have been.

- And then, if you have the time, to the Hungarian "Taos," the village of Szentendre less than an hour from Budapest (by suburban train or Danube River boat). Here is a preserved Hungarian hamlet of another age, now transformed into a mart for arts-and-crafts and paintings, and you'll at least want to return with one of those distinctive embroidered Hungarian blouses.

Those are visits that I'd schedule on a first trip to Budapest; they combine reality with fantasy, contemporary life with history, sheer aesthetic pleasure with a few lasting lessons. The author of this guide has suggested many more, and I'm impressed by the depth of his research.

A final thought. Of all the nations of Eastern Europe, Hungary affords us the most comfortable means of glimpsing an era of European life around the turn of the century, when people were generally optimistic and content with their lot. If such a picture causes us to reflect on how cruelly their hopes were dashed, and converted into a century of warfare and upheaval, well, such is the function of travel. It puts into perspective the human condition, our precarious roles, our need to pursue realistic hopes for the future.

INVITATION TO THE READERS

In researching this book, I have come across many fine establishments, the best of which I have included here. I am sure that many of you will also come across appealing hotels, inns, restaurants, guesthouses, shops, and attractions. Please don't keep them to yourself. Share your experiences, especially if you want to comment on places that have been included in this edition that have changed for the worse. You can address your letters to:

Joseph S. Lieber
Frommer's Budapest
c/o Prentice Hall Travel
15 Columbus Circle
New York, NY 10023

A DISCLAIMER

Readers are advised that prices fluctuate in the course of time, and travel information changes under the impact of the varied and volatile factors that affect the travel industry. Neither the author nor the publisher can be held responsible for the experiences of readers while traveling. Readers are invited to write to the publisher with ideas, comments, and suggestions for future editions.

SAFETY ADVISORY

Whenever you're traveling in an unfamiliar city or country, stay alert. Be aware of your immediate surroundings. Wear a moneybelt and keep a close eye on your possessions. Be particularly careful with cameras, purses, and wallets—all favorite targets of thieves and pickpockets.

INTRODUCING BUDAPEST

For much of the 20th century, Budapest languished in relative obscurity, off the itinerary and out of the minds of most European travelers. The dramatic political changes of 1989 have altered the state of the Hungarian capital irreversibly; awakened after its long slumber behind the Iron Curtain, Budapest is now one of Europe's hottest travel destinations and is reclaiming its place among the great cities of Central Europe.

Budapest came of age in the 19th century, at the start of which the two towns of Buda and Pest were little more than provincial outposts on the Danube. Indeed, despite its Roman ruins and reconstructed medieval Castle District, Budapest is very much a fin-de-siècle city, its characteristic coffeehouse and music-hall culture attesting to this. Unfortunately, the decades after World War I were not kind to Hungary's charming capital, and Budapest's turn-of-the-century glory seemed irretrievably lost. How fitting it is that Budapest's post–Cold War renaissance comes when it does: By the time the 21st century arrives, Budapest will have re-established itself as one of Central Europe's centers of new culture.

Budapest retains an exotic feeling seldom experienced in other European capitals. This is partly due to the complex and unusual *Magyar* language. As you listen to people conversing on a bus, as you attempt to read the labels in the grocery store, you will indeed know that you have arrived in a different and new place. The Hungarian language will always be a mystery to the great majority of those outside its borders. This has always been one of the country's greatest obstacles; nevertheless, the Hungarian people are intensely proud of their language and its charms.

Budapest's extraordinary ambience can also be felt on the city streets. Take a turn off any of the main boulevards some morning and quickly find yourself in a quiet residential neighborhood. The scent of a hearty *gulyás* (soup) wafts from a kitchen window. A woman with a brightly colored kerchief tied about her head sweeps the sidewalk with a homemade broom. Cigarette smoke fogs the cavelike entryway of the corner pub where a sign on the door states that beer is served as early as 7am. In the little park across the way, men play chess in the shade of chestnut trees, young lovers kiss on a bench, and

WHAT'S SPECIAL ABOUT BUDAPEST

Historic Buildings

- ☐ The vast Neo-Gothic Parliament, the very symbol of Pest, where democracy is now in practice for the first time.
- ☐ The magnificently ornate Opera House, one of the finest in all Europe.
- ☐ The Chain Bridge, the first permanent span across the Danube, which is lit up like a chandelier every night.

Museums

- ☐ The Royal Palace of Buda, home to no fewer than four museums, including the Hungarian National Gallery, where the country's greatest artists are represented, and the Budapest History Museum, which features excavated rooms from the medieval palace.
- ☐ The Hungarian National Museum, where the country's long and eventful history is on display, along with the priceless crown jewels of King Stephen.
- ☐ The Museum of Fine Arts, with one of Central Europe's most distinguished collections of Old Masters.

Parks

- ☐ Margaret Island, a summer playground in the middle of the Danube.
- ☐ City Park, home to the Fine Arts Museum, the circus, the zoo, the amusement park, and Gundel, Budapest's finest restaurant.

Churches and Synagogues

- ☐ Matthias Church, colorful symbol of the Castle District, where King Matthias Corvinus was twice married.
- ☐ The Dohány Synagogue, a Byzantine-style wonder which is Europe's largest and the world's second-largest synagogue.
- ☐ The Inner City Parish Church, embodying all the architectural styles of historic Hungary.

Districts

- ☐ Buda's Castle District, an intact—if largely reconstructed—medieval town.
- ☐ Pest's Inner City, the commercial center of the capital, with it's distinctive fin-de-siècle architecture.

Thermal Waters

- ☐ The fabulously ornate baths of the Hotel Gellért, with pools of varying temperatures, steam rooms, massage, and an outdoor artificial-wave pool.
- ☐ The Palatinus Beach, a huge pool complex on Margaret Island, with outdoor thermal baths, water slide, and a children's pool.
- ☐ The Király Baths, for Turkish-style thermal bathing, housed inside the original Turkish bath house.

the Hungarian pedigree dog, the *vizsla*, can be glimpsed darting through the trees. Inside the courtyards of apartment buildings one of the city's great secrets is told: Budapesters are villagers at heart. Fruit trees and flower gardens flourish, cats lounge in the tall grass, and jars of pickled vegetables sit on the sunny window ledges; bee-keeping boxes or a small chicken coop might even be seen.

The imagery of Budapest is endlessly alluring. Explore it, photograph it, indulge in it.

1. CULTURE, HISTORY & BACKGROUND

GEOGRAPHY & PEOPLE

GEOGRAPHY Budapest is the capital and in every way the cultural, economic, and more or less geographical center of Hungary. The city encompasses 525 square kilometers (203 square miles), of which just over two-thirds lies on the right bank in predominantly flat Pest. Buda, on the other hand, is distinguished by its hills—its highest is 529-meter (1,735-foot) János Hill—and wooded areas.

Budapest, the capital of a landlocked country, is, oddly, a city defined by water. The Danube River cuts a wide swath through Buda and Pest, and over 100 natural hot springs bubble beneath the city. The river flows through the city at an average width of 400 meters (1,312 feet), and its 28-kilometer (17.4-mile) stretch at Budapest represents almost 1% of its total length. Several Danube islands are also part of the city, the largest of which is Csepel Island. To the north of Budapest, the Danube alters its west–east course sharply in a series of curves at the celebrated Danube Bend, an area famous for its historic towns and lovely scenery.

PEOPLE With a population of approximately 2.1 million, Budapest is home to one in five Hungarians. Compared to the capital, every other Hungarian city is no more than a provincial town: Few capitals so dominate the life of their country.

Hungarians are a predominantly Catholic people; in fact, with the Poles and Lithuanians, they represent the eastern frontier of European Catholicism. Today Hungary is more or less ethnically homogeneous, the 1920 Treaty of Trianon having delegated most minorities to other countries. Scarcely a generation later, the destruction of Hungarian Jewry in World War II, and the departure of thousands of ethnic Germans after the war, further homogenized the population. Hungary's 500,000 Gypsies comprise the country's largest minority today, while other minority populations include ethnic Germans, Slovaks, South Slavs (Serbs and Croats), Jews (Budapest is home to the largest Jewish population of any European city outside Russia), and Romanians. Budapest embodies this ethnic mix fairly well.

DATELINE

HISTORY & POLITICS

- **3rd century B.C.**
Celtic tribes establish settlements in the area around Budapest

- **1st–5th century A.D.** Roman Empire extends to the Danube; Aquincum (present-day Óbuda) chosen as capital of Roman province of Pannonia

- **5th century** Huns take over Pannonia, soon to be replaced by migratory tribes

- **6th–9th century** Avars control Hungary

- **896** Magyar (Hungarian) Conquest of Carpathian Basin

- **1000** Stephen I becomes Hungary's first Christian king. The House of Árpád is established. The capital is first at Esztergom, and later at Visegrád and Székesfehérvár

- **12th century** Buda and Pest develop as trading towns

- **1241–42** Mongol armies under Batu Khan overrun Hungary, leaving it in ashes when they suddenly depart

- **1242–70** King Béla IV rebuilds the country; a fortress is built in Buda

(continues)

THE ROMANS AND THEIR SUCCESSORS Although Celtic tribes established themselves in the area around Buda in the 3rd century B.C., it was the Romans who built the first extensive settlements. After conquering present-day western Hungary (Transdanubia), the Romans extended their empire east to the Danube and occupied the Celtic settlement of Ak-Ink (Abundant Waters), renaming it Aquincum. The military camp of Aquincum was near where the Árpád Bridge now stands, while the civilian town was further north; ruins of both can be seen today. By the early 2nd century Aquincum had become the capital of the Roman province of Lower Pannonia. It was the seat of the Imperial Governor; the future emperor Hadrian was the first to fill the position in this Roman outpost. The Romans ruled Transdanubia for four centuries, building impressive fortifications along the Danube's west bank. They were the first to develop the thermal waters of Buda, building a number of bath houses. At its height, Aquincum had a population of 50,000 people. As the empire waned, however, the garrisons on the Danube were increasingly subject to attacks from "barbarians" from the east, and Rome evacuated Aquincum in the early 5th century.

THE AGE OF MIGRATIONS The Huns succeeded the Romans, but their rule here was to be brief. After the death of their great leader Attila in 453, the Hun empire crumbled and present-day Hungary became the domain of a succession of these mostly Teutonic tribes. A conquering tribe from central Asia, the Avars, moved into the area in the 6th century. Under their sponsorship, commerce-oriented Slavic tribes now settled in the area of present-day Budapest.

THE MAGYAR CONQUEST Led by Prince Árpád, whose family line (the House of Árpád) would rule Hungary until 1301, the seven allied Magyar tribes took the entire Carpathian Basin (a natural geological formation incorporating parts of present-day Romania, Serbia, Croatia, Slovenia, Austria, Slovakia, and Ukraine) in 896. Legend has it that the tribes fanned out, each taking control of a different part of the country. Árpád and his tribe are believed to have settled on Csepel Island in present-day Budapest, and another tribe settled in Óbuda, refortifying the Roman town. Once established, the Magyars engaged in a series of successful 10th-century raids on Western Europe, penetrating as far west as the Pyrenees. It was during these raids that they earned their lasting reputation as skilled horsemen; the tricky "feigned withdrawal" was their most famous ploy. The raids ended with a decisive defeat at Augsburg in southwest Germany in 955.

THE DEVELOPMENT OF THE STATE A feudal state was forged under Hungary's first Christian king, István (Stephen) I (later Saint Stephen), who was crowned by the pope in 1000. The forced conversion of the Magyars was not without its darker side: Those who preferred to maintain their traditional ways were treated with the utmost cruelty; religious tolerance was not a concept of Stephen's day. Nevertheless, Stephen succeeded in organizing a feudal state apparatus, without which the fledgling Hungarian kingdom certainly would not have survived. After Stephen's death there was a period of renewed strife between the Christians and the pagans. The iron-fisted Bishop Gellért, who had served Stephen for many years, was killed in 1046 when he was rolled in a barrel into the Danube from the hill in Buda that now bears his name. Despite this, and a number of succession crises in the following centuries, the feudal, Christian state remained intact.

In this period Esztergom, then Székesfehérvár, and briefly Visegrád had served as the capital of Hungary. It was not until the 12th century that Buda and Pest began to develop into major towns, populated in large part by German, French, and Walloon settlers. But in 1241 disaster struck: Rampaging out of Asia, the Mongols overran Hun-

DATELINE

- **14th century** Royal court is moved to Buda; late in the century King Sigismund of Luxembourg builds a great Gothic palace at Buda
- **1458–90** Reign of King Matthias Corvinus; who initiates Golden Age of Buda and introduces ideas and culture of the Renaissance
- **1541** 150-year Turkish occupation of Buda and Pest begins
- **1686** United Christian armies drive Turks from Buda; the city is destroyed in the liberation. Habsburg occupation of Hungary commences
- **1703–11** Ferenc Rákóczi II's War of Independence against Austria defeated
- **Late 18th century** Buda and Pest begin to undergo rapid growth; in 1777 the University of Nagyszombat moves to Buda and then to Pest in 1784
- **1825–48** Age of Reform; rise of neo-classical style in Budapest; building of National Theater (1837) and National Museum (1848)

(continues)

gary. Pest was destroyed, and after crossing the frozen Danube in the winter of 1241–42, the Mongols conquered Buda and all of Transdanubia beyond, burning and looting everything in their path. King Béla IV was forced to flee the country. During his brief exile he vowed his daughter would become a nun if he could return to rebuild Hungary. The Mongols retreated in 1242, and Princess Margit was duly sent to the convent on "Rabbit Island": this island in the Danube, now Budapest's most popular park, bears Margit's name today.

Because only hilltop fortresses had withstood the Mongol onslaught, King Béla had a series of new ones built around the country. Buda was one of the spots chosen; in addition to the fortification of Castle Hill, a royal palace was constructed (though it was not Béla's primary residence). German settlers were invited to replace the Hungarians who had been wiped out by invasion. These Germans gave the name *Ofen* (oven) to the town on the Danube's right bank, probably because of the presence there of a lime kiln industry. The Slavic name *Pest,* also meaning oven, is believed to derive from this time. In 1255, Castle Hill was made a city, usurping the name Buda from the former Buda to its immediate north, which was henceforth known as Óbuda (Old Buda). Buda became the residence of an increasing number of aristocrats and burghers, while the medieval walled city of Pest continued to develop across the river. In 1301 the male line of the House of Árpád died out; Hungary would be ruled henceforth by a mixed succession of foreign-born and Hungarian kings.

THE GOLDEN AGE OF BUDA King Charles Robert (1308–42), of the House of Anjou, moved his court from Visegrád to Buda, and his son Louis the Great (1342–82) expanded the palace. The town began to blossom at the turn of the 15th century under the rule of King Sigismund of Luxembourg (also Holy Roman Emperor), who had a glorious Gothic palace built on Castle Hill. But it was King Matthias Corvinus (1458–90), influenced by the Italian Renaissance, who oversaw the Golden Age of Buda. Matthias' palace was expanded in Renaissance style by Italian architects and decorated with the finest European art, while his court became one of the centers of European culture and learning. He amassed an enormous and fabled library, filled with the famous Corvinae manuscripts. The András Hess Press, one of Europe's earliest, was operating in Buda at this time as well. Called "Matthias the Just," the king remains one of the best-loved figures of Hungarian history, and the largest church of the Castle District bears his name.

THE TURKISH PERIOD After Matthias' death, a divided nobility and the bloody suppression of a peasant revolt severely weakened Hungary. The Ottoman armies swept north up the Danube, and in 1526 routed the Hungarians at the Battle of Mohács. The fortified city of Buda fell in 1541. The 150-year Turkish period that followed is rued by Hungarians as one of stagnation and decay. Little new building, aside from fortification of existing walls and bath house construction, was undertaken. Everywhere churches were converted into mosques, and Buda's skyline filled with minarets.

THE HABSBURG PERIOD: LIBERATION BY FIRE The wry joke "the operation was successful, but the patient died" might describe the liberation of Buda and Pest by the united Christian armies in 1686. The two towns were utterly destroyed, with only a few thousand people remaining alive inside the walls by the time the Turks were vanquished. Having survived the Turkish period intact, the royal palace was destroyed in the siege.

Resettlement and rebuilding were gradual, and formerly Gothic Buda took on a decidedly baroque appearance during the process. Though it would never again be a royal seat, the palace was rebuilt and expanded over the years.

Hungary was to be ruled by the victorious House of Habsburg until the collapse of

DATELINE

- **1918–19** Country in chaos; Hungarian Republic established. Béla Kun forms a short-lived Communist government, which is succeeded by the reactionary regime of Admiral Miklós Horthy
- **1920** Treaty of Trianon codifies the enormous territorial losses suffered by Hungary in the aftermath of World War I
- **1941** Hungary, obsessed with revision of Trianon, enters World War II, joining Germany's unprovoked attack on Yugoslavia
- **1944–45** Nazis occupy Hungary; Budapest Jews are forced into a walled ghetto. Bitter Soviet-German fighting leaves Budapest in ruins; Soviets liberate—and occupy—the country
- **1945–56** Brief Parliamentary democracy is followed by the establishment of a Stalinist state
- **1956** Hungarian uprising, led by Imre Nagy and centered in Budapest, is crushed by Soviet troops; János Kádár

(continues)

DATELINE

installed as new Communist leader

● **1968** Period of internal Communist reform is capped by the New Economic Mechanism, which decentralizes the economy and allows limited private enterprise

● **1988–89** Kádár ousted by reformers in the party and Hungary begins transition to multi-party government; Eastern European Communism collapses in the summer and fall of 1989

● **1990** First free elections since 1945 bring Hungarian Democratic Forum to power

● **1991** Last Soviet troops leave country; Pope John Paul II visits

● **1994** Elections scheduled

the Habsburg empire in World War I. Relations with the new Viennese rulers were strained from the outset, flaring into open conflict for the first time when the Transylvanian prince Ferenc Rákóczi II led a series of valiant, but ultimately unsuccessful, rebellions between 1703 and 1711. The beginnings of modern Hungarian nationalism, which would explode into revolution in 1848, can be detected in this period.

The population of Budapest grew steadily throughout the 18th century, while the university was moved from Nagyszombat (now Trnava, Slovakia) first to Buda, in 1777, and subsequently to Pest, in 1784. Pest expanded beyond its medieval city walls in the late 18th century with the development of Lipótváros (Leopold Town, now considered part of the Inner City).

THE 19TH CENTURY: REFORM, RE-VOLUTION & COMPROMISE By the early 19th century Pest and Buda had become the centers of political, economic, and cultural life in Hungary. Habsburg Archduke Joseph, longtime palatine of Hungary (1796–1847), was a leading force in the development of Pest in the early part of the century. The great Danube Flood of 1838 would destroy much of Pest, but it also provided an opportunity for the town to be rebuilt along more contemporary and progressive lines. For the first time, Pest began to surpass Buda as the center of commerce and industry, a role it has never relinquished. Jews played a major part in the early development of Pest, a part they would continue to play until World War II.

The second quarter of the century is known as the Age of Reform in Hungary. Concomitant to the development of modern nationalism, this period saw the construction of many important and grand buildings; first among them are the National Theater (1837) and the National Museum (1848). Emblematic of the era was the construction of the first permanent bridge across the Danube, the Chain Bridge (1839–49). Like the Academy of Sciences, founded in 1825, this project was the brainchild of Count István Széchenyi. One of the leading figures of the period, Széchenyi argued for increased Hungarian independence within the Habsburg empire and was the first to call for the union of Buda and Pest. His more radical rival, and the other giant figure of the mid-19th century, was Lajos Kossuth, a lawyer of Slovak ethnic origins, who demanded full independence from Austria in addition to the abolition of Hungary's feudal structure.

Hungary's nationalistic and anti-Habsburg sentiments culminated in the revolutionary events of 1848. Legend has it that the poet Sándor Petőfi rallied the radical forces of Pest by reciting his incendiary "National Song" from the steps of the National Museum. Students seized the university and City Hall. A revolutionary body, the Budapest Committee of Public Safety, was formed. Weakened by revolts spreading throughout their empire, the Austrians initially agreed to Hungarian independence, but as they consolidated power in the summer it became increasingly clear that Hungary would have to defend its independence militarily. Despite Lajos Kossuth's passionate leadership, the defeat of the revolution was eventually insured by the defection of most minorities living within Hungary— who saw that their own national aspirations had no future in an independent, ultra-nationalist Hungary—and the willingness of the Russian tsar to aid the Habsburgs. The tragic heroes of the day— Kossuth, who spent his remaining years in exile; Széchényi, who went mad; the prime minister Lajos Batthyány, who was executed by his captors; and the poet Petőfi, who was killed in battle—remain among the most revered figures in the land.

The defeat of the revolution was followed by a brief but painful period of absolutism, during which the Citadel on Gellért Hill was built as an overt symbol of Austrian supremacy. The 1867 Compromise, engineered by Ferenc Deák, established the dual Austro-Hungarian monarchy and brought a lasting peace and a measure of independence to Hungary. Following the coronation of the Habsburg emperor Franz Joseph, the union of the three cities—Buda, Pest, and Óbuda—became a reality in 1873.

PEST'S GOLDEN AGE: 1873–1914   The most intense period of development in the history of Budapest was now under way. The national railway system was developed, with all lines converging in the capital. The distinctive ring boulevards of Pest were designed, as well as the radial road, now called Andrássy út, on which the lovely State Opera House opened in 1884. The City Park was laid out, with Heroes' Square as its entrance, and more bridges were built over the Danube. The first metro on the continent was built underneath Andrássy út; this antique line is still functioning today. Much of this development culminated in the 1896 Hungarian millennial celebration, the greatest expression to date of Hungarian national pride. The

---

IMPRESSIONS

In the city of Buda, which is extraordinarily high, lies the king's palace, which reaches to the sky.
—Dzhelalshade Mustapha, Turkish Chronicler, 16th Century

predominantly Neo-Gothic Parliament building, modelled on London's, was completed in 1902, although only two democratically elected legislatures have thus far convened in its great hall (one in 1945, the second in 1990).

Hungarian nationalism fueled this period of frenetic expansion. Under the policy of 'Magyarization,' ethnic assimilation was encouraged, and even coerced, throughout the country. The use of the Hungarian language by ethnic minorities became more widespread; Jews, adopting it for the first time as their mother tongue, continued to play a leading role in the city's rapid expansion.

The population growth in the combined cities gives some hint of the magnitude of Budapest's expansion in this period: in 1867 the city had 270,000 residents; by 1890, there were 500,000 people living in the now unified city; and only 20 years later, in 1910, there were almost 900,000.

If King Matthias Corvinus' day was Buda's Golden Age, the turn of the century was certainly Pest's. The distinctive eclectic and art nouveau buildings which still define the city today date from this brief period when some of the country's greatest architects labored to create a singular Hungarian style. Cafe society was at its peak, rivalling that of Vienna. In the first heady days of the new century, Budapest seemed poised to take its place among Europe's great capitals. But as Matthias introduced the Italian Renaissance to a city in the path of the Turkish army, so too did the burgeoning of Pest occur under the gathering clouds of World War I.

THE WORLD WARS: DESTRUCTION, DESOLATION & LOSS The advent of war in 1914 and Hungary's alliance with the Central Powers was greeted with great shows of patriotism in the capital. Almost from the outset, however, the civilian population suffered great hardships, a factor which served to dim initial enthusiasm. Under the pressures of wartime production, the nascent worker's movement gained new ground in Hungary.

After Emperor Franz Joseph's death in 1916, the last Habsburg emperor, Charles IV, was crowned in Matthias Church. Juxtaposed against the steadily deteriorating situation in the war and desperate shortages of food and fuel in the city, the coronation became the last gasp of a dying empire. The winter of 1917–18 was a particularly difficult one for the Hungarians, both on the battlefield and at home. Anti-war protests, usually met by police repression, increased, and opposition forces rallied around Count Mihály Károlyi, a vocal opponent of the war.

The total defeat of the Central Powers in 1918 led to the collapse of the Austro-Hungarian empire, and the new Hungarian Republic was declared on November 16 of that year. Károlyi was elected president, but his position was untenable from the start. Chief among his domestic problems was the increasingly radical position of the labor movement, inspired by the recent Russian Revolution. His unwillingness to enact a land reform program caused unrest in the

IMPRESSIONS

*And when day dawned mournfully on a sea swarming with the
remains of a ruined city and hundreds and hundreds of the
drowned, the carcasses of cows and horses floated in the pale
rays of the rising sun.*
—MIKLÓS WESSELÉNYI, HERO OF THE 1838 DANUBE FLOOD.

countryside. The international situation was even grimmer. The victorious powers insisted on treating Hungary as a vanquished nation, much to the delight of the other newly formed successor states, (particularly Romania, Czechoslovakia, and Yugoslavia) who were competing with Hungary for disputed territory. Hungary suffered enormous territorial losses (later codified by the Treaty of Trianon) during these post-war days as the country's new leaders stood by helplessly. Károlyi's fall was ultimately caused by the French demand that Hungarian troops withdraw a further 50 kilometers from the Romanian border, in order to create a so-called "neutral zone": Unwilling to comply, he resigned.

In 1919, the Hungarian Communist Party leader Béla Kun formed a new government and declared a "Republic of Councils." Allied with Bolshevik Russia, the Kun administration initially enjoyed popular support in Hungary. Industry was nationalized, and the leading figures of Hungarian culture were enlisted to champion the regime. Much of the initial enthusiasm waned with the advent of a Red Terror on the Bolshevik model, and the rural population turned against Kun when it became clear that collectivization was his version of land reform.

A counter-revolution was centered in the town of Szeged, from where Admiral Miklós Horthy launched a "White Terror" of his own, massacring leftists and Jews. In June a rightest coup was attempted in Budapest, but was defeated. In the end it was the Romanian army, entering the city on August 3, which overwhelmed the short-lived Republic of Councils; after this brief flirtation with radicalism Hungary was to be ruled throughout the inter-war period by the reactionary Horthy, who was "elected" Regent in 1920 by a rubber-stamp parliament.

As Hungary drifted inexorably to the right in the inter-war period, many of the country's greatest minds would seek their fortunes elsewhere. Nevertheless, the inter-war period was one of enormous, uncontrolled growth for Budapest, its numbers swelled by refugees from the lost territories and the countryside. While the city expanded in all directions, it also suffered the effects of the worldwide recession: Social problems ballooned, hand in hand with increasing poverty.

The 1920 Treaty of Trianon confirmed the massive territorial losses of the past few years: 70% of the former Hungary was ceded to its neighbors, while 60% of the population found itself living beyond Hungary's new borders. Hungarians across all class and political lines were united in considering the treaty unjustly punitive, and every Hungarian government of the inter-war period was concerned chiefly with reversing it. This national obsession had the unfortunate consequence of inducing Hungary to ally itself in the 1930s with a Nazi Germany that endorsed Hungary's revisionist claims. It was a reckless path, and one about which the Hungarian people remain deeply troubled to this day.

As the war progressed, Horthy began to have second thoughts about the alliance with Germany. The Nazis, unwilling to accept anything other than total commitment to the war effort, occupied Hungary in March of 1944. Adolf Eichmann arrived with the Nazi forces and immediately set up a ghetto for the city's Jews in the historic Erzsebetváros district. While relatively few Hungarian Jews outside the capital survived the deportations (most perished in Auschwitz in the last year of the war), at least half of Budapest's Jews were saved, many through the intervention of Swedish diplomat Raoul Wallenberg, who at great personal risk issued thousands of false passports and established dozens of "safe houses."

In October, the Horthy regime, caught red-handed by the Germans in a clumsy attempt to negotiate a separate peace with the Allies, was replaced by Hungary's fascist Arrow Cross party. The next four months saw bizarre and wanton acts of cruelty in Budapest, elevated to a level unseen since the middle ages. Heavily armed Arrow Cross gangs wandered the scarred city, and hundreds of Jews were taken to the Danube that winter to be shot on its bank or thrown alive into its icy waters.

Meanwhile, the Red Army had penetrated eastern Hungary by late summer, and by Christmas had surrounded the capital. The war all but over, and Germany itself breached by allied forces, the Nazis stubbornly refused an invitation to quit the city honorably. Pest fell to the Russians on January 18, insuring the survival of those who remained alive in the Jewish ghetto. Retreating to Buda, the Nazis blew up all the Danube bridges and retrenched on Castle Hill. In one of the most bitter sieges of World War II, Soviet artillery pounded the Castle District from the top of Gellért Hill, until the Germans were finally driven from the capital on February 13. Budapest was again in

---

IMPRESSIONS

Bandits are skulking around the city beating, looting, and shooting people. Among my staff, I have already had forty cases of people being carried off and abused. . . . We hear the thundering cannons of the approaching Russians day and night.
—Raoul Wallenberg, Swedish diplomat, in a letter to his mother, 1945.

ruins; 75% of its buildings (including the Royal Palace and most of the Castle District) were damaged or destroyed in the war.

THE STALINIST ERA After the war, reconstruction was the primary task facing Budapest and the country. In the absence of clear central authority a civic spirit characterized the immediate post-war period, as newly formed local organizations assumed control of rebuilding projects, chief among them the reconstruction of the Danube bridges. The post-war days also saw Hungary suffering the most dramatic inflation in the history of the world; between January and July of 1946, the price of a standard postage stamp soared from 100 pengő to 100,000 quadrillion pengő! The introduction of a new currency, the Forint, halted the runaway inflation.

Soviet forces remained in the country as an occupation army. The Allied Powers at Yalta relegated Hungary to the Soviet sphere of influence, and by 1949 a Stalinist state was in place. A "cult of personality" surrounded Communist Party leader Mátyás Rákosi, now known as Stalin's "wise Hungarian disciple." The next few years would be an oppressive period of secret police activity and party in-fighting. The first Soviet-style Five Year Plan was introduced in 1950 and emphasized heavy industry and massive construction projects. Peasants, forced onto collective farms, became bitter opponents of the regime.

In Hungary, as elsewhere in the East Bloc, Stalin's death in 1953 led to pronounced swings between reform and retrenchment. Rákosi continued to play a major role, although the popularity of reformist Imre Nagy also rose. Following Khrushchev's "Secret Speech" at the Twentieth Party Congress in February 1956 denouncing the crimes of Stalin, the stage was set for political and social upheaval throughout the disenchanted Bloc.

1956–1989: REVOLUTION, REACTION & REFORM
Almost all the key events of the 1956 Hungarian uprising occurred in Budapest. The spark that lit the fire was an October 23 student demonstration in support of reforms unfolding in Poland. Tens of thousands marched from Petőfi Square in Pest to Bem Square in Buda. Spontaneously, the students decided to march on Parliament, where they lit torches and called for the reinstatement of the increasingly popular Nagy as prime minister (a post he had held briefly in the aftermath of Stalin's death). Another, smaller, group collected in front of the Budapest Radio Station, near the National Museum and were fired upon by the secret police. Shortly thereafter, outraged crowds toppled the enormous Stalin statue near the City Park and paraded through the darkened streets with the fallen dictator in tow. Army units, called out to protect key buildings, turned their weapons over to the rebels.

The events of the next twelve days would capture headlines around the world, though the simultaneous outbreak of war in the Middle East, at the Suez Canal, significantly detracted Western attention. In the end, the lack of Western assistance to the Hungarians gave unmistakable notice that the West, in the grip of the Cold War, essentially accepted the division of Europe as defined by Yalta.

Reappointed prime minister on October 24, Nagy found events moving beyond his control. The revolt was no longer aimed at reforming the system, but at overthrowing it. On October 25 the police again fired on unarmed demonstrators, this time at the Parliament. Two days later, a beleaguered Nagy announced the formation of his new government with most of the hard-line Stalinists excluded. Nagy announced the removal of Soviet military units from Budapest, the dissolution of the secret police, and his desire to negotiate with the Soviet Union regarding full military withdrawal from Hungary. In his boldest act, Nagy announced Hungary's unilateral withdrawal from the Warsaw Pact and pleaded for assistance from the west.

There was optimism in the capital as Nagy formed yet another new government. But by November 4 a Soviet invasion was in full swing. Facing little resistance, the Soviets crushed what they were now calling a "counter-revolution," and Nagy and several of his associates were executed. Budapest was heavily damaged by the fighting, and altogether about 2,000 Hungarians died in the uprising while another 200,000 fled the country.

János Kádár was now placed in control of the government, a position he would maintain for 30 years. A short period of hard-line rule was used to break the spirit of the uprising, but during his long rule Kádár achieved a level of public popularity enjoyed by few East Bloc leaders. Due to the many reforms he carried out, Hungary earned the nickname of "the happiest barracks" in Eastern Europe. By and large, Hungarians accepted the "goulash communism" practiced by Kádár, but no longer required to express their support, most people withdrew into political apathy.

Kádár's best-known reform, the 1968 New Economic Mechanism (NEM), encouraged limited private enterprise and partially decentralized the economy, foreshadowing "perestroika" a generation before Gorbachev. Hungary became known as the most liberal country of the Bloc, and Budapest became a magnet for the youth of

---

IMPRESSIONS

From the rooftop of my flat in Buda I saw the silent crowds sweeping across the city, torches flashing in every hand. . . . By the tens of thousands they congregated in sprawling Kossuth Square, milling about beneath the glistening red star atop the dome of the Hungarian Parliament. . . . I huddled in the damp October air, aware of the momentousness of what I was witnessing, giddy and exhilarated, but also apart from it and somehow unable to share in the ominous jubilation of Budapest's long suffering thousands.
—PESHOJ EBERLI, ALBANIAN JOURNALIST, 1956

the East Bloc. Western tourists, too, found Budapest to be a hospitable place in comparison to other Eastern European cities, and its proximity to Vienna placed it on many itineraries.

Despite economic difficulties caused by inflation and foreign debt, Hungary continued throughout the 1970s and 1980s to lead a sluggish Eastern Europe in gradual reforms. The advent of Gorbachev in the Soviet Union emboldened the most radical elements within the Party; while the world watched the 1989 events in Moscow and Warsaw, Hungary was quietly playing a key role in the drama.

In May 1989, a half year before the opening of the Berlin Wall, Hungary began dismantling portions of the barbed-wire frontier with Austria, becoming the first country to open a hole in the "Iron Curtain." Thousands of East Germans gathered in Hungary, hoping for permission to flee to the West; permission was granted in September, and over 50,000 crossed over to Austria. The year would conclude with the toppling of the East German, Czechoslovak, and Romanian Communist systems. As for the collapse of Communism in Hungary itself, it was far less dramatic and unaccompanied by violence.

POST-COMMUNIST BUDAPEST Hungary's first free elections since 1945 were held in April 1990, marking the end of nearly half a century of Communist rule. The new center-right coalition government was led by Prime Minister József Antall's Hungarian Democratic Forum (MDF), a party which used overtly nationalist themes in its campaign. The last Soviet troops left the country in June 1991, and Pope John Paul II visited Hungary in August of that year.

Trianon still strikes a deep chord of resentment and discontent in Hungarian society. The twin questions of national borders and Hungarian ethnic minorities abroad dominate politics with nearly all neighboring states. Hungary's relations with Romania remain bitter; regarding former Yugoslavia, Hungarian concern is over the very survival of Serbia's large Hungarian minority; and relations with newly independent Slovakia are strained at best. A disturbing new manifestation of Hungarian nationalism at home is the growth of a small but vocal neo-fascist right whose most visible spokesman is István Csurka.

Other pressing issues have moved to the forefront of public consciousness as Hungary endeavors to build a more open, democratic society: compensation for those who suffered under the previous Communist and fascist regimes; concern over steadily rising inflation and unemployment rates; and the question of integration into Europe. Unaccustomed to having a voice in their country's future, Hungarians look ahead to the second free election of the post-Communist era, scheduled for spring 1994, with mixed emotions. A number of Hungarians (mainly the elderly) rue the loss of financial and social security provided by the old regime. This pervasive sense of loss is a notable feature of the social landscape.

Among Hungarian cities, Budapest is the clear leader in the rapid Westernization process. For example, Budapest's fast-food market, as recently as 1991 cornered by McDonald's, is now crowded with outlets of Burger King, Kentucky Fried Chicken, Dairy Queen, Dunkin' Donuts, and Pizza Hut; Wendy's and Taco Bell are reputedly on the way. The opening of each successive establishment is mourned by a small minority intent on seeing Budapest retain its individuality, but is welcomed by the great majority of Hungarians, eager to "catch up with the West." Most consumer products are now available in the Hungarian capital, but some things do not change so fast: Salaries have not kept pace with inflation, and as a result most citizens can only look longingly through shop windows at these new goods. A certain amount of bitterness has thus accompanied the rapid development. For their part, Western visitors are pleased to see new standards of efficiency, service, and cleanliness in Hungary. Tourists are flocking to Budapest in numbers no one could have imagined even a few years ago. One estimate ranked Hungary as the fifth-most-visited country in the world!

LOOKING TO THE FUTURE In 1996 Budapest will be on display when it hosts the World Expo, the theme of which will be "Communications for a Better World." Many feel that resources used in preparing for the show could be better spent elsewhere and that Budapest is not ready—socially or environmentally—for the burst of expansion needed to prepare for Expo. Expo supporters, on the other hand, laud the exposure and economic boost the show will bring. Strangely, few comment on the significance of the year 1996: Exactly 1,100 years earlier the Magyars arrived in the Carpathian Basin, establishing the country of Hungary; 1,000 years later, in 1896, Budapest had its greatest party in celebration of the Magyar millennium. Whatever Expo '96 brings, it seems clear that life can only improve for the Hungarians.

FAMOUS BUDAPESTERS

Béla Bartók (1881–1945) The giant figure of 20th-century Hungarian music, Bartók's greatest achievement was the systematic collecting and cataloguing—along with his colleague Zoltán Kodály—of Hungarian folk music: For this project, he is considered one of the founders of Hungarian ethnomusicology. A composer and teacher of international fame, Bartók drew creative inspiration from the folk music he so laboriously studied. A refugee from fascism, he died a lonely death in New York.

Matthias Corvinus (1443–1490) Crowned King of Hungary as a teenager, Matthias (born Mátyás Hunyadi) oversaw Buda's Golden Age. His Renaissance court flourished as a center of European arts and culture, and his famed Biblioteca Corvinae was one of the continent's finest libraries. "Matthias the Just" was twice married in Buda's Church of Our Lady, which has since been known as the Matthias Church.

Theodore Herzl (1860–1904) Widely considered the

founder of modern Zionism, Herzl was born in Budapest, but spent most of his life in Vienna. The Zionist movement which his writings helped to inspire did not, incidentally, find fertile ground in his native Hungary, where a deeply assimilated Jewry resisted the pull of a separate homeland.

Attila József (1905-1937) A revolutionary poet, and one of the country's best-loved authors, József was born in Budapest and grew up in extreme poverty, abandoned by his father. A brilliant but intensely lonely man, he committed suicide by jumping under a train near Lake Balaton. The university in Szeged from which he was expelled now bears his name.

János Kádár (1912-1989) One of Eastern Europe's longest standing Communist rulers, Kádár was installed by the Soviets after the 1956 Hungarian uprising was crushed; he ruled the country until 1988. At first despised as a Hungarian quisling, he soon demonstrated his eagerness for genuine reform, evolving into one of the region's more popular leaders. He was ousted shortly before the collapse of Communism in Eastern Europe.

Zoltán Kodály (1882-1967) Along with Béla Bartók, Kodály traveled the country collecting and cataloguing a vast amount of Hungarian folk music, becoming in the process one of the founders of Hungarian ethnomusicology. Like Bartók, he was inspired by Hungarian folk music, whose influence can be seen in his own compositions. Internationally, Kodály is best known as the developer of the Kodály Method, a widely used system of musical education for children.

Lajos Kossuth (1802-1894) Lawyer, politician, and journalist, Kossuth was perhaps the best known leader of the 1848-49 Revolution. He spent the second half of his long life wandering in exile, alone among his associates in resolutely refusing to accept the compromise with the Habsburgs. A giant statue of him graces Kossuth Square, site of the Hungarian Parliament.

Ödön Lechner (1845-1914) One of Hungary's most influential architects, Lechner used colorful Zsolnay tiles and unusual Eastern motifs to create a uniquely Hungarian variant of the art nouveau style popular in Europe at the turn of the century. His most impressive buildings in Budapest are the Applied Arts Museum, the Geological Institute, and the Postal Savings Bank.

Ferenc (Franz) Liszt (1811-1886) A towering figure of 19th-century classical music, Liszt, though he lived most of his life abroad, was born in Hungary, and spent most of his later years living in Budapest, where he was one of the founders and the first president of the Academy of Music. A virtuoso performer as well as a world-renowned composer, Liszt was the founder of the symphonic poem. His "Hungarian Rhapsodies" and "Coronation Mass" are among the best-known pieces of Hungarian classical music.

Sándor Petőfi (1823-1849) A radical poet whose "National Song," supposedly recited on the steps of Pest's National Museum, helped inspire the 1848 Revolution, Petőfi is presumed to have died at the battle of Segesvár in 1849, though his body was never identified. Interestingly, this great Hungarian nationalist was of Slovakian descent, serving as a reminder of the complicated ethnic history of Hungary and the surrounding region.

István Széchenyi (1791–1860) Revered today as "the Greatest Hungarian," Széchenyi was a nobleman at the center of Hungarian intellectual life during the Age of Reform. He founded Hungary's Academy of Sciences (1825) and personally financed the building of Budapest's famous Chain Bridge (completed in 1848), which is named for him. An influential writer on subjects ranging from economics to horse breeding, he sought reform within the Habsburg monarchic system, and viewed the outbreak of revolution in 1848 with mixed emotions. After it ended in failure and destruction, he went mad.

Raoul Wallenberg (1912–?) The only non-Hungarian listed here, Wallenberg achieved his fame as a Swedish diplomat stationed in Budapest during World War II. At great personal risk, he saved the lives of thousands of Hungarian Jews during the Nazi occupation. Shortly after the Red Army liberated Budapest, Wallenberg was arrested, disappearing into the vast system of Soviet prison camps. His arrest has never been properly explained by the Russians, nor has his death been confirmed. There is a statue of him on Szilágyi Erzsébet fasor in Buda, and a street named for him in Pest.

Miklós Ybl (1814–1891) Ybl was one of the greatest figures of Hungarian architecture during the eclectic period of the late 19th century. Among his many buildings in Budapest the State Opera House, the Main Customs House, and St. Stephen's Basilica stand out. He also extended the Royal Palace in Buda, though his work was destroyed in World War II.

ARCHITECTURE, ART, LITERATURE & MUSIC

ARCHITECTURE The present architectural landscape of Budapest has been shaped by it's periodic destruction in war and conquest. Because of this unfortunate history, the architectural legacy of present-day Budapest is peculiarly and wonderfully 19th century. Few cities can boast a comparable wealth of 19th-century and fin-de-siècle architecture. Many of the city's finest buildings are in a state of woeful disrepair, reminders of a vanished age of imperial grandeur; this particular charm, however, is fleeting, as one by one the great buildings of Budapest are restored.

Examples of Roman architecture remain in present day Óbuda, but these are exclusively the result of excavation and reconstruction. The best ruins are the two amphitheaters and the buildings of the civilian town.

Supplanting the Romanesque style of the 11th and 12th centuries (of which nothing remains in Budapest), the Gothic style appeared in Buda in the late 13th century, becoming dominant during the 14th century. Little survives in an unreconstructed state from this period.

Perhaps the most notable architectural development of post–World War II Budapest was the painstaking reconstruction of Castle Hill, during which many wonderful examples of past glories were excavated and rebuilt.

ART Hungary has produced several artists whose works measure up to the highest international standards; many of their finest paintings (including most of those mentioned below) can be seen in the Hungarian National Gallery in Budapest. Smaller museums around the country focus on the works of individual artists, usually in their home towns.

Until the 19th century, Hungarian art was essentially ecclesiastical, heavily under the influence of Austrian and Italian styles. It wasn't until the advent of modern Hungarian nationalism in the 19th century that a uniquely Hungarian art began to emerge. Even then, however, Hungarian artists almost without exception followed—rather than established—international trends. Indeed, many of the country's best artists lived abroad, particularly in Paris, Munich, or Vienna, where they were able to be in closer contact with the schools to which they adhered. Thus, despite the creative flowering of Hungarian artists in the 19th century, it remains difficult to pinpoint a specifically Hungarian Art.

The Hungarian nationalism in the 19th century manifested itself in the arts most forcefully in the development of the historicist genre, whose best known practitioners were Viktor Madarász (1830–1917), Bertalan Székely (1835–1910), and Gyula Benczúr (1844–1920). Their paintings, based usually on events from Hungary's past, tended to be very large and yet with great attention to detail. Madarász is perhaps best known for his *Mourning of László Hunyadi*, which, in depicting the unjustly executed 15th-century nobleman, evokes the tragic nature of Hungarian history; Székely's *Women of Eger* celebrates the heroic women who defended Eger Fortress alongside their husbands against the 16th-century Turkish siege; and Benczúr's *Baptism of Vajk* (Stephen I) celebrates the beginning of Christianity in Hungary.

The artist Károly Lotz (1833–1904) is best known as a fresco painter. Among his most famous works are the ceiling frescoes of the Opera House and the wall frescoes of the National Museum.

Pál Szinyei Merse (1845–1920), a contemporary of the French Impressionists, is the outstanding figure of the Hungarian plein-air school. Szinyei Merse lived in Munich, not Paris, and his development was independent of the great French artists whose work his own so admirably resembles. His *Picnic in May* is widely considered one of the finest Hungarian paintings of the century.

Mihály Munkácsy (1844–1900), who lived in Paris, was a contemporary of Szinyei Merse. Munkácsy, heavily influenced by Courbet, was the unrivalled master of the Hungarian folk-genre and enjoyed an international reputation unequalled by any of his countrymen. Among his finest paintings are *The Condemned Cell, Woman Churning Butter, Woman Carrying Wood,* and *The Lint Makers.*

All show a profound empathy with the common folk who were the subjects of most of his paintings.

Advancing beyond studio-painted art, many of the best Hungarian plein-air painters gathered at Nagybánya (now in Romania) after 1896, where they established a thriving colony ("the Hungarian Barbizon"). Simon Hollósy (1857–1918) and Károly Ferenczy (1862–1917) were the colony's leading figures; many of the latter's finest paintings can be seen in the Ferenczy Museum, near Budapest at Szentendre.

One of Hungary's most unusual and most cherished artists was the post-Impressionist Tivadar Csontváry Kosztka (1853–1919), whose mystical landscapes and portraits reflect a unique personal vision. He was little known in his own lifetime, but by the mid-20th century even Picasso was calling him a genius.

"The Eight," a group which included Dezső Cigány (1883–1931) and Lajos Tihany (1855–1939), was formed in Budapest in the early years of the 20th century. It was to Cubism and the German Expressionists that The Eight, Hungary's first avant-garde school, looked for inspiration. The journal *Ma* (Today), edited by painter and writer Lajos Kassák (1887–1967), became the movement's mouthpiece. Other important 20th-century artists include László Moholy-Nagy (1895–1946), Hungary's leading Bauhaus artist; Victor Vasarely, the founder and leading figure of op-art who fled the country in 1919; and the Expressionist Gyula Derkovits (1894–1934).

Another leading 20th-century figure in Hungarian art is the ceramic artist Margit Kovács (1902–1977), whose unique works combined Hungarian folk themes with elements of modern art. She represents one of the most successful in a long series of Hungarian artists—including writers, musicians, and architects—who drew inspiration from the richness of Hungarian folk life and customs. A museum dedicated to her work is in Szentendre, near Budapest (see "Szentendre" in Chapter 10 for more information about the museum). Finally, Imre Varga (b. 1923) is the leading contemporary sculptor in Hungary. His works are on display throughout Budapest, as well as in a small museum in Óbuda (see "More Attractions" in Chapter 6 for information about the museum).

LITERATURE Latin was the written language of church-dominated early Hungary, and most surviving texts from this period are of a religious nature. The best known Latin text is the *Gesta Hungarorum,* written by a 12th-century cleric named Peter; much of what is known about the Magyar migration and conquest comes from this historiography.

Péter Bornemissza (1535–1584) was the outstanding prose writer of the Reformation period in Hungary. His collected sermons (including the best-known *The Temptations of the Devil*) amount to thousands of pages. Péter Pázmány (1570–1637), archbishop of Esztergom and founder of Hungary's first university, was the greatest literary figure of the counter-reformation. Pázmany's disciple was Miklós Zrínyi (1620–1664), whose *Peril of Sziget* described his grandfather's heroic defense of Sziget Castle against the Turkish onslaught. Zrínyi, who himself would lead raids against the Turks, became the model of the poet-patriot which pervades Hungarian literary history, its most celebrated example being Sándor Petőfi.

The first Hungarian literary school was based in the imperial capital Vienna; playwright György Bessenyei (1747–1811) was its leading figure. At the turn of the 19th century, decades before movements of a similar nature were initiated by architects, musicians, and painters, Hungarian writers endeavored to create a distinctly Hungarian literature through the celebration of both past national glories and simple peasant culture. Coming generations of Hungarian writers would add to this overtly nationalistic literature, creating a body of work much loved in Hungary. The first outstanding figure of the literary revival of the late 18th century was Ferenc Kazinczy (1759–1831), a prose writer, poet, and translator who led the language reform movement, an attempt to modernize the Hungarian literary language. Ferenc Kölcsey (1790–1838), considered the founder of Hungarian literary criticism, was a strong proponent of the creation of a Hungarian populist style, first fully realized in Mihály Vörösmarty's (1800–1855) *The Flight of Zalán,* which celebrated the early Magyars. Vörösmarty would achieve his lasting fame, however, from his later lyric poems.

The populist themes which dominated the middle of the 19th century are best represented by the poet Sándor Petőfi (1823–1849). Petőfi, one of the most revered figures in Hungarian history, was a leading figure in the anti-Habsburg Revolution of 1848; his "National Song" served to inspire the crowds, while he himself died in battle.

Hungary's most important writers and poets of the early 20th century gathered around the radical literary journal *Nyugat* (Occident), founded in 1908. The writers of *Nyugat* sought to revitalize Hungarian letters, at the same time integrating Hungarian literary culture into the European arena; the most prominent figures were Endre Ady (1877–1919), Zsigmond Móricz (1879–1942), and Mihály Babits (1883–1941). Ady, a towering figure of modern Hungarian poetry, was a radical whose uncompromising views and brutal honesty made him a highly controversial figure. Móricz, a novelist and short story writer, wrote about peasant life, but unlike the pretty picture painted by the 19th-century romantic populists, his was a stark, naturalistic—though not unaffectionate—portrayal of the countryside; some of his finest stories are compiled in *Seven Pennies.* Babits was a poet somewhat less fiery than Ady, but it was he who, as longtime editor of the journal, exerted the greatest influence over the next generation of Hungarian poets. Another *Nyugat* writer, Gyula Krúdy (1878–1933), is known for bringing the legendary character Sinbad to Hungary in a series of novels.

The influence of Zsigmond Móricz can be seen in the work of Gyula Illyés (1902–1983), "the Grand Old Man of Hungarian Letters." Illyés' classic novel is the semi-autobiographical *People of the Puszta,* an unromanticized vision of life on the Great Plain. Ferenc Molnár (1878–1952) was the most popular playwright of the

Nyugat period; his plays, known at the time throughout Europe, are distinguished by their sharp wit.

Two Hungarian poets of the inter-war period stand out: Attila József (1905–1937) and Miklós Radnóti (1909–1944). József, Hungary's greatest "proletarian poet," was attacked by the right and left alike, ultimately spurned by the Communist Party, of which he was a member, for his refusal to follow any party line in his poetry. His stark, desolate poetry is about the alienation of the working class. Impoverished and alone for much of his short life, he committed suicide by throwing himself under a train near Lake Balaton. Hero worship by several generations of alienated youth has elevated him to near mythic status. Radnóti, a Jew, was a scholarly poet whose life was cut short by the Nazis during a brutal forced march. Antal Szerb (1901–1945) was another martyred inter-war writer. A leading essayist whose *Hungarian Literary History* remains a classic in the field, he was murdered in a labor camp.

The magical realist Géza Csath (1887–1919) is widely read outside Hungary: *Opium and Other Stories* is a representative collection of his short stories. Hungarian-born Arthur Koestler (1905–1983) is known the world over for *Darkness at Noon,* in which he attempted to make sense of the brutal Stalinist purges of the 1930s. To this day critics are divided between those who call it a masterpiece and those who condemn it as overly simplistic. György Lukács (1885–1971) was a Marxist theoretician and philosopher who enjoyed a level of international respect and recognition shared by very few of his colleagues.

Noted living writers include Géza Ottlik (b. 1912); Ferenc Sánta (b. 1927); Iván Mándy (b. 1918); Erzsébet Galgóczi (b. 1930); Ádam Bodor (b. 1936); and György Konrad (b. 1933), a former dissident who enjoys an international reputation. The younger generation of contemporary writers is best represented by Péter Esterházy, Ákos Kertész, and Péter Nádas.

MUSIC It is probably in the realm of music that Hungary has contributed most to world culture. Musical life flourished in medieval Hungary. An integral part of court life, it followed general European Gothic trends, achieving its highest point during the 15th-century reign of Matthias Corvinus, the great patron of the Renaissance.

There were two important musical figures in 16th-century Hungary: Bàlint Bakfark (1507–1576) was a composer and lute player who spent much of his life at the royal courts of Paris and Vienna, while Sebestyén Tinódi Lantos (?–1556) was the greatest master of the sung poem, a dominant musical style of the Hungary of his time.

The 17th century saw the development of the *kuruc* songs, named for the kuruc soldiers who fought against Habsburg rule. The most famous of the kuruc songs—which still today strikes a deep patriotic chord in many Hungarians—was arranged by Berlioz, and is universally known as the "Rákóczi March" after revolutionary Ferenc Rákóczi.

In the 18th century Josef Haydn spent 30 years living and composing in the Esterházy Palace in western Hungary, while at the same time the Hungarian *verbunkos* genre arose, originally as music composed to accompany the recruitment of soldiers. The influence of the verbunkos can be seen in the works of the best of the early 19th century Hungarian composers, János Bihari (1764–1827), János Lavotta (1764–1820), and Antal Csermák (1779–1822).

Ferenc Erkel's (1810–1893) almost single-handed development of Hungarian opera was, like the rise of neo-Classicism in architecture and the historicist genre in painting, part of a self-conscious attempt to create a unique and grandiose national culture. His two most famous operas are *László Hunyadi* and *Bánk Bán*. He also composed Hungary's national anthem, setting to words the poetry of Ferenc Kölcsey. Budapest's second opera house is today named after Erkel.

The greatest Hungarian composer of the 19th century, and one of the country's most famous sons, was undoubtedly Ferenc (Franz) Liszt (1811–1896), who spent most of his life abroad but maintained a deep interest in Hungarian culture and musical traditions. His well known "Hungarian Rhapsodies" are evidence of his continued commitment to his homeland. In addition to being a composer of worldwide stature he was one of the great virtuoso pianists of his century. Liszt was the founder of the symphonic poem, its first manifestation being *Les Preludes* (1848). Budapest's Academy of Music, of which he was the first president, is named after him.

If Liszt was the towering figure of 19th-century Hungarian music, Béla Bartók (1881–1945) and Zoltán Kodály (1882–1967) were the giants of the 20th century. The founders of Hungarian ethnomusicology, Bartók and Kodály traveled the back roads of the country in the early years of the century systematically recording Hungarian and Gypsy folk music. Peasant folk music had for hundreds of years been an important part of rural Hungarian culture, but by the turn of the century it was in danger of being lost. In addition to saving an enormous wealth of music from oblivion, Bartók and Kodály made some important discoveries in their research, noting both the differences and the interrelationships between Hungarian and Gypsy folk music, which had over time fused considerably. Both men were composers, and the influence of the folk music they so cherished can be heard in their work. Kodály established the internationally acclaimed Kodály method of musical education, and lived to become the grand old man of Hungarian music, while Bartók died relatively young in the United States, an impoverished, embittered refugee from fascism.

Though Hungarian folk music no longer survives as a thriving part of rural life (except, perhaps, in Transylvania, now part of Romania), recent years have seen the growth of an urban-centered folk revival movement known as the *táncház* (dance house). The best táncház group is Muzsikás, whose lead singer is the incomparable Márta Sebestyén. Gypsies, otherwise an oppressed and largely impoverished minority in Hungary, continue to maintain their role as honored members of the country's musical culture.

2. FOOD & DRINK

FOOD Hungary's renowned paprika, the red powder ground from peppers, comes in as many varieties as the peppers themselves. Ranging from sweet (*édes*) to hot (*csípős*), it can be found in countless Hungarian dishes.

Lunch, the main meal of the day, begins with soup. *Gyümölcs leves,* a cold fruit soup, is excellent when in season. *Babgulyás,* a hearty bean soup, or *halaszle,* a fish soup popular at river and lakeside eateries, constitute meals in themselves.

The main course is generally a meat dish. Try the *paprikás csirke,* chicken cooked in a savory paprika sauce. It is especially good with *galuska,* a pasta dumpling. *Pörkölt* is a stewed meat dish, which comes in many varieties. *Töltött káposzta,* whole cabbage leaves stuffed with rice, meat, and spices, is another favorite. Vegetarians will mystify Hungarian waiters, but they would do well to order *lecsó tojással* (eggs scrambled in a thick tomato-onion-paprika sauce), *rántott sajt* (batter-fried cheese with tartar sauce), or *túrós csusza tepertő nélkul* (a macaroni-and-cheese dish).

Snack foods include *lángos,* a slab of deep-fried bread served with your choice of toppings: sugar and whipped cream, or garlic sauce and cheese. *Palacsinta,* a paper-thin crêpe stuffed with cheese or draped in hot chocolate sauce, is a treat that should not be missed. Ice cream (*fagylalt*) is the national street food; even early in the morning you'll see people standing in line for cones. The scoops are small, so order more than one. Fruit flavors are produced seasonally; in the spring try strawberry (*eper*) and sour cherry (*meggy*); in the fall, plum (*szilva*) and pear (*körte*). Another summer regular is the delicious cinnamon (*fahéj*).

Hungarian pastries are very good and cost a fraction of what they do in Vienna, so indulge. The light, flaky *rétes* are filled with fruit or cheese. *Csoki torta* is a decadent chocolate layer cake, and a *Dobos torta* is topped with a shiny caramel crust. *Mákos* pastry, made with poppy seeds, is a Hungarian specialty. *Gesztenye,* chestnuts, are another popular ingredient in desserts.

Picnickers should pick up a loaf of Hungarian bread (baked without preservatives) and sample any of Hungary's world-famous salamis. A number of fine cheeses are produced in Hungary as well: *Karaván füstölt* (a smoked cheese), *Edami,* and *márvány* (similar to blue cheese). In season, fresh produce is delightfully cheap and of high quality. You won't find much fresh fruit or vegetables in the winter or in traditional dishes served in restaurants, but there are wonderful markets where you will be amazed at the abundance and variety. Sour cherries in July are out of this world.

Hungary's cuisine is delicious and various, although restaurants tend to offer only the most traditional dishes. An invitation to a home-cooked meal should not be refused; it will surely prove to be a savory and satisfying experience.

BEER, WINE & SPIRITS   Hungary does not have a beer culture like the neighboring Austrians, Czechs, and Slovaks, and as a result its beer is unexceptional. Beers from the latter countries, as well as Germany, can now be found everywhere in Budapest, so the connoisseur has no reason to sample the mediocre Hungarian brews (of which, incidentally, Dreher is the best one). Hungarian wines, on the other hand, are excellent. The most renowned are the red *Egri Bikavér* (Eger Bull's Blood); and the white *Tokaj* wines, *száraz* (dry) or *édes* (sweet). *Soproni* wines also enjoy an international reputation.

Unicom, the richly aromatic bitter which some call "Hungary's national drink," is a taste worth acquiring. *Pálinka* is another variety of Hungarian "fire water" which is often brewed at home from apricots, plums, or pears; in folk wisdom, it's acclaimed for its medicinal value.

COFFEE & TEA   Hungarians drink coffee (*kávé*) throughout the day, either at stand-up coffee bars or in elegant coffeehouses. Until recently, Hungarian coffee drinking borrowed from the Turkish tradition: Alarmingly strong, unfiltered espresso was served straight up, generally without cream or sugar. These days, coffee drinking has expanded to include milder and more refined tastes. In general, though, when ordering coffee in Hungary, you are still ordering espresso. If you ask for coffee with milk (*kávé tejjel*) you are served espresso with cream on the side. Cappuccino (and its variant *cappuciner,* with chocolate shavings on top) is now available in most coffeehouses, as is decaffeinated coffee (*koffein mentes*). *Tejeskávé,* a Hungarian version of café au lait, is another option.

Tea drinkers will have a difficult time in restaurants; if tea is available at all, it is generally of the strong black variety. For more variety and a peek at Hungary's burgeoning world of herbal medicine, look for teas in any of the numerous shops: *gyógynövény, herbárium,* or *gyógytea.*

WATER   While tap water (*csapvíz*) is safe to drink in Budapest, it is not offered in restaurants, and few Hungarians request it. Instead they drink *ásványyvíz,* a carbonated mineral water, or *szóda víz,* carbonated tap water.

3. RECOMMENDED BOOKS & FILMS

BOOKS   A good number of the best books on Hungary are now out of print. If you can't find a given book in a bookstore, your best bet is to check in a university library. A small bookstore in New York called Puski Corvin (251 E. 81st St., New York, NY 10028; tel. 212/879-8893) specializes in Hungary. Corvina is a Budapest-based English-language press, many of whose books are recommended below. They can be purchased at English-language bookstores in Budapest, or you can write for a free catalog: Corvina kiadó, P.O. Box 108, Budapest H-1364, Hungary.

History & Politics For a general history of Hungary, there is still nothing better than C. A. McCartney's *Hungary: A Short History* (Aldine, 1962). Unfortunately it is out of print, and difficult to find. *A History of Hungary* (Indiana University Press, 1990), edited by Peter Sugar, is an anthology with a number of good essays. *The Habsburg Monarchy, 1809–1918* (Hamish Hamilton, London, 1948), by A. J. P. Taylor, one of the great historians of the 20th century, is a readable analysis of the final century of the Austro-Hungarian empire.

Two memoirs of early 20th-century Budapest deserve mention: *Apprentice in Budapest: Memories of a World That Is No More* (University of Utah Press, 1988) by the anthropologist Raphael Patai; and *Budapest 1900* (Weidenfeld & Nicolson, 1989), by John Lukacs, which captures the feeling of a lively but doomed imperial city at the turn of the century.

The Holocaust in Hungary: An Anthology of Jewish Response (University of Alabama Press, 1982), edited and translated by Andrew Handler, is notable for the editor's excellent introduction. Elenore Lister's *Wallenberg: The Man in the Iron Web* (Prentice Hall, 1982) is a readable account of the heroic life of Raoul Wallenberg, written against the chilling backdrop of Nazi-occupied Budapest.

Joseph Rothschild has written two excellent surveys of 20th-century Eastern European history, both of which contain large sections on Hungary. They are *East Central Europe Between the Two World Wars* (University of Washington Press, 1974) and *Return to Diversity: A Political History of East Central Europe Since World War II* (Oxford University Press, 1989).

Culture *The Cuisine of Hungary* (Bonanza Books, 1971), by the famous Hungarian-born restaurateur George Lang, contains all you need to know about the subject. Tekla Domotor's *Hungarian Folk Beliefs* (Corvina and Indiana University Press, 1981) covers witches, werewolves, giants, and gnomes.

Julia Szabo's *Painting in Nineteenth Century Hungary* (Corvina, 1985) is a large book with a fine introductory essay and over 300 plates. Of the many tourist-oriented coffee-table books available in Budapest, the best is *Budapest Art and History* (Flow East, 1992) by Delia Meth-Cohn, whose scholarly narration accompanies the fine photographs.

Architecture buffs should get their hands on a copy of K. Pintér Tamás' *Századeleji Házak Budapesten* (Magyar Építőművészek Szövetsége, 1987), a wonderful guidebook to turn-of-the-century architecture in Budapest. Available only in the ETK Bookstore on

Rumbach Sebestyén utca in Pest, it is in Hungarian but has an English-language introduction and lists the addresses of all buildings pictured. Other architecture-oriented guides more generally available in Budapest include András Török's *Budapest: A Critical Guide* (Park Books), notable for its walking tours, and István Wellner's *Budapest: A Complete Guide* (Corvina).

Fiction Not all of the best examples of Hungarian literature are available in translation, but look for the following: Gyula Illyés' *The People of the Puszta* (Corvina, 1979), an unabashedly honest look at peasant life in the early 20th century; Gyorgy Konrád's *The Case Worker* (Penguin, 1987), a portrayal of a political system in disrepair; Péter Esterházy's *Helping Verbs of the Heart* (Weidenfeld & Nicolson, 1991), a gripping story of grief following a parent's death; István Örkény's *The Toth Family and The Flower Show* (New Directions, 1966), the first an allegorical story about fear and authority, the second a fable about different types of reality in modern life; Zsolt Csalog's *Lajos M., Aged 45* (Maecenas, Budapest, 1989), an extraordinary memoir of life in a Soviet labor camp; Kálmán Mikszáth's *St. Peter's Umbrella* (Corvina, 1962); and Zsigmond Móricz's *Seven Pennies* (Corvina, 1988), a collection of short stories by one of Hungary's most celebrated authors.

Corvina publishes three good anthologies of modern Hungarian short stories and poetry: they are *Present Continuous: Contemporary Hungarian Writing* (1985), edited by István Bart; *Nothing's Lost: Twenty-Five Hungarian Short Stories* (1988), edited by Lajos Illyés; and *Today: An Anthology of Contemporary Hungarian Literature* (1987), edited by Éva Tóth. Another good anthology is *Ocean at the Window: Hungarian Prose and Poetry Since 1945* (University of Minnesota Press, 1980), edited by Albert Telzsa.

Poetry The translation situation is even worse with poetry than with prose, but some works are available. In addition to the anthologies noted in "Fiction," above, look for *Modern Hungarian Poetry* (Columbia University Press/Corvina, 1977), edited by Miklós Vajda. Works of individual poets in translation include: *János Pilinszky: Selected Poems* (Manchester, 1976); *Attila József: Selected Poems* (Carcanet Press, 1973); Imre Madách's dramatic poem *The Tragedy of Man* (Corvina, 1988); and *Sándor Weöres: Selected Poems* (Penguin, 1970).

FILMS Several Hungarian-born directors, working abroad, had a tremendous impact on the development of cinema: Alexander Korda, George Cukor, and Michael Kertész are giant names in film history. And Hungarian-born actors like Tony Curtis and the Gábor sisters achieved international fame on the silver screen.

But not all the best talent emigrated. Some Hungarian directors whose films are worth looking for include (in rough chronological order) Zoltán Fábri, whose *Merry Go-Round* is a recognized masterpiece of socialist realism; Péter Bacsó, whose classic *The Witness* is a well-loved parody of Stalinist-era terror; Miklós Jancsó, of whose many well known films *Confrontation,* about the first post–World War II generation, is his most famous; Péter Gothar, whose *Time Stands Still,* a dark vision of alienated youth in post-1956 Budapest, is a cult classic in Hungary; and the contemporary filmmaker István Szabó, whose most internationally acclaimed films have been *Mephisto* (1981), filmed in Berlin; and *Meeting Venus* (1991), the story of a conductor and the diva with whom he falls in love.

One Hollywood film, *Music Box* (1989, starring Jessica Lange and Armin Mueller-Stahl), should be mentioned. It is a haunting tale of a daughter's dawning awareness of her father's past identity as a Hungarian fascist; it includes some interesting Budapest footage.

CHAPTER 2

PLANNING A TRIP TO BUDAPEST

Now that you've decided to travel to Budapest, you must have dozens of questions. Do I need a visa? What currency do they use there? Are there any festivals occurring during my trip? How can I get there? This chapter is devoted to providing answers to these and other questions.

1. INFORMATION, ENTRY REQUIREMENTS & MONEY

SOURCES OF TOURIST INFORMA-TION Ibusz, the former state-owned travel agency and one of the first Hungarian companies to be privatized, continues to play a dominant role in the tourist industry. Ibusz has several offices abroad; on request, they will send you a mailing with various free pamphlets and maps. In the **United States:** One Parker Plaza, Suite 1104, Fort Lee, NJ 07024. Tel. 201/592-8585; fax 201/592-8736; telex 428187. 233 North Michigan Ave., Suite 1308, Chicago, IL 60601. Tel. 312/819-3150; fax 312/819-3151. In **Britain:** c/o Danube Travel Ltd., 6 Conduit St., London W1R 9TG. Tel. 071/493-0263; fax 071/493-6963; telex 23-541.

The Los Angeles–based **Hungarian Hotel Sales Office** handles reservations for hotels of the three major Hungarian chains: Pannonia, Danubius, and HungarHotels; contact them at 6033 West Century Blvd., Suite 670, Los Angeles, CA 90045. Tel. toll free 800/448-4321 (in California 800/231-8704; in Los Angeles 800/649-5960); fax 213/649-5852. A similar reservations service **Hun-**

garian Air Tours Limited, is based in London: Kent House, 87 Regent St., London W1R 7HF. Tel. 071/437-9405; fax 071/287-7505; telex 296536 WWT HAT.

See "Tourist Information" in Chapter 3 for sources of information in Budapest.

ENTRY REQUIREMENTS Documents Citizens of the United States, Canada, and the United Kingdom need only a valid passport to enter Hungary. Citizens of Ireland, Australia, and New Zealand need a visa as well as a passport; contact the nearest Hungarian Embassy for details.

Customs You are allowed to bring duty-free into Hungary 250 cigarettes, 2 liters of wine, and 1 liter of spirits. There is no limit to the amount of currency you may bring in, but import or export of more than 500 Hungarian Forints is forbidden. Most tourists report that there is no customs check at either rail or airport border points.

MONEY The basic unit of currency in Hungary is the Forint (Ft). There are 100 fillérs (almost worthless and soon to be taken out of circulation) in a Forint. Coins come in denominations of 10, 20, and 50 fillers; and 1, 2, 5, 10, 20, 100, and 200 Ft. Newly issued coins, without the symbols of the previous regime, have recently been introduced and should eventually phase out the older ones. Banknotes come in denominations of 50, 100, 500, 1,000, and 5,000 Ft.

Artificially bolstered by the government, the Forint has remained fairly steady against the dollar in recent years despite Hungary's annual inflation rate of about 20% to 30%. Thus, dollars (and other hard currencies) are worth less in real buying power each year in Hungary. Nonetheless, Hungary is still considerably less expensive than most Western countries.

Because of the non-convertibility of the Forint, its import and export (above 500 Ft) are forbidden, and foreigners have reported having Forints siezed by customs agents. Technically you are allowed to reexchange into hard currency up to half the amount of Forints you originally purchased. This is sometimes harder in practice than in theory; inquire at Budapest's Tourinform office if you have any difficulty. Keep all exchange receipts (you will need to produce them to reexchange currency) and don't exchange more than you'll be likely to spend.

As of this writing (summer 1993) $1=90 Ft; or 1 Ft=1.1¢; this is the rate used to calculate the dollar values below and all the dollar prices in this book. Presstime rates stood at 136 Ft to the pound sterling, and 68 Ft to the Canadian dollar. Exchange rates do change over time. The impending changes in Hungarian monetary policy, particularly a decision that would allow the value of the Forint to be determined by free market forces (to be "convertible"), may have a profound effect on exchange rates.

CURRENCY CONVERSION

Ft	U.S.$	£
5 Ft	.05	.03
10 Ft	.11	.07
25 Ft	.27	.18
50 Ft	.55	.37
75 Ft	.83	.55
100 Ft	1.11	.74
150 Ft	1.66	1.10
200 Ft	2.22	1.47
250 Ft	2.77	1.84
300 Ft	3.33	2.20
400 Ft	4.44	2.94
500 Ft	5.55	3.68
750 Ft	8.32	5.51
1,000 Ft	11.10	7.35
2,000 Ft	22.20	14.70
5,000 Ft	55.50	36.75
10,000 Ft	111.00	73.50
25,000 Ft	277.50	183.80
50,000 Ft	555.00	367.60

WHAT THINGS COST IN BUDAPEST   U.S. $

Taxi from Ferihegy I to the city center	8.90
Metro from Nyugati Station to Deák tér	.28
Local telephone call	.06
Double room at the Hilton (very expensive)	203.10
Double room at Vadvirág Panzió (moderate)	51.05
Double room at Hotel Express (budget)	16.65
Lunch for one at Kispipa Vendéglő (moderate)	4.75
Dinner for one, without wine, at Kis Buda Gyöngye (very expensive)	12.75
Dinner for one, without wine, at Sipos Halászkert (moderate)	6.10
Dinner for one, without wine, at Kiskacsa Vendéglő (inexpensive)	3.05
Half liter of beer	1.25
Coca-Cola	.60
Cup of coffee	.55
Roll of ASA 100 Kodacolor film, 36 exposures	5.00
Admission to the Hungarian National Museum	.45

	US$
Movie ticket	1.35
Opera ticket	.65–13.65

Traveler's Checks   Traveler's checks are accepted for exchange at most banks and exchange offices, including the American Express office. Many hotels (but not stores) also accept them as payment. In lieu of the difficulties of reexchanging unused Forints, consider bringing traveler's checks in small denominations.

Hard Currency   It's impossible to overstate the importance of having some cash on hand if you plan to do any traveling in Eastern Europe. When buying international train tickets in Hungary, for instance, you will generally be required to pay for the "international" section of the trip (the section which is outside Hungary) in hard currency—cash only.

Following is an example of the trouble you can have without enough cash on hand. We met Taeku Lee, from Chicago, in Budapest's Keleti Station. He had arrived at the station several hours before his Prague-bound train was due to depart, with an adequate supply of both Hungarian Forints and traveler's checks in U.S. dollars. After losing time in various lines, he found he had to pay in hard currency for the section of the trip between the Slovak border and Prague. The amount was a mere $12, but only cash was accepted. Mr. Lee tried all the exchange booths in the station, again losing time, in an attempt to cash a traveler's check for dollars. Unfortunately, the booths could only offer him Forints for his checks. He had no time to go to one of the downtown banks where this kind of transaction is possible (albeit for a ruinous 6% commission). Only a quick black-market exchange with a kind fellow traveler, who was willing to trade precious dollars for the Forints, enabled him to make his train.

Credit Cards   Credit cards are accepted at all first-class hotels, and at many cheaper hotels and pensions. Most of the more expensive restaurants in Budapest also accept credit cards, while the cheaper ones generally do not. Boutiques, art galleries, antiques stores, crystal and china stores, and other shops in the city center accept credit cards, but most other shops in Budapest do not.

Exchange   The best official rates for both cash and traveler's checks are obtained at banks. Exchange booths, however, are located throughout the city center and in most hotels and so may prove more convenient for you.

Black Market   As long as the Forint remains non-convertible there will be a **black market** in Hungary. On the black market (cash only, of course) you can get an exchange rate about 8% higher than in a bank or exchange office. Partly to prevent flight from the Forint, the State Bank prohibits Hungarians from purchasing more than $500 worth of hard currency annually; if a Hungarian wants to travel abroad, he or she may need far more than $500. So he or she goes to the black market (centered in the main waiting room of Keleti Station, near Track 6) and buys dollars from a black marketeer, who has acquired those dollars in exchange for Forints from tourists. The state knows the black market serves a necessary function in the economy, and therefore tolerates it.

Tourists have reported being ripped off by money changers on the street, but no one has told us of trouble in Keleti Station. Before doing business on the black market, you should know the bank rate: You can expect roughly 8% better. The black marketeer will ask you how much you want to exchange; the rate offered may depend on the size of the deal. Take it or leave it, but don't expect a better offer from a nearby exchanger; the system is highly organized, and these entrepreneurs cooperate with each other rather than compete.

The protocol, obeyed by all honest money changers, is as follows: The black marketeer counts out the Forints for you, while you keep your own money in your pocket. After receiving the Forints, take your time counting them. Then take your money out of your pocket, hand it over, and wait while the money changer counts it.

Some travelers have reported that when staying in private rooms, their host has asked to change money. While the rates offered are probably a little lower than the Keleti Station rates, you may feel more comfortable making the deal in such a setting.

2. WHEN TO GO — CLIMATE, HOLIDAYS & EVENTS

CLIMATE The climate in Hungary is generally pleasant: cool in winter and warm in summer, with few temperature extremes. The annual mean temperature is 50°F, and summer temperatures rarely exceed 80° to 85°F, although hot, dusty summer days are not unusual. January is the coldest month, averaging 30°F. Spring is usually mild and, especially in May and June, wet, and autumn is usually pleasant with mild weather through October.

Budapest's Average Daytime Temperatures

	Jan	Feb	Mar	Apr	May	June	July	Aug	Sept	Oct	Nov	Dec
Temp. (°F)	30	34	38	53	62	68	72	71	63	52	42	35
Temp. (°C)	−1	1	3	12	17	20	22	22	17	11	6	2

HOLIDAYS Hungarian holidays are: New Year's Day (January 1), National Holiday (March 15), Easter Sunday and Easter Monday, May Day (May 1), Whitmonday, St. Stephen's Day (August 20), Republic Day (October 23), and Christmas (December 25 and 26). Shops, museums, and banks are closed on all holidays.

BUDAPEST
CALENDAR OF EVENTS

With good fortune, your trip to Budapest will coincide with one of the city's cultural events. Keep in mind, though, that during some of them, particularly the Spring Festival and the Formula One Grand Prix, hotel rooms are particularly hard to come by. All inquiries about ticket availability and location of events should be directed to Budapest's main tourist information office, **Tourinform,** at 1052 Budapest, Sütő u. 2. (tel. 36-1/117-9800, fax 36-1/117-9578).

MARCH

✪ *BUDAPEST SPRING FESTIVAL Two weeks of performances of everything from opera to ballet, from classical music to drama. Simultaneously, temporary exhibitions open in many of Budapest's museums. **Where:** All the major halls and theaters of Budapest. **When:** Mid to late March. **How:** Tickets available at the Spring Festival Box Office, V. Vigado tér 2 (tel. 117-5067) and at venues.*

MAY OR JUNE

☐ **Book Week** During the last week of May or first week of June, publishers set up kiosks throughout central Pest to display the year's newly released titles. Most books are in Hungarian of course, but there are always beautiful books on art, architecture, and other subjects.

JUNE–AUGUST

☐ **Open-air Theater Programs** Throughout the summer, there is a rich variety of open-air performances in Budapest. Highlights include opera and ballet at the Margaret Island Open Air Theater, folklore and dance at the Buda Park Theater, musicals in Városmajor Theater, and classical music recitals in the Dominican Courtyard at the Hilton Hotel.
☐ **Organ Concerts** Concerts are given in the Matthias Church, in

the lovely Castle District of Buda, June through August. Budapest's largest church, St. Stephen's Basilica, also hosts organ concerts July through August.

JULY OR AUGUST

✪ *SUMMER OPERA AND BALLET FESTIVAL* Except for this 10-day festival, the wonderful Hungarian State Opera House has no summer performances. *Where:* Opera House. *When:* Date varies, but falls in July or August. *How:* Tickets available at the Opera House box office or at the National Philharmonic Ticket Office, V. Vörösmarty tér 1 (tel. 117-6222).

AUGUST

☐ **Formula One Grand Prix** One of the European racing circuits most important annual events, this race is held at the HungaroRing the second weekend in August.
☐ **St. Stephen's Day** (August 20) Hungary's patron saint is celebrated with fireworks over the Danube.

SEPTEMBER

☐ **Budapest International Fair** For 10 days in the middle of September the HungExpo grounds are filled with Europe's latest consumer goods.

SEPTEMBER–OCTOBER

☐ **Budapest Art Weeks** In celebration of the opening of the season, three weeks of special classical music and dance performances are held in all the city's major halls. September 25, the day of Béla Bartók's death, is the traditional starting day for the festival.
☐ **Contemporary Music Weeks** Held in conjunction with the Budapest Art Weeks, this three-week festival also features performances in all the city's major halls.

3. HEALTH & INSURANCE

HEALTH No shots or inoculations are required for entry to Hungary. Hungarian pharmacies are generally not well-stocked, so try to bring enough of any medication you may need. In case you do run out, take along a copy of all prescriptions.

INSURANCE Emergency medical treatment is provided free of charge in Hungary, but you will have to pay for prescription medications and for non-emergency care. Check with your insurance company before leaving home to see if you are covered for foreign travel. If not, it might be a good idea to take out a special short-term travel policy. Some homeowner's insurance policies cover items like cameras even when you are traveling abroad. You might look into this, too, before your departure.

If you feel that you need to purchase extra travel insurance, contact **Travel Guard International,** 1145 Clark St., Stevens Point, WI 54481 (tel. 715/345-0505, or toll free 800/826-1300), which offers policies that protect you against trip cancellation and include provisions for medical coverage and lost luggage as well. Prices start at $52 for one week of coverage. Other companies to consider include **Travelers Insurance Co.,** 1 Tower Square, 10NB, Hartford, CT 06183-5040 (tel. 203/277-2318, or toll free 800/243-3174); and **Mutual of Omaha (Tele-Trip),** Mutual of Omaha Plaza, Omaha, NE 68131 (tel. toll free 800/228-9792), both of which offer similar protection.

Insurance for British Travelers Most big travel agents offer their own insurance, and will probably try to sell you their package when you book a holiday. Think before you sign. Britain's Consumers' Association recommends that you insist on seeing the policy and reading the fine print before buying travel insurance. You should also shop around for better deals. Try **Columbus Travel Insurance Ltd.** (tel. 071/375-0011) or, for students, **Campus Travel** (tel. 071/730-3402). If you're unsure about who can give you the best deal, contact the **Association of British Insurers,** 51 Gresham St., London EC2V 7HQ (tel. 071/600-333).

4. WHAT TO PACK

Hungarians do not dress formally; casual, comfortable clothing will see you through your days and nights in Budapest. You might bring one dressy outfit for a visit to the opera or to one of Budapest's classiest restaurants, although even there dress is more or less at your discretion.

Budapest has a generally mild climate, although if you're visiting in the summer you should be aware that it can get very hot. A baseball cap or sun hat is good to protect you from the bright sun. Sunglasses are another essential item. Sunscreen is generally unavailable in Budapest, so bring some along. A light sweater and raincoat are recommended for cool spells that may occur even in the middle of the summer. In winter, although temperatures rarely dip below freezing, be prepared for damp and chilly weather.

For a visit in any season, remember to pack a bathing suit so you won't have to rent a vintage 1970 model when you visit Budapest's famous thermal baths. Tennis players should probably also bring along their own gear. Tennis is cheap in Budapest, but equipment is not always available for rent; when it is available, it's usually primitive. Tennis whites are not compulsory.

A money belt is recommended to visitors in light of the pickpocketing incidents reported by unhappy tourists. The best kind can be worn inside your clothing without too much discomfort or bulkiness.

If you wish to take gifts along, you will rarely go wrong with T-shirts—the more "American" the better. Professional and college sports logos are particularly coveted. Decals are also very popular; again, the more Western the better.

5. TIPS FOR THE DISABLED, SENIORS, SINGLES, FAMILIES & STUDENTS

FOR THE DISABLED   Before you go, there are many agencies to check with about information for the disabled.

Travel Information Service, MossRehab Hospital, 1200 W. Tabor Rd., Philadelphia, PA 19141-3099, supplies names and addresses of accessible hotels, restaurants, and attractions through a telephone referral service (tel. 215/456-9603).

Names and addresses of organizations offering tours for travelers with disabilities can be obtained by writing to the **Society for the Advancement of Travel for the Handicapped,** 347 Fifth Ave., Suite 610, New York, NY 10016 (tel. 212/447-7284); send a self-addressed stamped envelope to receive a general information sheet. The yearly membership fee of $45 ($25 for senior citizens and students) includes information sources and a quarterly newsletter.

FedCap Rehabilitation Services, Inc., 211 W. 14th St., New York, NY 10011 (tel. 212/727-4200), offers tours for members who pay a yearly fee of $14.

For the blind, the best source is the **American Foundation for the Blind,** 15 W. 16th St., New York, NY 10011 (tel. 212/620-2000, or toll free 800/232-5463).

For Disabled British Travelers   **RADAR** (the Royal Association for Disability and Rehabilitation) publishes an annual holiday guide for the disabled, "Holidays and Travel Abroad" (£3.50 in the U.K., £5 in Europe, £7 in other destinations). RADAR also provides a number of holiday fact sheets on such subjects as sports and outdoor holidays, insurance, financial arrangements, and accommodations with nursing care for groups or for the elderly. There is a nominal charge for all these publications, which are available by calling 071/637-5400 or by writing RADAR, 25 Mortimer St., London W1N 8AB.

Another good resource is the **Holiday Care Service,** 2, Old Bank Chambers, Station Road, Horley, Surrey RH6 9HW (tel. 0293/774-535; fax 0293/784-647), a national association that advises on vacations for the elderly and the disabled. It provides competitive travel insurance designed for people with pre-existing medical conditions.

FOR SENIORS   For pretrip information, write for a free booklet, "101 Tips for the Mature Traveler" from **Grand Circle Travel,** 347 Congress St., Suite 3A, Boston MA 02210 (tel. 617/350-7500, or toll free 800/221-2610).

Mature Outlook, 6001 N. Clark St., Chicago, IL 60660 (tel. toll free 800/336-6330), is a travel club operated by Sears Roebuck & Co. for people over 50. Annual membership of $9.95 includes a bimonthly newsletter featuring hotel discounts.

SAGA International Holidays, 222 Berkeley St., Boston, MA 02116 (tel. toll free 800/343-0273), is known for all-inclusive tours for seniors (mostly 60 and older).

The best U.S. organization for seniors is the **American Association of Retired Persons,** 601 E St. NW, Washington, DC 20049 (tel. 202/434-AARP). Members are offered discounts on car rentals and hotels. The association's group travel is provided by the AARP Travel Experience from American Express. Tours may be purchased through any American Express office or travel agent or by calling toll free 800/927-0111.

Information is also available from the nonprofit **National Council of Senior Citizens,** 1331 F St. NW, Washington, DC 20005 (tel. 202/347-8800). For $12 per person or couple, you receive a monthly newsletter partly devoted to travel tips and discounts on hotels and auto rentals.

For British Seniors   **Wasteels,** 121 Wilton Rd., London (tel. 071/834-7066), currently provides an over-60s Rail Europe Senior Card, and **Scandinavian Sea Ways** offers 50% discounts to senior citizens for any sailing (except those on Fridays and Saturdays). Proof of age is necessary, so take along your passport or driver's license when you book and when you board the ship. Coach tours also cater to those over 60, with excellent offerings available from **Wallace Arnold** (tel. 081/464-9696) and **Cosmos Tourama** (tel. 081/464-3477).

FOR SINGLES   There is one company that has made heroic efforts to match single travelers with like-minded companions, and it is now the largest and best-listed such company in the United States. New applicants desiring travel companions fill out a form stating preferences and needs; they receive a minilisting of potential partners who might be suitable. There is a charge of between $36 and $66 for a six-month listing. A bimonthly newsletter also gives numerous money-saving travel tips of special interest to solo travelers; a sample copy is available for $4. For an application and more information, write to Jens Jurgen, **Travel Companion Exchange,** P.O. Box P-833, Amityville, NY 11701 (tel. 516/454-0880). Another agency to check is **Grand Circle Travel,** 347 Congress St., Boston, MA 02210 (tel. 617/350-7500, or toll free 800/221-2610), which offers escorted tours and cruises for retired people, including singles.

Singleworld, 401 Theodore Fremd Ave., Rye, NY 10580 (tel. 914/967-3334, or toll free 800/223-6490), is a travel agency that operates tours geared to singles.

For British Singles   In Britain, **Explore** (tel. 0252/344-161) has a well-justified reputation for fascinating offbeat tours for singles. **HF Holidays** (tel. 081/905-9388) also runs a range of packages throughout Europe for travelers aged 18 to 35.

Dedicated independent travelers may want to check out the **Globetrotters Club,** BCM/Roving, London WC1N 3XX, which enables members to exchange information and generally assist each other in traveling as cheaply as possible. The fee to join is £3 for British and European residents (U.S. $5 for others), and a one-year subscription to *Globe* magazine will run £9 (U.S. $18).

FOR FAMILIES   If you have a very small child, you will probably want to take along such standard items as children's aspirin, a thermometer, Band-Aids, and similar supplies.

On airlines, you must request a special menu for children at least 24 hours in advance. If baby food is required, however, bring your own and ask a flight attendant to warm it to the right temperature. Arrange ahead of time for such necessities as a crib, bottle warmer, and car seat.

"Family Travel Times" is published 10 times a year by TWYCH (Travel With Your Children) and includes a weekly call-in service for subscribers. Subscriptions ($55 a year) can be ordered from **TWYCH,** 45 W. 18th St., 7th floor, New York, NY 10011 (tel. 212/206-0688). TWYCH also publishes two nitty-gritty information guides, *Skiing with Children* and *Cruising with Children* which sell for $29 and $22, respectively, but are discounted to newsletter subscribers. An information packet, including a sample newsletter, is available for $2.

For British Families   The best deals for families are often package holidays. **Skytours** (tel. 081/200-8733) offers thousands of free holidays for children under 18, on a first-come, first-served basis. After those spots are filled, reduced fares are available for children. **Airtours** (tel. 0706/26000) operates a similar program for children under 19. Both companies have clubs for children between the ages of 3 and 11 running for several hours each day in many popular destinations.

FOR STUDENTS   **Council Travel** (a subsidiary of the Council on International Educational Exchange) is America's largest student, youth, and budget travel group, with more than 60 offices worldwide.

The main office is at 205 E. 42nd St., New York, NY 10017 (tel. 212/661-1414). Council Travel's London Centre is located at 28A Poland St., W1V 3DB, just off Oxford Circus (tel. 071/287-1565 for European destinations, 071/437-7767 for other destinations). International Student Identity Cards, issuable to all bona fide students for $15 (£5) entitle holders to generous travel and other discounts. Discounted international and domestic air tickets are available. Eurotrain rail passes, YHA passes, weekend packages, overland safaris, and hostel/hotel accommodations are also bookable. Council Travel sells a number of publications for young people, including *Work, Study, Travel Abroad; The Whole World Handbook; Volunteer: The Comprehensive Guide to Voluntary Service in the U.S. and Abroad;* and *The Teenager's Guide to Study, Travel, and Adventure Abroad.*

To keep down costs, membership in the **International Youth Hostel Federation** (IYHF) is recommended. Many countries have branch offices, including **American Youth Hostels (AYH)/ Hostelling International,** 733 15th St. NW, Suite 840, Washington, DC 20005 (tel. 202/783-6161) (walk-in office, 1108 K St. NW, Washington, DC; tel. 202/783-0717). Membership costs $25 annually, except for those under 18, who pay $10, and those over 54, who pay $15.

For British Students   In Britain, you can purchase the IYHA card from the youth hostel store at 14 Southampton St., London (tel. 071/836-8541) or Campus Travel (tel. 071/730-3402). Take both your passport and some passport-sized photos of yourself, plus your membership fee. In England and Wales, this is £3 (for those under 18) or £9 (for those over 18). In Scotland, the fee is slightly less: £2.50 for those under 18, and £6 for everyone else. See above for information on **Council Travel's** London office.

6. GETTING THERE

BY PLANE   **Delta Air Lines** (tel. toll free 800/241-4141; from eastern Canada 800/361-9783) is the leading North American carrier to Eastern Europe. In peak season, they have 13 flights a week from North America to Budapest, including the only three non-stop flights from New York to Hungary. There are also three weekly direct (same plane, one stop) flights from New York to Budapest via Amsterdam. All flights leave New York in the evening, arriving in Europe the next morning. Connecting flights link passengers from almost all American cities with Budapest-bound planes. Connecting flights are routed through Frankfurt's Flughafen Main, an efficient and hassle-free transit point.

Other airlines serving Budapest include **Malév** (the former Hungarian state airline, now partially owned by Alitalia) (tel. toll free 800/223-6884 or 800/877-5429); **Lufthansa** (tel. toll free 800/

**FROMMER'S SMART TRAVELER:
AIRFARES**

1. Shop all the airlines that fly to Budapest.
2. Consider a flight to Vienna. If it's significantly cheaper, you can easily get a train from Vienna to Budapest. You won't have to spend a night in the wallet-busting Austrian capital if you don't want to.
3. Reserve your ticket at least three weeks in advance for the best prices.
4. Read the advertisements in newspaper travel sections. Look for special deals and packages and discount fares.

654-3880); and **British Airways** (tel. toll free 800/247-9297). None offer non-stop flights from North America.

BY TRAIN   Countless trains arrive in Budapest from the corners of Europe. Many connect through Vienna, where 11 daily trains depart for Budapest from either the Westbahnhof or Sudbahnhof stations. Six daily trains connect Prague and Budapest, while one connects Berlin with Budapest, and two connect Warsaw with Budapest.

Thomas Cook's International Timetable has the most complete schedule information. The Eurail and InterRail timetables are also helpful. Contact the Austrian National Tourist Board for more information on the Vienna trains: 500 Fifth Ave., New York, NY 10110 (tel. 212/944-6917); 30 St. George St., London W1R 0AL (tel. 071/629-0461); 2 Bloor St. East, Suite 3330, Toronto, Ontario M4W 1A8 (tel. 416/967-4101).

BY BUS   Although buses do ply the main routes to Budapest, they are generally no cheaper than the train and a lot less enjoyable. From Vienna, there are two buses daily to Budapest (7am and 5pm) departing from Wien Mitte bus station. The ride takes 3½ to 4 hours. You can get tickets and information from Blaguss Reisen, Wiedner Haupstrasse 15 (tel. 50-18-00 or 712-04-51) or from the bus station (tel. 71101). The price of a one-way ticket is 394 AS ($33.70).

BY CAR   There are several major highways linking Hungary to nearby European capitals. The E60 connects Budapest with Vienna and points west; the E65 connects with Prague and points north. The border crossings from Austria and Slovakia (from which countries most westerners enter Hungary) are hassle-free. In addition to your passport, you may be requested to present your driver's license, vehicle registration, and proof of international insurance (the so-called "Green Card"). Hungary no longer requires the International Driver's License. If you plan to drive a rental car across the border, make sure you request a Green Card from the rental agent. Cars entering Hungary are required to have a decal indicating country of registration, a first-aid kit, and an emergency triangle. For traffic regulations, see "Getting Around," in Chapter 3.

Driving distances are: from Vienna, 248 km (154 miles); from Prague, 560 km (347 miles); from Frankfurt, 952 km (590 miles); and from Rome, 1,294 km (802 miles).

BY HYDROFOIL   Two companies, the Hungarian **MAHART** and the Austrian **Donau Dampfschiffarts Gesellschaft,** operate hydrofoils on the Danube between Vienna and Budapest in the spring and summer months. It is an extremely popular route; you should book your tickets well in advance. In North America or Britain contact Ibusz (see "Sources of Information," above), or the Austrian National Tourist Board. In Vienna, contact MAHART, Karlsplatz 2/8 (tel. 53-26-86 or 51-55-50); or DDSG Donaureisen, Handelskai 265 (tel. 0222/217 50-0).

From early April through mid-October the MAHART hydrofoil departs Vienna at 8:10am daily, arriving in Budapest at 12:30pm. June through mid-September an additional hydrofoil makes the daily passage, departing Vienna at 2:30pm, and arriving in Budapest at 7pm. The fare is 730 AS ($62.40) one way, and 1,100 AS ($93.95) round trip. ISIC card holders pay 590 AS ($50.40) one way, and 900 AS ($76.85) round trip. Children under 4 ride free; children between 4 and 14 pay 410 AS ($35) one way, and 620 AS ($52.95) round trip. The Budapest office of MAHART is at V. Belgrád rakpart (tel. 118-1704).

DDSG, a slightly more expensive line, has a daily hydrofoil in operation from late April through mid-September, departing Vienna at 8:10am and arriving in Budapest at 12:30pm. From mid-September through mid-October, the DDSG hydrofoil operates three times weekly. The one-way fare is 830 AS ($70.90); the round-trip fare is 1,200 AS ($102.50). Eurailpass holders get 50% off. Children under 6 ride free; children between 6 and 15 receive a 50% discount. DDSG is represented in Budapest by Blue Danube Travel, V. Régiposta u. 19. II/1 (tel. 118-3980).

If you enjoy traveling by hydrofoil, but can't get reservations or find the price a bit too stiff, you can always take an inexpensive hydrofoil excursion up the Danube from Budapest to Esztergom, taking in the glories of the Danube Bend, Hungary's most scenic stretch of the river, along the way. For details, see "Easy Excursions from Budapest," in Chapter 10.

PACKAGE TOURS   The **Hungarian Hotel Sales Office** (in Los Angeles), **Hungarian Air Tours Limited** (in London), and **Ibusz** organize package tours of Budapest, of Hungary, and of the region (see "Sources of Information," above).

Budapest Express Tours & Travel, 80 Richmond St., Suite 1502, Toronto, Ontario M5H 2A4 (tel. toll free 800/268-4155 or 416/653-6600; fax 416/362-8020), specializes in spa packages (Hungary, Czech and Slovak Republics, and Bulgaria), but offers a number of non-spa tours as well.

Hunting is popular in Hungary. **Wingshooting Adventures** is one company which offers a variety of hunting tours. Contact them at 4320 Kalamazoo Ave. SE, Grand Rapids, MI 49508 (tel. 616/455-7810; fax 616/455-5212).

GETTING TO EUROPEAN DESTINATIONS FROM THE U.K.

BY PLANE There are no hard and fast rules about where to get the best deals for European flights, but do bear the following points in mind.

Daily papers often carry advertisements for companies offering cheap flights. London's *Evening Standard* has a daily travel section, and the Sunday editions of almost any newspaper will run many ads. Highly recommended companies include **Trailfinders** (tel. 071/938-3366) and **Platinum Travel** (tel. 071/937-5122).

In London, there are many bucket shops around Victoria and Earls Court that offer cheap fares. Make sure that the company you deal with is a member of the IATA, ABTA, or ATOL. These umbrella organizations will help you out if anything goes wrong.

BY TRAIN Many different rail passes are available in the U.K. for travel in Europe. Stop in at the **International Rail Centre,** Victoria Station, London SW1V 1JY (tel. 071/834-2345); or **Wasteels,** 121 Wilton Rd., London SW1V 1JZ (tel. 071/834-7066). They can help you find the best option for the trip you're planning.

BY CAR & FERRY Taking your car abroad gives you maximum flexibility to travel at your own pace and to set up your own itinerary. You can make ferry/drive reservations with any good travel agent. There are many different options, so as always, it's advisable to shop around for the best deals.

CHAPTER 3

GETTING TO KNOW BUDAPEST

1. ORIENTATION
2. GETTING AROUND
• **FAST FACTS: BUDAPEST**
3. NETWORKS & RESOURCES

This chapter is full of practical information you will need during your stay in Budapest—from neighborhood orientation to listings of the cheapest rental-car agencies, from how to use a payphone to how to avoid taxi hustlers. Glance through this chapter before your arrival, and consult it during your stay.

---

1. ORIENTATION

ARRIVING

BY PLANE Budapest's two airports, **Ferihegy I** and **Ferihegy II,** are adjacent to each other in the XVIII district in southeastern Pest. Malév and Lufthansa flights land at Ferihegy II (tel. 157-7831 or 157-7000); all other flights land at Ferihegy I (tel. 157-2122 or 157-7755). Both airports are quite small, and each has only one exit from Customs (there is no domestic air service in Hungary, so all arriving flights are international). Ferihegy II has been modernized recently, while Ferihegy I is a bit run-down (although plans are afoot for renovation in the near future).

Both airports have a number of accommodation offices, rental-car agencies (see "Getting Around," below), shops, and exchange booths. Exchange rates are generally a little worse than in the city, so you may not want to change very much money at the airport.

Getting Into Town The easiest and most reliable way into the city is the **Airport Minibus** (tel. 157-6283), a public service of the LRI (Budapest Airport Authority). The minibus, which leaves every 10 or 15 minutes throughout the day, takes you directly to any address in the city. From Ferihegy I it costs 400 Ft ($4.45); from Ferihegy II it costs 500 Ft ($5.55). In both airports the Airport Minibus desk is easily found in the main hall. Minibuses also provide the same efficient service returning to the airports; arrange for your pick-up several hours in advance.

LRI also runs an **Airport-Centrum** bus. It leaves every half hour from both airports. Passengers are dropped off at Pest's Erzsébet tér bus station, just off Deák tér, where all three metro lines converge. The price is 200 Ft ($2.20). You can also take the LRI Airport-

Centrum bus to return to the airports; pick up is at Erzsébet tér bus station.

The private **taxi** drivers who hang out at the airport are notorious rip-off artists. Foreigners have been charged as much as $50 for a ride that would cost $6 to $10 in a reliable fleet taxi. The fleet known as "Airport Taxi" charges grossly inflated fares, too, although it is hard to call them "dishonest" since their fares are on a meter (albeit a fast one). However, for three or more people traveling together, an honest taxi to the city will be cheaper than the combined minibus fares. Our advice is to take only taxis of the recommended fleets (see "By Taxi," below). If you don't see any taxis from these reliable outfits, call for one. In both airports there is a Fő Taxi phone at the Hertz desk in the main arrivals hall. They'll call a cab for you; it rarely takes more than 5 minutes for one to arrive.

It is also possible to get to the city by **public transportation.** From either airport, take the red bus 93 to the last stop, Kőbánya-Kispest. From there, the Blue metro line runs to the Inner City of Pest. The cost is two transit tickets (50 Ft/55¢); tickets can be bought from any newsstand in the airport.

BY TRAIN Budapest has three major train stations: Keleti pályaudvar (Eastern Station), Nyugati pályaudvar (Western Station), and Déli pályaudvar (Southern Station). The stations' names, curiously, correspond neither to their geographical location in the city nor to the origins or destinations of trains serving them. Each has a metro station beneath it and an array of accommodation offices, currency exchange booths, and other services.

Most international trains pull into bustling **Keleti Station** (tel. 155-8657), located in Pest's Baross tér, beyond the Outer Ring on the border of the VII and VIII districts. Tourists are met here by various hustlers offering rooms, youth hostels, and taxis. Budapest's black market in currency is currently centered in the main international waiting room at Keleti (see "Money," in Chapter 2 for information and advice on black-market exchange). The Red line of the metro is below the station; numerous bus, tram, and trolleybus lines serve Baross tér as well.

Some international trains arrive at **Nyugati Station** (tel. 149-0115), a gem of a station designed by the Eiffel company and built in 1874–77. It's located on the Outer Ring, at the border of the V, VI, and XIII districts. There is a station for the Blue line of the metro beneath Nyugati, and numerous tram and bus lines serve busy Nyugati tér (formerly Marx tér).

Few international trains arrive at **Déli Station** (tel. 155-8657), an ugly modern building in central Buda; the terminus of the Red metro line is beneath the train station.

BY BUS Most international buses pull into the **Erzsébet tér bus station** (tel. 117-2966), just off Deák tér in central Pest. All three metro lines converge on Deák tér. Tourinform, Budapest's main tourist office, is also at Deák tér.

BY BOAT & HYDROFOIL Boats and hydrofoils from Vienna

arrive at the **Belgrád rakpart** (tel. 118-1704), on the Pest side of the Danube, between the Szabadság and Erzsébet bridges.

TOURIST INFORMATION

Budapest is a rapidly changing city and a lot of published tourist information is out of date. Incredibly, there are still thousands of

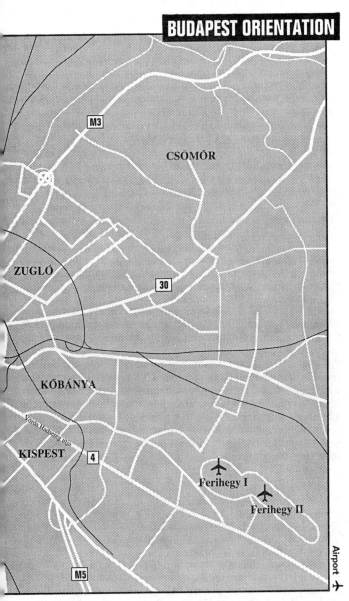

maps floating around with the old pre-1990 street names. The best source of information in the city is **Tourinform** (tel. 117-9800), the office of the Hungarian Tourist Board. It is centrally located at Sütő utca 2, just off Deák tér (reached by all three metro lines) in Pest. The helpful staff all speak English. Advice is given on all tourist-related subjects, from concert tickets to pension rooms, from train schedules to horseback riding. Many free pamphlets are available, the most useful of which are the monthly *Program in Hungary* and *Budapest Panorama*. They are open from 8am to 8pm daily.

Budapest Week and the *Budapest Sun*, the two English-language weekly newspapers, have extensive listings for concerts, theater, dance, movies, and other events; they are available at most hotels and newsstands.

CITY LAYOUT

You'll understand this section much better with a map in hand. The city of Budapest came into being in 1873, the result of a union of three separate cities, **Buda, Pest,** and **Óbuda.** Budapest, like Hungary itself, is defined by the **River Danube (Duna).** The stretch of the Danube flowing through the capital is fairly wide (average width, 400 meters), and most of the city's historic sites are on or near the river. Eight bridges connect the two banks, including five in the city center. The Széchenyi Chain Bridge (Lánchid), built in 1849, was the first permanent bridge across the Danube. Although blown up by the Nazis, it was rebuilt after the war.

MAIN STREETS & SQUARES Pest   On the right bank of the Danube lies Pest, flat as a *palacsinta* (pancake), spreading far into the distance. Pest is the commercial and administrative center not just of the capital, but of all Hungary. Central Pest, the term used in this guide, is that part of the city between the Danube and the semi-circular **Outer Ring** boulevard (Nagykörút), stretches of which are called by the names of former monarchs: Ferenc körút, József körút, Erzsébet körút, Teréz körút, and Szent István körút. The Outer Ring begins at the Pest side of the Petőfi Bridge in the south and wraps itself around the center, ending at the Margit Bridge in the north. Several of Pest's busiest squares are found along the Outer Ring, and Pest's major east–west avenues bissect it at these squares.

Central Pest is further defined by the **Inner Ring** (Kiskörút), which lies within the Outer Ring. It starts at Szabadság híd (Freedom Bridge) in the south and is alternately named Vámház körút, Múzeum körút, Károly körút, Bajcsy-Zsilinszky út, and József Attila utca before ending at the Chain Bridge. Inside this ring is the **Belváros,** the historic Inner City of Pest.

Váci utca (different from Váci út) is a popular pedestrian shopping street between the Inner Ring and the Danube. It spills into Vörösmarty tér, one of the area's best-known squares and site of Gerbeaud's coffee house. The Dunakorzó (Danube Promenade), a popular evening strolling place, runs along the river in Pest, between the Chain Bridge and the Erzsébet Bridge. The historic Jewish district of Pest is in the **Erzsébetváros,** between the two ring boulevards.

Margaret Island (Margit-sziget) is in the middle of the Danube. Accessible via the Margaret Bridge or Árpád Bridge, it is an enormously popular park without vehicular traffic.

Buda and Óbuda On the left bank of the Danube is Buda; to its north, beyond the city center, lies Óbuda. Buda is as hilly as Pest is flat, while Óbuda is less hilly. Streets in Buda, particularly in the hills, are not as logically arranged as those in Pest.

The two most dramatic points in central Buda are **Castle Hill** and **Gellért Hill.** Castle Hill is widely considered the most beautiful part of Budapest. There are a number of steep paths, staircases, and small streets going up to Castle Hill, but no major roads. Easiest access is from Clark Ádám tér (at the head of the Chain Bridge) by funicular, or from Várfok utca (near Moszkva tér) by foot or bus. Castle Hill consists of the royal palace itself, home to numerous museums, and the so-called **Castle District,** a lovely neighborhood of small, winding streets, centered around Holy Trinity Square (Szentháromság tér), site of Gothic Matthias Church. There is very little traffic on Castle Hill, and the only industry is tourism.

Gellért Hill, to the south of Castle Hill, is named after the martyred Italian Bishop who aided King István I (Stephen I) in his conversion of the Hungarian nation to Christianity in the 10th and 11th centuries. There is a giant statue of Gellért on the side of the hill, and on top is the Citadella, a fortress built by the Austrians.

Below Castle Hill, along the Danube is a long, narrow neighborhood known as the **Watertown** (Víziváros). The main street of Watertown is Fő utca (Main Street).

Central Buda, the term used in this guide, is a collection of mostly lowlying neighborhoods below Castle Hill. The main square of central Buda is Moszkva tér, just north of Castle Hill. Beyond Central Buda, mainly to the east, are the **Buda Hills.**

Óbuda is on the left bank of the Danube, north of Buda. Although the greater part of Óbuda is modern and drab, it can boast both a beautiful old city center and the impressive Roman ruins of Aquincum. Unfortunately, the old city center has been sliced in half by the road coming off the **Árpád Bridge,** destroying its integrity. The historic center of the old city is Fő tér (Main Square), a square as lovely as any in Hungary. **Óbuda Island** (Óbudai-sziget) is home to a huge, and underused, park.

FINDING AN ADDRESS Finding addresses in Budapest can be daunting at first, largely because of the strangeness of the Hungarian language. However, with a little practice and a good map, you should meet with success.

Budapest is divided into 22 districts, called *kerülets* (abbreviated as *ker*). A Roman numeral followed by a period precedes every written address in Budapest, signifying the kerület, for example, XII. Csörsz utca 9 is in the twelfth kerület. Because many street names are repeated in different parts of the city it is very important to know which kerület a certain address is in. If the address you seek does not have a Roman numeral preceding it, you can also tell the kerület from the four-digit zip code. The middle two digits represent the kerület; Csörsz utca 9, 1123 Budapest will be in district XII.

Navigating in Budapest will be easier if you are familiar with the following words: *utca* (abbreviated as u.)—street; *út*—road; *útja*—road of; *körút* (abbreviated krt.)—boulevard; *tér*—square; *tere*—square of; *köz*—alley or lane; *liget*—park; *sziget*—island; *híd*—bridge; *sor*—row; *part*—riverbank; *pályaudvar* (abbreviated pu.)—railway station; *állomás*—station. *Note:* These words are never capitalized in Hungarian.

A common mistake made by tourists is to mistake Váci út, the uninteresting road which goes from Nyugati station to the city of Vác, with Váci utca, the shopping street in the Inner City. Similarly, tourists are known to mistake Vörösmarty utca, a station on the Yellow metro line, with Vörösmarty tér, the terminus of the same Yellow metro line. Read signs carefully. Hungarian is a language with a fine sense of detail.

Street signs are posted on buildings and give the name of the street, or square, the kerület, and the building numbers found on that block. Even- and odd-numbered buildings are on opposite sides of the street. Numbers are seldom skipped; often you'll end up walking longer than you expected to reach a given number.

Many street names have been changed since 1990, reverting for the most part back to their pre–World War II names, but maps with old street names are still floating around. The best way to check if you have an up-to-date map is to look for Pest's Outer Ring: if a section of it is called Lenin, you have an old map; if Teréz is there, you have a new map.

Floors in buildings are numbered European style, that is to say the first floor is one flight up from the ground floor (*földszint*), and so on. Addresses are usually written with the floor number in Roman numerals and the apartment number in Arabic numerals. Example: XII. Csörsz utca 9, IV/3 is on the 4th floor, apartment 3.

MAPS   A good map can save you much frustration in Budapest. Western-made maps are sold throughout Budapest, but **Cartografia,** a Hungarian company, makes two maps which are substantially cheaper and cover Budapest in great detail. The Cartografia fold-out map is fine, but if you find its size awkward you should pick up the Cartografia *Budapest Atlas*. Both maps are available throughout central Pest at kiosks and bookstores. Public transportation lines are shown on the maps, but in places the map is too crowded to make the lines out clearly. The **BKV térkép** (Budapest Transportation Authority map), available from metro ticket windows, is therefore recommended as a complement (see "Getting Around," below). If you plan on any hiking excursions in the Buda Hills, you should pick up the A Budai Hegység map, no. 6 of the Cartografia Turistatérképe (Touring Map) series.

There are two map stores in Pest, where you can buy maps of other cities in Hungary and elsewhere. Again, look for Cartografia maps; they are always cheaper than Western-made maps and equal in quality. One store is at VI, Bajcsy-Zsilinszky út 37 (tel. 112-6001), open weekdays from 9am to 5pm (the closest metro station is Arany János utca on the Blue line). The other store is at VII, Nyár u. 1 (tel.

122-0438), open weekdays from 9am to 5:30pm (the closest metro station is Blaha Lujza tér on the Red line). You can also find maps in most of the bookstores recommended in Chapter 8 of this guide.

NEIGHBORHOODS IN BRIEF

Pest

Inner City (Belváros) The historic center of Pest, the Belváros is the area inside the Inner Ring, bounded by the Danube to the west. Many of Pest's historic buildings are found in the Belváros, as well as the city's showcase luxury hotels and most of it's best-known shopping streets.

Leopold Town (Lipótváros) Just to the north of the Belváros, Lipótváros is considered a part of central Pest. Development began here at the end of the 18th century; it soon emerged as a center of Pest business and government. In addition to Parliament, a number of government ministries, courthouses, banks, and the former stock exchange are all found here. Before the war, it was considered a neighborhood of the "high bourgeoisie."

Theresa Town (Terézváros) The character of Terézváros is defined by the great boulevard running the length of it, Andrássy út, formerly the best address in Budapest, now the center of the embassy district. The Teréz körút section of the Outer Ring cuts through Terézváros; Oktogon is its major square. The area around Nagymező utca is the city's theater district.

Elizabeth Town (Erzsébetváros) Directly to the southeast of Terézváros, Erzsébetváros is the historic Jewish neighborhood of Pest. During the German occupation of 1944–45, a ghetto was constructed here. It's still the center of Budapest Jewish life, though by no means is it as vibrant a place as it once was.

Joseph Town (Józsefváros) One of the largest of the central Pest neighborhoods, Józsefváros is to the southeast of Erzsébetváros. It has long had a reputation of being the seediest part of Pest, and for all appearances this reputation is a deserved one. József körút, the neighborhood's segment of the Outer Ring, is a center of prostitution and pornography.

Buda

Castle District (Várnegyed) The city's most beautiful and historic district, it dates to the 13th century. On a plateau above the surrounding neighborhoods and the Danube beyond, the Castle District is defined by its medieval walls. The southern end of the Castle District is filled by the immense Buda Palace and its grounds. The northern end is home to small winding streets, as well as Matthias Church, the Fisherman's Bastion, and the Hilton Hotel.

Watertown (Víziváros) The long narrow neighborhood wedged between the Castle District and the Danube, the Víziváros is historically a quarter of fishermen and small artisans. Built on the steep slope of Castle Hill, it has narrow alleys and stairs instead of roads in many places. Its main street, Fő utca, runs the north–south length of the Víziváros, parallel to and a block away from the river.

Buda Hills The Buda Hills are numerous remote neighborhoods that feel as if they are nowhere near, let alone within, a capital city. By and large, the hills are considered a classy place to live. Neighborhoods are generally known by the name of the hill on which they stand. **Rose Hill** (Rózsadomb) is the part of the Buda Hills closest to the city center and one of the city's most fashionable neighborhoods.

Óbuda

Óbuda is a mostly residential area now, its long Danube coastline once a favorite spot for worker's resorts under the old regime. Most of the facilities have by now been privatized, explaining the large number of hotels found here. The extensive Roman ruins of Aquincum are Óbuda's chief claim to fame.

2. GETTING AROUND

BY PUBLIC TRANSPORTATION

Budapest has an extensive, efficient, and inexpensive public transportation system. If you have enough patience and you enjoy reading maps, you can easily learn the system well enough to use it wisely. The system, however, is not without its drawbacks. The biggest disadvantage is that except for 17 well-traveled bus and tram routes, all forms of transport shut down for the night at around 11:30pm (see "Night Service," below); certain areas of the city, most notably the Buda Hills, are beyond the reach of this night service, and taxis are thus required for late-night journeys. The second problem with the system is that travel can be quite slow, especially during rush hour. The third disadvantage, pertinent mostly to tourists, is that Castle Hill can be reached in only three ways by public transportation, all of which are crowded in busy tourist seasons.

FARES All forms of public transportation in Budapest require the self-validation of pre-purchased yellow tickets (*jegy*) costing 25 Ft (28¢) each; they can be bought from metro ticket windows, kiosks, and the occasional tobacco shop. There are also automatic machines (requiring exact change) in most metro stations and at major transportation hubs, but these are not always reliable. On weekends and at night it can be rather difficult to find an open ticket window, so

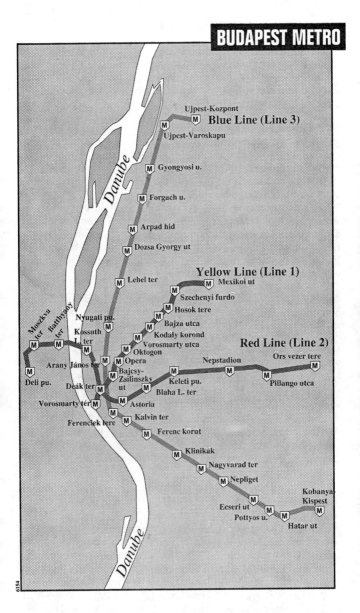

BUDAPEST METRO

Blue Line (Line 3)

- Ujpest-Kozpont
- Ujpest-Varoskapu
- Gyongyosi u.
- Forgach u.
- Arpad hid
- Dozsa Gyorgy ut
- Lehel ter

Yellow Line (Line 1)

- Mexikoi ut
- Szechenyi furdo
- Hosok tere
- Bajza utca
- Kodaly korond
- Vorosmarty utca
- Oktogon
- Opera

Red Line (Line 2)

- Ors vezer tere
- Pillango utca
- Nepstadion
- Keleti pu.
- Blaha L. ter

Moszkva ter
Bathyany ter
Nyugati pu.
Kossuth ter
Arany Janos ter
Deli pu.
Bajcsy-Zsilinszky ut
Deak ter
Vorosmarty ter
Ferenciek tere
Astoria
Kalvin ter
Ferenc korut
Klinikak
Nagyvarad ter
Nepliget
Ecseri ut
Pottyos u.
Hatar ut
Kobanya-Kispest

Danube

buy a stack of them to avoid the trouble of constantly replenishing your stock.

Day passes (*napijegy*) (200 Ft/$2.20), bought from metro ticket windows and validated by the clerk at the time of purchase, are valid until midnight of the day of purchase. A three-day *turistajegy* costs 400 Ft ($4.45); same validation procedure as with the day pass. For longer stays in Budapest, it might be worth buying a monthly pass (*bérlet*) for 1,100 Ft ($12.20). These are available only at major metro stations. You need a regulation passport photo.

Inspectors occasionally come around checking for valid tickets. On the spot fines (600 Ft/$6.65) are assessed to fare dodgers; pleading ignorance generally does not work.

SCHEDULES & MAPS All public transport operates on rough schedules, which are posted at bus and tram shelters and in metro stations. The schedules are a little confusing at first, but you'll get used to them. The important thing to note is when the last ride of the night departs: Many a luckless tourist has waited late at night for a bus that won't be coming until 6am!

The transportation map produced by the Budapest Transport Authority (*BKV térkép*) is available at most metro ticket windows for 65 Ft (70¢). Since transportation routes are extremely difficult to read on most city maps, you are advised to buy one of these handy maps. In addition, on the reverse side of the map, there is a full listing of routes, including the all-important night bus routes.

USING THE SYSTEM "Subway" means underpass in Europe. Subways are found under most major boulevards in Budapest. A subway may have as many as five or six different exits, each letting you out onto a different part of the square or street. Signs direct you to bus, tram, trolleybus, and metro stops, often using the word *fele*, meaning "toward." (Note that although Budapest is a very safe city, especially when compared to American cities of comparable size, subways tend to be among the more menacing places late at night; various lowlifes enjoy hanging out in these subterranean confines.)

Directions given throughout this book use a metro station as a starting point whenever possible. In cases where that is simply impossible, other major transportation hubs, such as Móricz Zsigmond körtér in southern Buda, are used as starting points.

BY METRO

You will no doubt spend a lot of time in the Budapest metro. The system is clean and efficient, with trains running every 3 to 5 minutes from about 4:30am until about 11:30pm. The only problem with the system is that there are just three lines, only one of which crosses under the Danube to Buda. The three lines are universally known by color—Yellow, Red, and Blue. Officially they have numbers as well (1, 2, 3 respectively), but all Hungarians refer to them by color and all signs are color coded. All three lines converge at Deák tér, the only point where any meet.

The **Yellow line** is the oldest metro on the European continent. Built in 1894 as part of the Hungarian millennial celebration, it looks more like an underground tram than a metro. Signs for the Yellow line, lacking the distinctive colored *M*, are harder to spot than signs for the Blue and Red lines. Look for signs saying *Földalatti* (literally, "underground"). At each station there are two entrances, one for each direction. The Yellow line runs from Vörösmarty tér, site of Gerbeaud's Cukrászda in the heart of central Pest, out the length of Andrássy út, past the Városliget (City Park), ending at Mexikói út, in a part of Pest known as Zugló. So, depending on the direction you are heading, enter either the side marked *Irány Mexikói út* or *Irány Vörösmarty tér*. Incidentally, somewhere in the middle of the line is a stop called Vörösmarty utca; this is a small street running off Andrássy út, and should not be confused with the terminus, Vörösmarty tér. Tickets for the Yellow line are self-validated on the train itself. Even if you have no business which takes you on the Yellow line it is worth a ride, as it is the continent's oldest underground, and seems little changed since the 19th century.

The **Blue** and **Red lines** are modern metros and to reach them you descend long, steep escalators. The Blue line runs from Kőbánya-Kispest, in southeastern Pest, through the center, and out to Újpest-Központ in northern Pest. Nyugati station is along the Blue line. The Red line runs from Örs vezér tere in eastern Pest, through the center, and across the Danube to Batthyány tér, Moszkva tér, and finally Déli Station. Keleti Station is also along the Red line.

On the street above stations of both the Red and Blue lines are distinctive colored *M* signs. Tickets should be validated at automatic boxes before you descend the escalator. When changing lines at Deák tér, you are required to validate another ticket. The validating machines are in the hallways between lines, but are easy to miss, particularly if there are big crowds. Metro tickets are good for one hour, for any distance along the line you are riding. Though it is not officially allowed, you are able to get out en route and reboard going in the same direction as long as your trip is completed within an hour of your first entry.

BY BUS

There are about 200 different bus (*busz*) lines in greater Budapest. Many parts of the city, most notably the Buda Hills, are best accessed by bus. Although buses are the most difficult to use of Budapest's transportation choices, with patience (and a BKV map) you'll be able to get around by bus in no time. With the exception of night buses, most lines are in service from about 4:30am to about 11:30pm. Some bus lines run far less frequently (or not at all) on weekends, while others run far more frequently (or only) on weekends. This information is both on the reverse of the BKV transportation map and on the schedules posted at every bus stop.

Budapest's buses are blue. Black-numbered local buses constitute the majority of the city's lines. Red-numbered buses are express; generally, but not always, the express buses follow the same routes as local buses with the same number, simply skipping some stops along the way. If the red number on the bus is followed by an *E* the bus runs non-stop between terminals (whereas an *É*—with an accent mark—signifies *észak,* meaning night). Depending on your destination, an express bus may be a much faster way of traveling. A few buses are labelled by something other than a number; one which you'll probably use is the *Várbusz* (Palace Bus), a minibus which runs between Várfok utca, off Buda's Moszkva tér, and the Castle District.

Bus tickets are self-validated on board by the mechanical red box found by each door. Unlike metro tickets, bus tickets are valid only for one line. Tickets cannot be purchased from the driver. You are allowed to board the bus by any door. There is a new, experimental policy being tested by the BKV, which may or may not be made permanent: After 8pm, you may only board through the front door, and you must show your ticket to the driver.

The biggest problem for bus-riding tourists is the drivers' habit of skipping stops when no one is waiting to get on and no one has signalled to get off. To signal your intention to get off at the next stop, press the button above the door (beware: Some drivers open only the doors which have been signalled). Most stops do not have their names posted; a list of stops is posted inside all buses, but if stops are skipped you may lose track. Chances are, though, that the Hungarians riding a given bus will know exactly where your stop is, and they are generally enthusiastic about helping foreigners on buses. You can also ask the driver to let you know when he's reached your stop.

Avoid buses in central areas during rush hours, since traffic tends to be quite bad. It pays to go a bit out of your way to use a metro or tram at these times instead.

BY TRAM

You'll find Budapest's 33 bright yellow trams (known as *villamos* in Hungarian) very useful, particularly the 4 and 6 which travel along the Outer Ring (Nagykörút).

Tickets are self-validated on board. As with buses, tickets are valid for one ride, not for the line itself. Trams stop at every station, and all doors open, regardless of whether anyone is waiting to get on. The buttons near the tram doors are for emergency stops, not stop requests. Frommer's reader Elizabeth White of Saugerties, New York, likes to tell of the minor international incident caused by her weary husband, Arnie, who, afraid of missing his stop, accidentally pushed the emergency stop button. Despite this, Ms. White is an advocate of tram riding in Budapest: "Tram riding is more comfortable for foreigners than bus riding."

BY TROLLEYBUS

Red trolleybuses are electric buses which receive power from a cable above the street. There are only 14 trolleybus lines in Budapest, all in Pest. Of particular interest to train travelers is the 73, the fastest route between Keleti Station and Nyugati Station. All the information in the "By Bus" section above regarding boarding, ticket validation, and stop skipping applies to trolleybuses.

BY HÉV

The HÉV is a suburban railway network which connects Budapest to various points along the city's outskirts. There are four HÉV lines; only one, the Szentendre line, is of serious interest to tourists (see Chapter 10, "Easy Excursions from Budapest").

The terminus for the Szentendre HÉV line is Buda's Batthyány tér, also a station of the Red metro. The train makes 10 stops in northern Buda and Óbuda, en route to Szentendre. Most hotels, restaurants, and sights in those areas are best reached by the HÉV (so indicated in the directions given throughout this book). To reach Óbuda's Fő tér (Main Square), get off at the Árpád híd (Árpád Bridge) stop.

The HÉV runs regularly between 4am and 11:30pm. For trips within the city limits, the cost is one transit ticket, self-validated as on a bus or tram. Tickets to Szentendre cost 64 Ft (70¢), minus 25 Ft if you have a valid day pass. They are different from the standard transportation tickets, and are punched by conductors on board. Tickets are available at special HÉV ticket windows at the Batthyány tér station or from the conductor on board (no penalty assessed for such purchase).

BY COGWHEEL RAILWAY & FUNICULAR

Budapest's **cogwheel railway** (*fogaskerekű*) runs from Város-major, across the street from the Hotel Budapest on Szilágyi Erzsé-bet fasor in Buda, to Széchenyi-hegy, terminus of the Children's Railway (Gyermek Vasút) and site of Hotel Panoráma. The cogwheel railway runs from 4:30am to midnight, and normal transportation tickets (self-validated on board) are used. The route is a pleasant one, twisting high into the Buda Hills; at 25 Ft (25¢), it might be worthwhile to take it just for the ride.

The **funicular** (*sikló* in Hungarian) connects Buda's Clark Ádám tér, at the head of the Széchenyi Chain Bridge, with Dísz tér, just outside the Buda Castle. The funicular is one of only two forms of public transportation which serves the Castle District (the Várbusz, bus 16, and bus 116 are the other possibilities; see "By Bus," above). An extremely steep and short ride, the funicular runs from 7:30am to 10pm. Tickets cost 60 Ft (65¢) for adults and 40 Ft (45¢) for children.

BY BOAT

From May through September a BKV boat carries passengers between Pest's Boráros tér and Pünkösdfürdő in Óbuda, with 10 stops en route—in Pest, Buda, Margaret Island, and Óbuda Island. Centrally located landing points include Batthyány tér, Petőfi tér, and Szent Gellért tér. Twelve boats run daily, between 9am and 7pm. From terminus to terminus, the trip is around 90 minutes. Depending on the distance traveled, the fare for adults is from 14–100 Ft

(15¢–$1.10); for children it is 7–50 Ft (8¢–55¢). Schedules and maps are posted at every station. BKV also charters boats, and offers a "water taxi" service. For all BKV boat information, call 129-5844.

NIGHT SERVICE

Most of the transportation system in Budapest closes down between 11:30pm or midnight and 5am. There are, however, 17 night routes (12 bus and 5 tram), and they are generally quite safe. Though they share the same number as normal routes (with an *É* suffix, meaning *észak,* or night), they actually run different routes. A full listing appears on the BKV transportation map. Night buses require the standard, self-validated ticket. Stop skipping is prevalent on night buses so pay attention.

BY TAXI

Budapest taxis are unregulated, so fares vary tremendously between the different fleets and among the private, unaffiliated drivers. Perhaps because there are more taxi drivers than the level of business can support, many drivers are experts at fleecing foreigners. However, if you watch out for yourself, taxis are substantially cheaper than in the West; a ride from Castle Hill to central Pest, for example, should cost about 200–300 Ft ($2.20–$3.35). Here are a few rules of thumb to consider before riding taxis in Budapest:

There are several **fleet companies** with good reputations in Budapest. These fleets have honest drivers and competitive rates. The most recommended company is **Fő Taxi** (tel. 122-2222). Other reliable fleets include: **Volántaxi** (tel. 166-6666); **Tele 5** (tel. 155-5555); **Gábriel Taxi** (tel. 155-5000); **Palota Taxi** (tel. 164-5722); **City Taxi** (tel. 153-3633); **Budataxi** (tel. 120-0200); and **Intertaxi** (tel. 180-4040).

If someone at a hotel or restaurant offers to call you a taxi, ask for one of these companies; it is your right to decide which company to use.

Many **private drivers** are undoubtedly honest, but your best bet is to avoid them altogether. Be especially wary of drivers known to Hungarians as "hyenas." They hang around at the airports and tourist sites. Their tricks include fast meters, meters with unusually high base rates, and return-trip surcharges. Don't pay in hard currency. A driver who asks to be paid in anything but Forints is most likely a dishonest driver. And avoid flat rates, any driver who offers you a flat rate is most likely naming a price well above the one that the meter would register.

Tipping is usually around 10%. But, it is important to note, you have no obligation to give a tip: If you feel cheated by the driver, then don't tip.

Though most people call for a taxi or pick one up at a taxi stand, it is possible to **hail** one on the street. The risk is that an undesirable one will stop for you. It is your right to wave him on if he is not a fleet cab.

At **taxi stands** in Budapest, the customer has the right to choose with whom to do business; look for a cab from one of the recommended fleets, even if it is at the back of the line.

All these warnings notwithstanding, you'll find the majority of the fleet drivers to be polite, honest, and pleasant. Some even speak a little English and enjoy chatting with passengers and pointing out sights.

BY CAR

RENTALS There is no reason to use a car for sightseeing in Budapest. You may, however, wish to rent a car for trips out of the city. Although Hertz, Avis, and Budget offices can be found in town and at the airports, much better deals can be had from local companies. A 25% VAT tax is charged for all car rentals in Hungary. The tax is not included in the rates quoted by companies, nor is it included in the rates listed below. You are urged to reserve a rental car as early as possible. If you reserve from abroad by fax, ask for written confirmation. If you don't receive confirmation, its wise to assume the reservation has not been made.

We have quoted rates for the cheapest car currently listed by each of these recommended agencies. All agencies list their prices in U.S. dollars.

V.I.P., with offices at Ferihegy I (tel. 157-8392) and Novotel (tel. 166-7466, fax 166-5636), offers a Lada 2107 for $15 per day ($90 per week), plus 15¢ per kilometer. **X-Car,** with offices at Ferihegy I (tel. 157-8670, fax 127-1969) and Ferihegy II (tel. 157-8680, fax 127-1969), offers the Toyota Starlet for $17 per day ($104 per week), plus 17¢ per kilometer. **LRI Airport Rent-A-Car,** at Ferihegy II (tel./fax 157-7170), offers the Volkswagen Polo for $22 per day, ($132 per week), plus 22¢ per kilometer.

PARKING Parking is very difficult in central Pest and parts of central Buda, but no problem elsewhere in the city. You'll notice that people park anywhere—on the sidewalk, in crosswalks, etc. Parking regulations are not regularly enforced, but cars do get towed on occasion (to Szent István Park). If your car has been towed, call 157-2811. On many central streets a *fizető* sign indicates that there is a fee for parking in that area. The fee is collected by the agent who approaches you as you park. Some neighborhoods, notably Buda's Castle District, allow vehicular access only to cars with special resident permits.

DRIVING REGULATIONS Hungarian police impose on-the-spot fines for driving violations. The speed limit in Hungary is 50 kmph in built-up areas; 80 kmph on main roads; and 120 kmph on motorways. Safety belts must be worn in the front seat and, when available, in the back seat; children under 6 may not sit in the front seat. Horns may not be used in built-up areas, except in emergency. Drunken driving laws are strictly enforced; any alcohol content in the driver's blood is illegal.

Cars are required to have in them at all times a first aid kit and a reflective warning triangle. A decal indicating country of registration is also required. These items should be included in all rental cars. If you are driving a rental car from another country, make sure you have the so called "Green Card" (proof of international insurance), not automatically given by all rental agencies. Hungarian police set up random checkpoints, where cars are pulled over and drivers made to present their papers. It's totally arbitrary, and makes some people nervous, but if all your papers are in order you'll have no trouble.

BREAKDOWN SERVICES   The **Magyar Autóklub** has a 24-hour emergency breakdown service; in Budapest, call 169-1831 or 169-3714. A private company, **Budasegély,** also provides break-down assistance; in Budapest, call 188-6201 or 180-3996.

BY BICYCLE

Budapest is not a city that lends itself to bicycle riding, and very few bikers are in evidence. Bicycles are nonetheless available for rent on Margaret Island and from a few bicycle shops in the city. Ask at Tourinform for a list of the shops; also ask for the free *Cycling Tours in Hungary* pamphlet. One of the best deals in Hungary, about which few foreigners know, is the MÁV (Hungarian State Railways) bike rentals; bikes are available for a pittance at 19 train stations in scenic areas of Hungary (Budapest not included). The price is 270 Ft ($3) for one day; 360 Ft ($4) for two days; and 420 Ft ($4.65) for three days. Ask at Tourinform about how to book a bicycle.

FAST FACTS: BUDAPEST

American Express   Hungary's only American Express office is between Vörösmarty tér and Deák tér in central Pest, at V. Deák Ferenc u. 10, 1052 Budapest (tel. 266-8680, fax 251-5220, telex 22-2124). All American Express travel services are provided—client mail, money exchange, ticketing, traveler's check and credit card replacement. Hours are weekdays from 9am to 6pm, Saturday from 9am to 1pm. There is an express cash ATM on the street in front. The 24-hour emergency telephone number is in London: dial U.K. Direct at 00 (wait for tone) 800-44011 for a British operator. The American Express number is then (00-44) 273/675975 for lost traveler's checks or (00-44) 273/696933 for lost credit cards; you can reverse the charges.

Area Code   The country code for Hungary is 36; the city code for Budapest is 1.

Babysitters   There are no organized babysitter services. Ask at your hotel.

Bookstores   See "Bookstores" in Chapter 8 for stores selling English-language books.

Business Hours   Most stores are open from 10am to 6pm

on weekdays, and 9 or 10am to 1 or 2pm on Saturday. Many shops close for an hour at lunchtime, and almost all stores are closed on Sunday. On weekdays, food stores open early, at around 6 or 7am, and close at around 6pm. A few grocery stores, called "non-stops," are open 24 hours; there is a non-stop in Nyugati Station. Banks are usually open weekdays 8am to noon and 1pm to 3pm. The hours of private currency-exchange booths vary greatly, but those in hotels and travel agencies are generally open weekdays 8am to 6pm and weekends 8am to 1pm. Museums in Budapest are usually open Tuesday through Sunday, 10am to 6pm.

Car Rental   Local companies offer much better deals than Avis, Budget, or Hertz; see "Getting Around," above.

Crime   By Western standards, Budapest is a very safe city. Nevertheless, tourists are always prime targets. While muggings and violent attacks are almost unheard of, there are skilled pickpockets operating mainly on crowded buses, trams, and metros. Be particularly careful on bus 26 (Margaret Island), and trams 4 and 6. One way to avoid being victimized is by wearing a money belt instead of carrying a wallet or purse. Sadly, non-white people need to be wary of racist gangs, who, though small in number, have made some highly publicized attacks in the past few years. Their crimes are usually committed late at night.

Doctors & Dentists   IMS, a private outpatient clinic at XIII. Váci út 202 (tel. 129-8423), has English-speaking doctors, and is used by many foreigners living in Budapest; it is reached via the Blue metro line (Gyöngyös utca). You might also contact your embassy for recommendations. Many luxury hotels have a staff dentist or a private dentist with rented office space.

Electricity   Hungarian electrical current is 220 volts, AC. If you plan to bring any North American electrical appliances, you'll need both a 110–220 volt transformer/converter (built into the adapters of some appliances), and a small adapter to fit North American flat plugs into the round holes in the wall.

Embassies   U.S. Embassy: V. Szabadság tér 12 (tel. 112-6450). **U.K. Embassy:** V. Harmincad u. 6 (tel. 118-2888). **Canadian Embassy:** XII. Budakeszi út 32 (tel. 176-7711). **Australian Embassy:** VI, Délibáb u. 30 (tel. 153-4233). New Zealand and Ireland do not yet have representation in Hungary.

Emergencies   Dial 04 for ambulance; 05 for the fire department; 07 for police.

Etiquette   Though Hungarians are not always polite, they do take their old-fashioned Middle European system of etiquette quite seriously. Some basic rules: On public transit, always give up your seat to an elderly person or a pregnant woman; men always hold doors open for women, except when entering restaurants or other public places, where men enter first; women always order first in restaurants and are always served first. While you may find some of these rules a bit backward, you may be considered rude by Hungarians if you don't abide by them.

Eyeglasses   *Optika* is the Hungarian name for an optometrist's shop; Pest's Outer Ring Boulevard (Nagykörút) would be a good place to search one out. The word for eyeglasses is *szemüveg*.

Fax/Telex Faxes and telexes can be sent from the main telephone office, on Petőfi Sándor u. 17 (near Deák tér). It is open weekdays from 8am to 8pm, weekends from 9am to 3pm. A one-page fax to the U.S. costs 583 Ft ($6.45); two pages cost 922 Ft ($10.25). Downtown luxury hotels may also have fax services.

Hairdressers & Barbers *Fodrász* is the word for barber. *Női fodrász* is a women's hairdresser, while *férfi fodrász* is a men's. Hungarians make appointments the day before a haircut. You can try getting a haircut on the spot, or make an appointment and come back. Haircuts are very cheap outside of the main tourist areas, usually in the 150–450 Ft ($1.65–$5) range (plus 10% tip). Most barbers don't speak English, but rudimentary communication is never too difficult.

Hospital Szent János Kórház, XII Diós árok 1 (tel. 156-1122).

Language Hungarian (*Magyar*), a member of the Finno-Ugric family of languages, is unrelated to any of the languages of Hungary's neighboring countries. By and large, Hungarians know how obscure their language is and welcome and encourage any attempts made by foreigners to communicate. Almost all Hungarians have studied Russian, though many pretend not to understand it. Many Hungarians speak German, and a steadily increasing percentage speak English. In Budapest, most people involved in tourism speak at least a little English.

Colloquial Hungarian (Routledge, Chapman, Hall) is a good phrase book and comes with a cassette.

Laundry & Drycleaning Your best bet is to ask at your hotel or pension. Private room hosts are usually happy to make a little extra money doing laundry. Self-service laundromats (*patyolat*) are scarce in Budapest. *Budapest Week* occasionally publishes a list of laundromats. Dry cleaning is available only at luxury hotels.

Libraries The United States Information Service (USIS) has a public reading room at VI. Bajza u. 31 (tel. 142-4122), off Andrássy út (take the Yellow metro line to Bajza utca). There are periodicals, books, and videos. Open hours are weekdays from 11am to 5pm (until 7pm on Tuesday). The British Council library is at VII. Benczúr u. 26 (tel. 118-2888). It's open Monday to Thursday 11am to 6pm, Friday 11am to 5pm, and Saturday 9:30am to noon.

Lost Property The BKV (Budapest Transportation Authority) lost and found office is at VII. Akácfa u. 18 (tel. 122-6613). For items lost at Ferihegy I, call 147-2784 or 157-7690; for Ferihegy II, call 157-8381 or 157-8108. For items lost on a train or in a train station, call 129-8037. For items lost on an intercity bus (not on a local BKV bus), call 118-2122. And for items lost in a taxi, try 134-3199.

Luggage Repair Strikingly cheap in Hungary, luggage and handbag repair is done at any workshop called *Táska javítás*. Try Divat-Kellék, at Kálvin tér 2 (tel. 217-7736), near the Kálvin tér metro station (Blue line). Open weekdays 1 to 4pm.

Luggage Storage   There are left-luggage offices at all three major railroad stations. At Keleti, near the head of track 5, open 24 hours; at Nyugati, near the head of track 10, open 24 hours; and at Déli, behind the station on the street level, open 5am to midnight. The cost is 80 Ft (90¢) per day. There are also self-storage lockers in Keleti and Nyugati stations for 40 Ft (45¢) per day. The Erzsébet tér bus station, near Deák tér in central Pest, has a left-luggage office, charging only 25 Ft (30¢) per bag; it's open 6am to 6pm daily.

Mail/Post Office   Mail can be received by clients at American Express (see above); a single traveler's check is sufficient to prove you are a client. Others can receive mail c/o Poste Restante, Magyar Posta, Petőfi Sándor u. 17-19, 1052 Budapest, Hungary. This confusing office (open 8am to 8pm weekdays and 8am to 3pm Saturday), not far from Deák tér (all metro lines), is the city's main post office. There are 24-hour post offices near Keleti and Nyugati stations.

Postal rates in Hungary have risen above the rate of inflation. At press time, they had almost equalled Western levels: airmail postcard, 35 Ft (39¢); airmail letter, 50 Ft (55¢) and up. The rate for letters mailed within Budapest to a Budapest address is 10 Ft (postcards, 7 Ft), and for letters mailed to other parts of Hungary the rate is 17 Ft (postcards, 10 Ft).

Maps   Cartografia, a Hungarian company, produces good maps of Budapest. See "Orientation," earlier in this chapter for more information.

Money   See "Information, Entry Requirements, and Money," in Chapter 2.

Names   Hungarians write their names with the family name first, followed by the Christian name. When mentioning Hungarian names in this book we have employed the more common form of Christian name followed by family name. The only exception is with street names, where we have used the Hungarian style: hence Ferenc Deák, the man, but Deák Ferenc utca, the street.

Newspapers & Magazines   The *International Herald Tribune, USA Today,* the *Guardian,* the *Financial Times,* the *Times of London,* the *European, Newsweek,* and *Time* are all commonly found in luxury hotels and at newsstands, kiosks, and bookstores in the neighborhood around Váci utca. Look also for *Budapest Week* and the *Budapest Sun,* two English-language weeklies published in Budapest that are indispensable for the tourist (for subscription information in the United States tel. toll free 800/775-0578 for the *Budapest Sun,* and 800/878-5113 for *Budapest Week*). In addition to articles on current events and politics in Hungary, both papers provide weekly listings of theater, movies, exhibitions, and special events, and dozens of useful addresses. *The Daily News,* a small, somewhat dry paper published by the Hungarian News Agency, consists of English-language translations of Hungarian news articles and brief wire-service reports.

Pharmacies   The Hungarian word is *gyógyszertár,* or occasionally, *patika.* Generally, pharmacies carry only prescription drugs.

Some hotels advertise "drugstores"; these are really just shops with soap, perfume, aspirin, and other non-prescription items. There are a number of 24-hour pharmacies in the city—every pharmacy posts the address of the nearest one in its window. *Budapest Week* also lists the 24-hour pharmacies from time to time.

Photographic Needs Two successful private chains, Fotex and Sooters, have stores throughout Budapest and the country. They can meet all your normal photographic needs. The price of film is about the same as in the West.

Police The emergency police number is 07. You may not get an English speaker. For any other matters which require police attention, ask at Tourinform. They'll give you the appropriate number or address.

Radio Radio Bridge, at 102.1 FM, broadcasts Voice of America news bulletins in English every hour. Budapest Day & Night, a daily 30-minute news program in English with segments from National Public Radio (NPR), is broadcast on Radio Bridge at 8am and 8pm. If you have a short-wave radio, you can pick up the BBC, Voice of America, Radio Moscow, and other English-language stations.

Religious Services Both *Programme in Hungary* and *Panorama,* available at Tourinform and most hotels, list English-language religious services in Budapest.

Restrooms The word for toilet in Hungarian is *WC* (pronounced VAY-tsay). *Nöi* means women's; *férfi* means men's. Public facilities in Budapest are entirely inadequate. When you manage to find one, it will usually be rather unpleasant. You are advised to carry your own stash of toilet paper. Many tourists now regularly use the city's numerous McDonald's restaurants, which have free, delightfully clean, and well-stocked (i.e. paper) bathrooms. Management does not seem to mind, as this usage can only bring in more customers and improve public relations. Most McDonald's are open daily 7am to midnight in summer, to 11pm the rest of the year. Budapest's three Burger Kings can be utilized in similar fashion. There is also a clean, free bathroom in the lobby of the International Trade Center, in the heart of Pest, at Váci utca 19-21.

In many restaurants, theaters, and other public places you'll find an attendant parked outside the bathroom door. All users are required to pay a fee, usually no more than 5 Ft (5¢). If there is a plate outside the door but no attendant, it is up to you whether or not to make a donation.

Safety See "Crime," above.

Shoe Repair The Hungarian word is *cipész*. Like other labor-intensive services, shoe repair is very cheap in Hungary. There is scarcely a neighborhood in the city without a cipész. Ask your hotel reception for the nearest one.

Smoking The anti-smoking crusade has not yet reached Hungary, the land of harsh tobacco. Nevertheless, smoking is forbidden in many public places (including all public transport). *Dohányzás tilos* or *Dohányozni tilos* means "No Smoking."

Taxes   Taxes are included in all restaurant prices, hotel rates, and shop purchases. A 25% VAT tax is added to all car rentals.

Telephone   The Hungarian phone system is old and rickety; for best results, be patient and always dial slowly. The easiest way to call the United States or Canada is through **AT&T** or **MCI.** You can access the international operator from most public phones, though older phones are less reliable; a 20-Ft coin is required, but is returned after the call. The AT&T operator is reached at 00/360111; the MCI operator at 00/800-01411. You can bill calls to your account, or call collect. If you have an MCI card, you can call any country served by MCI, but calls to countries outside of North America are very expensive.

Other **country direct** access numbers connect you to operators in the country you are calling, with whom you can arrange your preferred billing. Australia Direct is 00/366111; Canada Direct is 00/361111; New Zealand Direct is 00/800 06411; and U.K. Direct is 00/800 44011.

You can also use **direct dial;** Hungarian telephone books list the numbers of all countries which can be directly dialed. Direct dial to the United States and Canada is 00/1 (150 Ft/$1.65 per minute), to the U.K. 00/44 (60 Ft/65¢ per minute), to Australia 00/61 (180 Ft/$2 per minute), and to Ireland 00/353 (60 Ft/65¢ per minute). A few Eastern European countries cannot be called by direct dial, and should be accessed from the post office. You can also call 1/118-6977 for information on international direct-dial calls, or 1/117-2200 for general information.

The **area code** for Budapest is 1, and all phone numbers in Budapest have seven digits, almost always starting with 1 or 2. All other towns in Hungary have a two-digit area code and six-digit telephone numbers. The only exceptions are tiny towns, where manual ("crossbar") switchboards are still in use. You must call the town operator in those cases, and he or she will put your call through. To make a call from one area code to another, first dial 06; when you hear a second dial tone, dial the area code and number. Remember, dial slowly.

Payphones charge 5 Ft (6¢) for a 3-minute local call, and 5 Ft for every additional 3 minutes. The same 3-minute call to a neighboring area code costs 15 Ft (17¢), and to all other area codes in Hungary 20 Ft (22¢). Payphones accept 5-, 10-, and 20-Ft coins and do not give change.

The **main telephone office** on Petőfi Sándor u. 17 (near Deák tér), is open weekdays 8am to 8pm, and weekends 9am to 3pm. Telephone calls, as well as faxes and telexes, can be made to anywhere in the world. It costs 150 Ft ($1.65) per minute to call the United States from this office. Hotels typically add a surcharge to all calls (although some allow unlimited free local calls), so you are advised to use public telephone booths (often found in hotel lobbies) or the post office.

Time   Hungary is on Central European Time, 2 hours ahead of GMT and 6 hours ahead of EST from 26 March to 26 September;

from 27 September to 25 March, the difference is 1 hour and 5 hours respectively.

Tipping Tipping is generally 10%. Among those who welcome tips are waiters, taxi drivers, hotel employees, barbers, cloakroom attendants, toilet attendants, masseuses, and tour guides.

Transit Information The BKV (Budapest Transportation Authority) number for lost property on public transportation is 122-6613. For other information your best bet is to call Tourinform (tel. 117-9800).

TV Many hotels and pensions offer satellite TV channels, including CNN, BBC, Super Channel, Euro-sport, and Sky.

Watch Repair Watch repair, like other labor intensive trades, is very cheap in Hungary. If your watch stops, or you just want a tune-up, look for an *órás* or *óra javítás* shop; they are found throughout Budapest.

Water Tap water in Budapest is generally considered safe for drinking. Mineral water, which many Hungarians prefer to tap water, is called *ásványvíz*.

3. NETWORKS & RESOURCES

FOR STUDENTS Express, the former state-run student travel agency, remains a valuable resource for students. In addition to selling the ISIC and IYHF cards (bring a photo), they offer discount travel fares for students and youths under 26. The main office of Express is located at V. Szabadság tér 16 (tel. 131-7777 or 111-1430). Hours are Monday through Thursday 9am to 5pm (Tuesday closing at 4pm), and Friday 9am to 2pm.

FOR GAY MEN & LESBIANS The Gay Students' Group, which consists mostly of men, meets every other Monday evening at Decentrum (XIII. Forgách u. 18, tel. 120-8440), a former trade union office now used as a kind of alternative community center. **The Lesbian Group** also meets at Decentrum, on Friday evenings. A number of group members (from both groups) speak English, and there is usually someone around answering the telephone. Forgách utca is a station of the Blue metro line.

FOR WOMEN The Feminist Network also uses Decentrum (XIII. Forgách u. 18, tel. 120-8440) as its base. Meetings are held on Tuesday evenings.

CHAPTER 4

WHERE TO STAY IN BUDAPEST

- **FROMMER'S SMART TRAVELER: HOTELS**
1. **VERY EXPENSIVE**
2. **EXPENSIVE**
3. **MODERATE**
- **FROMMER'S COOL FOR KIDS: HOTELS**
4. **INEXPENSIVE**
5. **PENSION ACCOMMODATIONS**
6. **PRIVATE ROOM ACCOMMODATIONS**
7. **YOUTH HOSTEL ACCOMMODATIONS**

Budapest hotels range from beautiful, historic turn-of-the-century gems to drab, utilitarian establishments typical of the city's socialist period. Although the most notable establishments—among them the stunning art nouveau Hotel Gellért and the city's other "thermal" hotels, the historic Palace Hotel (currently under renovation) and Hotel Béke, and Castle Hill's distinctive Hilton Hotel—are the city's priciest, accommodation rates in Budapest are some of the lowest of any major European city. Rooms in these top hotels cost no more than moderately priced accommodations in other European capitals, making Budapest a great place to splurge.

Despite the number of new hotels and pensions which have opened in recent years, Budapest retains its reputation as a city without enough guest beds. Indeed, in high season, it can be quite difficult to secure a hotel or pension room or hostel bed (although private rooms are always available), so make reservations and get written confirmation well ahead if possible. See "Sources of Information" in Chapter 2 for addresses and telephone numbers of organizations in North America and Britain that can help you make reservations before your trip.

When booking keep in mind that if you want a double-bedded room it should be specifically requested; otherwise you will get a room with two twin beds. Note also that Hungarian hotels use the word "apartment" to describe the kind of room we call a "suite" (i.e. connected rooms, without a kitchen). In these listings, we have called a suite a suite, so to speak.

BUDGET LODGINGS There is unfortunately a dearth of recommendable budget hotels in Budapest, but travelers can take advantage of the wealth of good alternative accommodations. Small pensions, rooms in private homes, and a number of good youth hostels, all listed in separate sections below, make the city inviting to travelers on any budget. Remember that location plays a significant role in cost, with inflated prices for centrally located accommodations the norm. Budapest's efficient public transportation means that reaching downtown from points outside will not be as difficult as you might expect;

**FROMMER'S SMART TRAVELER:
HOTELS**

1. Private rooms provide the best bargains in Budapest.
2. Most hotels have lower rates in the off-season; some reduce as much as 50%.
3. Pensions in the Buda Hills are far cheaper than downtown hotel rooms; what's more, the air is cleaner and most of them have lovely gardens.

QUESTIONS TO ASK IF YOU'RE ON A BUDGET

1. Is there a surcharge on telephone calls? Some hotels allow unlimited free local calls.
2. Is breakfast included?
3. Is parking free? Most downtown hotels charge for garage use, some as much as $15 per night.

if you are on a budget, consider staying outside the center in a room removed from the din and smog of inner Pest.

ACCOMMODATION AGENCIES Most accommodation agencies can secure private room rentals, help reserve hotel and pension rooms, and book you into a youth hostel. The most established agencies are the former state-owned travel agents Ibusz, Cooptourist, MÁV Tours, and Budapest Tourist. Although newer, private agencies have proliferated, the older ones tend to have the greatest number of rooms listed. There are agencies in both airports, all three major train stations, throughout central Pest, and along the main roads into Budapest for travelers arriving by car. The main Ibusz reservations office, at Petőfi tér 1 (tel. 118-5707 or 118-4842, fax 117-9099), is the only tourist agency in Hungary open 24 hours. It is located near the Intercontinental Hotel, a short walk from Deák tér (reached by all three metro lines), and they accept all major credit cards.

Be aware that tourists have reported agents urging them to take a more expensive room than they wanted. Stick to your guns; the agent will eventually help you reserve a room where you want it.

SEASONS Most hotels and pensions in Budapest divide the year into three seasons. **High season** is roughly from March or April through September or October. The week between Christmas and New Year's, Easter week, the period of the Budapest Spring Festival, and the weekend of the Grand Prix (second weekend in August) are also considered high season. **Mid season** is roughly March and October and/or November. **Low season** is roughly November through February, except Christmas week. Some hotels discount as much as 50% in low season (others offer no discount), so if you are traveling to Budapest during this season you might scan the more expensive hotel listings to see if there is a good winter deal.

PRICE CATEGORIES Many hotels and pensions in Budapest list their prices in German Marks (DM) and a few list them in U.S. dollars. This is done as a hedge against Forint inflation; all hotels in Budapest accept payment in Hungarian Forints as well as hard currencies.

In the following sections, hotels are separated into four price categories: **Very Expensive,** over $120 (DM 192/10,800 Ft); **Expensive,** $65–$120 (DM 104–192/5,850–10,800 Ft); **Moderate,** $40–$65 (DM 64–104/3,600–5,850 Ft); and **Inexpensive,** under $40 (DM 64/3,600 Ft).

Hotels in Hungary are rated by the international star system. The ratings, however, are somewhat arbitrary and are not included in our entries for that reason. (Note that a new law requires five-star hotels to charge a 25% VAT; this tax is calculated into the rates we quote if relevant.)

1. VERY EXPENSIVE

THE INNER CITY & CENTRAL PEST

FÓRUM HOTEL, V. Apáczai Csere J. u. 12-14, 1052 Budapest. Tel. 117-8088. Fax 117-9808. 408 rms (with bath). TV TEL MINIBAR A/C **Metro:** Deák tér (all lines).

$ Rates (including breakfast): DM 320 ($200) single, streetside; DM 360 ($225) single, riverside; DM 380 ($237.50) double, streetside; DM 420 ($262.50) double, riverside; DM 500–700 ($312.50–$437.50) suite; DM 70 ($43.75) extra bed. Rates 20% lower in low season. AE, DC, MC, V. **Parking:** 1,000 Ft ($11.10) per day.

Some aficionados consider the Fórum, a HungarHotel, the finest hotel in town. Built in 1981, the Fórum has some 285 rooms overlooking the Danube, with spectacular views of the Chain Bridge and Castle Hill. The rooms, decorated with contemporary Hungarian artworks, are plush and luxurious, without the depressing, claustrophobic feeling found in some of Budapest's modern hotels. There is a safe in every room. The bathrooms have a wide selection of toiletries in addition to built-in hairdryers and bathrobes for the guests. The Fórum offers video message retrieval and video check-out, accessed from the TV in your room.

Dining/Entertainment: László György, one of Budapest's better-known chefs, prepares international/Hungarian cuisine in the elegant Silhouette Restaurant. There is piano music nightly, and outdoor dining is possible on Pest's famous Dunacorso (Danube promenade). The Fórum Grill is a more modest place, suitable for lunch. The Viennese-style Wiener Kaffeehaus is said by some to offer the best pastries in Budapest. There is also a bar in the lobby.

Alba Hotel Budapest 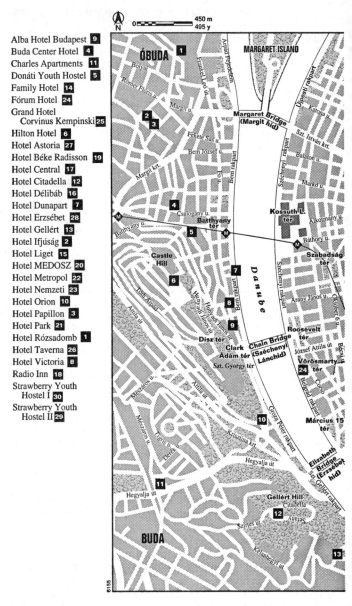9
Buda Center Hotel 4
Charles Apartments 11
Donáti Youth Hostel 5
Family Hotel 14
Fórum Hotel 24
Grand Hotel
  Corvinus Kempinski 25
Hilton Hotel 6
Hotel Astoria 27
Hotel Béke Radisson 19
Hotel Central 17
Hotel Citadella 12
Hotel Délibáb 16
Hotel Dunapart 7
Hotel Erzsébet 28
Hotel Gellért 13
Hotel Ifjúság 2
Hotel Liget 15
Hotel MEDOSZ 20
Hotel Metropol 22
Hotel Nemzeti 23
Hotel Orion 10
Hotel Papillon 3
Hotel Park 21
Hotel Rózsadomb 1
Hotel Taverna 26
Hotel Victoria 8
Radio Inn 18
Strawberry Youth
  Hostel I 30
Strawberry Youth
  Hostel II 29

Facilities/Services: 24-hour room service, laundry, sound-proof windows, non-smoking and handicapped rooms, business center, barber shop, hairdresser, drugstore, safe-deposit boxes, fitness center, swimming pool, sauna, massage, solarium, conference facilities.

GRAND HOTEL CORVINUS KEMPINSKI, V. Erzsébet tér

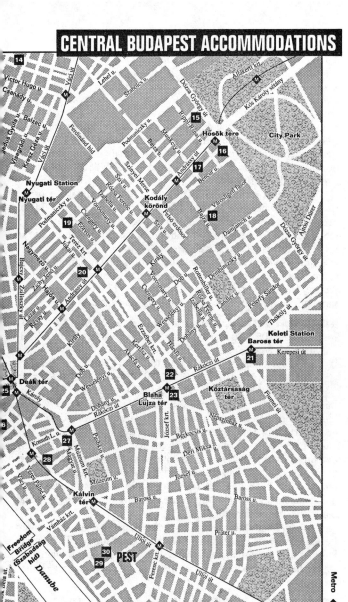

CENTRAL BUDAPEST ACCOMMODATIONS

7-8, 1051 Budapest Tel. 266-1000. Fax 266-2000. 368 rms (with bath). A/C TV TEL **Metro:** Deák tér (all lines).

$ Rates: DM 310–390 ($193.75–$243.75) single; DM 390–470 ($243.75–$293.75) double; DM 80 ($50) extra bed; DM 550–1,790 ($343.75–$1,118.75) suite. Breakfast costs DM 27 ($16.90). Rates 15% lower in low season. AE, DC, MC, V. **Parking:** DM 20 ($12.50) per day.

The Kempinski, opened in 1993, is Budapest's newest luxury hotel. It is located in the heart of Pest, just off Deák tér. A member of a well known German chain and under German management, it is gaining a reputation as the hotel of choice for corporate visitors to Budapest; the staff is already known for efficiency and politeness. The rooms are as luxurious as any in the city, and soundproof windows shield you from the noise of the busy traffic below. Children under 12 can stay free in their parents' room. The Kempinski chain maintains reservations numbers in Britain (tel. toll free 0-800/89-8588) and North America (tel. toll free 800/426-3135).

Dining/Entertainment: The hotel's Bistro Jardin is a gourmet restaurant serving international cuisine. Pub V offers four kinds of beer on draft; there is also an informal coffee shop in the hotel and a lobby bar. The American-style buffet breakfast (not included in the room price) has received rave reviews.

Facilities/Services: Swimming pool, sauna, solarium, fitness room, massage, business center, conference facilities, 24-hour room service, laundry and dry cleaning, newsstand, beauty parlor, barber shop, gift shop, boutiques, car rental, travel agency.

HOTEL ASTORIA, V. Kossuth Lajos u. 19. Tel. 117-3411. Telex 22-4205. 130 rms (half with bath, half with shower). TV TEL MINIBAR **Metro:** Astoria (Red line).

$ Rates (including breakfast): DM 167 ($104.35) single; DM 217 ($135.60) double; DM 265 ($165.65) triple. Rates 25% lower in low season. AE, DC, MC, V. **Parking:** Unavailable.

Built in the early years of the 20th century, the centrally located Hotel Astoria has a stormy history. In 1918 it served for a time as the headquarters of the Hungarian National Council. Hungary's first independent post–World War I government was declared from the hotel. During the 1956 Hungarian uprising it served as headquarters of the occupying Soviet army and suffered heavy damage. Completely renovated in 1986, the Astoria now recalls a bygone Budapest of quiet, stately luxury. The rooms are spacious and comfortable and most have period furniture.

Dining/Entertainment: The newly renovated Amstel Garden Restaurant serves Hungarian and International cuisine. The Amstel Pub has a more casual atmosphere. The hotel also has a nightclub.

Facilities/Services: Room service, car-rental agency, fitness center, sauna.

HOTEL BÉKE RADISSON, VI. Teréz krt. 43, 1067 Budapest. Tel. 132-3300. Fax 153-3380. 231 rms, 7 suites. TV TEL MINIBAR A/C **Metro:** Nyugati pu. (Blue line) or Oktogon (Yellow line).

$ Rates (including breakfast): DM 220–290 ($137.50–$181.25) single; DM 270–340 ($168.75–$212.50) double; DM 500 ($312.50) suite; DM 50 ($31.25) extra bed. Rates 25%–50% lower in low season. AE, DC, MC, V. **Parking:** 700 Ft ($7.75) per day.

★ The Béke Radisson, excellently situated on Pest's Outer Ring (Nagykörút), carries on a long tradition. In 1913 the Hotel Brittania opened on the same spot. It was an art nouveau gem and one of the most modern Budapest hotels of its time. Unfortunately, it was badly damaged in World War II, and it was not until 1955 that it was reopened under the name Béke (Peace). The hotel underwent renovations again in the 1980s and reopened in 1985 after a reconstruction notable for the respect it payed to the hotel's original design. The lobby is gracious and elegant (although who can say what effect the hotel's new casino will have), and rooms are neatly furnished in dark wood. Each room has a safe, and bathrooms have built-in hairdryers. Unfortunately, sound-proof windows do not muffle all the noise from the busy boulevard below. Non-smoking rooms and handicapped rooms are available.

Dining/Entertainment: The Shakespeare Restaurant serves breakfast and lunch. A bright, cheerful place, it is lit by a skylight, and features the Shakespearean frescoes of Jenő Haranghy, preserved from the original Hotel Brittania. The elegant Szondi Restaurant (named after a Hungarian hero who fought the Turks) serves Hungarian/International dinners accompanied by Gypsy music. The restaurant is decorated with Turkish weaponry and frescoes and stained-glass windows (also from the original hotel) depicting battle scenes and other scenes from Szondi's life. László Héjja, the chef, has an excellent reputation. In the Zsolnay Cafe, delicious pastries are served on hand-painted Zsolnay porcelain. The decor here is also carefully chosen, and pays respect to the original hotel: Venetian mirrors, chandeliers, a grand piano. The hotel recently opened the Casino Orfeum, just off the lobby.

Facilities/Services: Swimming pool, sauna, massage, solarium, business center, fitness center, drug store, gift shop, laundry and dry cleaning, Ibusz desk.

HOTEL ERZSÉBET, V. Károlyi Mihály u. 11-15, 1053 Budapest. Tel. 138-2111. Fax 118-9237. 123 rms (with bath). TV TEL A/C **Metro:** Ferenciek tere (Blue line).

$ Rates (including breakfast): DM 170 ($106.25) single; DM 200 ($125) double. Rates 20% lower in low season. AE, DC, MC, V.

Parking: Available for a fee in neighborhood garage.

The Erzsébet Hotel was originally built in 1872, when its namesake was queen of Austria-Hungary. The present hotel, a HungarHotel, is the result of a total reconstruction in 1985. Its central Pest location is excellent, just a few minutes by foot from Váci utca. The hotel has fewer facilities than most in this category, but it is also substantially cheaper, barely missing out on being classified as only "expensive." Rooms are fine, with all the standard features of a hotel in this category. If you want a modern, centrally located hotel at lower prices, this might be the place for you.

Dining/Entertainment: The János Pince is a Hungarian wine-cellar restaurant, and there is also a bar in the hotel.

Facilities/Services: Gift shop, banquet hall, garden, car rental, laundry, Ibusz desk.

HOTEL TAVERNA, V. Váci u. 20, 1052 Budapest. Tel. 138-4999. Fax 118-7188. 224 rms (half with bath, half with shower). TV TEL MINIBAR **Metro:** Deák tér.

$ Rates (including breakfast): DM 156 ($97.50) single; DM 199 ($124.40) double; DM 352 ($220) suite; DM 48 ($30) extra bed. Rates 15% lower in low season. AE, DC, MC, V. **Parking:** DM 20 ($12.50) a day.

The Taverna's location simply cannot be beaten, on bustling Váci utca, just minutes away from Vörösmarty tér, Pest's tourist center. The hotel is recessed a bit off the street, and since Váci utca is a pedestrian street the noise level is somewhat lower than you might imagine. The lobby is small and without distinction. The rooms are modern and clean. Take a room here for the location.

Dining/Entertainment: You'll find the Taverna Restaurant, the DAB Brasserie, the Kronenbourg Bowling Bar, and a wine saloon in the hotel.

Facilities/Services: Room service, safe, Ibusz desk, tours and tickets arranged, bowling, sauna, fitness room, solarium, massage.

JUST BEYOND CENTRAL PEST

HOTEL LIGET, VI. Dózsa György út 106, 1068 Budapest. Tel. 111-3200 or 111-7050. Fax 131-7153. 139 rms (with bath). TV TEL MINIBAR **Metro:** Hősök tere (Yellow line).

$ Rates (including breakfast): DM 159 ($99.40) single; DM 196 ($122.50); DM 50 ($31.25) extra bed. Rooms with A/C are about 5% more. Rates 25% lower in low season. AE, MC, V. **Parking:** Free in lot; DM 12 ($7.50) per day in garage.

Although unabashedly modern and somewhat out of touch with the surrounding architecture, the Hotel Liget is well located just off Heroes' Square and across the street from the Fine Arts Museum and the City Zoo. The Yellow metro line whisks you into the center of town in no time at all. There is a small, fast-paced lobby with a bar and coffee shop. All common spaces of the hotel and 55 guest rooms (see price differences above) are air conditioned. The rooms are comfortable and modern, though somewhat unimaginatively furnished. The American Embassy is said to put up guests here.

Dining/Entertainment: Although the hotel does not have a restaurant, there is a breakfast room, a coffee bar, and a cocktail bar on the premises.

Facilities/Services: Sauna, massage, solarium, travel agency, nonsmoking floor.

CENTRAL BUDA & THE CASTLE DISTRICT

ALBA HOTEL BUDAPEST, I. Apor Péter u. 3, 1011 Budapest. Tel. 175-9244. Fax 175-9899. 95 rms (half with bath, half with shower). TV TEL MINIBAR **Bus:** Many buses run to Clark Ádám tér, including the 16 from Deák tér.

$ Rates (including breakfast): DM 180–220 ($112.50–$137.50) single; DM 230–270 ($143.75–$168.75) double; DM 65 ($40.65) extra bed. Rates 10% lower in low season. AE, DC, MC, V. **Parking:** DM 17 ($10.65) per day.

Opened in 1990, the Alba Hotel Budapest belongs to a Swiss chain, and the Swiss influence is pervasive—from the buffet breakfast which features a half dozen kinds of Muesli to the crisp angles of the antiseptically clean rooms. The hotel is nestled in a tiny cobblestoned alley directly beneath Buda Castle. It has seven floors, but only rooms on the top floor have views; the two best are 706, which has a view of the castle, and 707, which overlooks Matthias Church. Other seventh-floor rooms offer a pleasing vista of red Buda rooftops.

Dining/Entertainment: There is no restaurant in the hotel, but there is a bar in the lobby.

Facilities/Services: Laundry service offered.

HILTON HOTEL, I. Hess András tér 1-3, 1014 Budapest.
Tel. 175-1000. Fax 156-0285. 323 rms & suites (with bath). AC TV TEL MINIBAR **Bus:** "Várbusz" from Moszkva tér, 16 from Deák tér, 116 from Március 15 tér, or funicular from Clark Ádám tér.

$ Rates: DM 250–330 ($156.25–$206.25) single; DM 325–405 ($203.10–$253.10) double; DM 450–710 ($281.25–$443.75) suite; DM 75 ($46.85) extra bed. Buffet breakfast costs DM 27 ($16.90) per person. Rates are the same all year. AE, DC, MC, V. **Parking:** DM 20 ($12.50) in garage; possible on street.

The only hotel in Buda's elegant Castle District, the Hilton, built in 1977, is widely considered the city's finest hotel. Its location, on Hess András tér, next door to Mátyás Church and the Fisherman's Bastion, is no less than spectacular. The hotel's award-winning design incorporates both the ruins of a 13th-century Dominican church (the church tower rises above the hotel) and the baroque facade of a 17th-century Jesuit college (the hotel's main entrance). The ruins were carefully restored during the construction of the hotel; the results are uniformly magnificent. Although the building is clearly modern, its tasteful exterior blends in well with the surrounding Castle District architecture. The more expensive rooms have views over the Danube, with a full Pest skyline, while rooms on the other side of the hotel have delightful views of the Castle District. All rooms are luxurious and well appointed, with complimentary bathrobes, built-in hairdryers, and loads of toiletries. Children stay free in a room with their parents.

Dining/Entertainment: The luxurious Dominican Restaurant has an international menu; dinner is accompanied by piano music. The colorful Kalocsa Restaurant has a Hungarian menu and nightly gypsy music. The Corvina Coffee Shop, off the lobby, is a more modestly priced place (with a good salad bar). The Margareeta Cafe, with outdoor tables behind the hotel by the Fisherman's Bastion, has coffee and pastries, in addition to afternoon barbecue lunches in the summertime. Drinks are served in the Faust Wine Cellar, the Codex Cocktail Bar, and the Lobby Bar. There is a casino in the hotel, and the lovely Dominican Courtyard is the site of summer concerts.

Facilities/Services: Business center, conference facilities, doctor/dentist on call, laundry, newsstand, free airport minibus, babysitter, room service, Malév desk, Ibusz desk, beauty salon, antiques shop, florist, photo shop, souvenir shop.

HOTEL DUNAPART, I. Szilágyi Dezső tér, Alsó rakpart, 1011 Budapest. Tel. 155-9001, 155-9201 or 155-9244. Fax 155-3770. 32 rms (with shower). TV TEL A/C **Metro:** Batthyány tér (Red line).

$ Rates (including breakfast): DM 120–150 ($75–$93.75) single facing the bank, DM 140–170 ($87.50–$106.25) single facing the river; DM 180 ($112.50) double facing the bank, DM 200 ($125) double facing the river; DM 220 ($137.50) suite for two or three people facing the bank, DM 240 ($150) suite for two or three people facing the river. Rates 25% lower in low season. AE, DC, MC, V. **Parking:** Free.

The Hotel Dunapart is a permanently moored boat, on the Buda side of the Danube just beneath the quiet Szilágyi Dezső Square. The cabins, though luxuriously outfitted, are smaller than rooms you would find in a comparably priced hotel. But if you don't mind the tight quarters, the Dunapart is a lovely place. It is definitely worth paying more for a room facing the river; without this view (which bank-side rooms lack) it hardly makes sense to sleep on a boat in Budapest. The suites have double beds. Sadly, the pleasures of river-side strolling, a favorite European pastime, are marred by the busy road which runs right alongside the river.

Dining/Entertainment: There is a bar and restaurant on board, the latter with an excellent reputation in Budapest. It's open noon to 11pm and offers a varied Hungarian menu that includes both fish and game specialties.

HOTEL GELLÉRT, XI. Gellért tér 1, 1111 Budapest. Tel. 185-2200 or 166-6867 (for reservations). Fax 166-6631. 239 rms (201 with bath, 38 with shower). TEL **Tram:** 47 or 49 from Deák tér.

$ Rates (including breakfast): DM 145–220 ($90.60–$137.50) single; DM 288–340 ($180–$212.50) double; DM 420 ($262.50) suite; DM 70 ($43.75) extra bed. Rates are the same all year. Spa package rates available. AE, DC, MC, V. **Parking:** Free.

First opened in 1918, this splendid, sprawling art nouveau hotel was most recently restored in 1970. It's a bit run-down now, but still one of the most elegant and charming hotels in Budapest. Located at the base of Gellért Hill in Buda, on the bank of the Danube, the Gellért is one of four thermal hotels in Budapest managed or owned by Danubius Hotels. While the majority of the guests do not come for the official spa treatment, there are a number of spa-related facilities which all guests can use free of charge: indoor swimming pool and outdoor swimming pool with waves; steam room; and the art nouveau Gellért Baths, perhaps the most popular of Budapest's thermal baths (most tourists visit them at least once during their stay).

The hotel lobby is circular with marble columns and a mezzanine level. The quality and size of the rooms vary greatly; if you choose to splurge for the Gellért, it may make sense to go for the higher priced rooms. Eighty percent of the rooms have TV and minibar, and some rooms have balconies. There are great views over the Danube from some rooms, though Gellért Square, in front of the hotel, is loud and busy.

Dining/Entertainment: The Duna Restaurant serves international/Hungarian cuisine; there is a nightly gypsy music and folklore program and terrace dining is possible. On the ground floor is the Söröző (beerhall), with a terrace; and the Coffeehouse, where delicious pastries are served, also with a terrace. There is a nightclub with live music nightly.

Facilities/Services: Spa facilities, laundry, gift shop, beauty salon/barber, babysitting, room service, newsstand, conference facilities, Malév desk, Ibusz desk, complimentary bathrobes.

HOTEL VICTORIA, I. Bem rakpart 11, 1011 Budapest. Tel. 201-8644. Fax 201-5816. 27 rms (18 with shower, 9 with bath). TV TEL MINIBAR A/C **Tram:** 19 from Batthyány tér to first stop.

$ Rates (including breakfast): DM 185 ($115.65) single; DM 195 ($121.90) double; DM 350 ($218.75) suite for two to four people; DM 60 ($50) extra bed for double room. Rates 25% lower in low season. AE, DC, MC, V. **Parking:** Free in garage.

⭐ The Hotel Victoria is separated from Buda's Danube bank only by the busy road which runs alongside the river. It is situated in a narrow building, with only three rooms on each of its nine floors. This design makes two-thirds of the rooms corner rooms with large double windows providing great views over the river to Pest's skyline beyond. Rooms are quite large and have spacious bathrooms. Middle rooms, though smaller than corner rooms, also have windows facing the river. Unfortunately, the busy road beneath your window may disturb your rest. The hotel is just minutes by foot from both Batthyány tér and Clark Ádám tér, with dozens of metro, tram, and bus connections.

Facilities/Services: Bar, sauna, 24-hour room service, safe, laundry.

MARGARET ISLAND

RAMADA GRAND HOTEL, XIII. Margitsziget, 1138 Budapest. Tel. 132-1100 or 111-1000. Fax 153-3029. 152 rms, 10 suites (with bath). TV TEL MINIBAR **Bus:** 26 from Nyugati pu.

$ Rates (including breakfast): DM 180–240 ($112.50–$150) single; DM 230–310 ($143.75–$193.75) double; DM 360–480 ($225–$300) suite for one or two people; DM 60 ($37.50) extra bed. Rates are the same all year. Spa package rates available. AE, DC, MC, V. **Parking:** DM 15 ($9.35) in garage; possible outside.

Situated on the northern tip of lovely Margaret Island, in the middle of the Danube, the Ramada Grand Hotel was originally built in 1873. Destroyed in World War II, it was restored and reopened in 1987. A Danubius Hotel, it is connected by an underground tunnel to the adjacent Thermal Hotel Margitsziget. While the majority of the guests do not come for the official spa treatment, a number of spa-related facilities of the Thermal Hotel can be used free of charge: swimming pool, sauna, thermal bath, and the "drinking cure." It's one of only two hotels on Margaret Island, Budapest's most popular park. Though two bridges connect the island with the rest of the city, vehicular traffic (except one city bus) is forbidden except for access to the hotels.

Dining/Entertainment: The Széchenyi Restaurant serves international/Hungarian cuisine; special dietetic dishes are offered and there is terrace dining. Other dining options include the Begonia Cafe Terrace, the Gösser Brasserie, the Eskimo Ice Salon, and the Victoria Drink Bar. Guests have access to Thermal Hotel Margitsziget's Thermal Star Night Club, with live shows nightly.

Facilities/Services: Free use of spa facilities in neighboring Thermal Hotel Margitsziget, laundry, safe, conference facilities, business center, souvenir shop, drug store, Ibusz desk, Danubius Travel Agency desk, room service, access to Thermal Hotel Margitsziget's barber/beauty salon.

2. EXPENSIVE

THE INNER CITY & CENTRAL PEST

HOTEL NEMZETI, VIII. József körút 4, 1088 Budapest. Tel. 133-9160 or 133-9169. Fax 114-0019. 76 rms (73 with bath, 3 with shower). TV TEL MINIBAR **Metro:** Blaha Lujza tér (Red line).

$ Rates (including breakfast): DM 140 ($87.50) single; DM 185 ($116.25) double; DM 35 ($21.90) extra bed. Rates 50% lower in low season. AE, DC, MC, V. **Parking:** Available for a fee in neighborhood garage.

The turn-of-the-century Hotel Nemzeti, just off Blaha Lujza Square, underwent a 1987 restoration that returned much of its original art nouveau splendor. The lobby is small but delightful, with comfortable chairs and a coffee shop. Half the rooms face the loud street, while the other half face into a lovely interior courtyard to which, sadly, there is no access. The rooms have high ceilings and sober decor, with spacious bathrooms. Rooms on the top floor (5th) are most interesting, with slanted ceilings and funky windows. This is perhaps Pest's most handsome and historic hotel, though it lacks the luxuries of the more modern hotels.

Dining/Entertainment: In addition to the lobby coffee shop, the hotel has a restaurant, once one of Budapest's fashionable eateries but now of little interest to anyone not staying in the hotel.

Facilities/Services: Room service, laundry, car rental available.

JUST BEYOND CENTRAL PEST

FAMILY HOTEL, XIII. Ipoly u. 8/b, 1133 Budapest. Tel. 120-1284. Fax 129-1620. 10 rms, 3 suites (with bath). TV TEL MINIBAR A/C **Trolleybus:** 79 from Keleti pu. to Ipoly utca.

$ **Rates** (including breakfast): DM 150 ($93.75) single; DM 180 ($112.50) double; DM 210 ($131.25) suite for up to three people; DM 30 ($18.75) extra bed. Rates 10% lower in low season. AE, DC, MC, V. **Parking:** Free.

A charming, elegant little place opened in 1991, Family Hotel stands two blocks from the Danube in a quiet mostly residential neighborhood in the Újlipótváros (New Leopold Town), just north of the Inner City of Pest. Szent István Park, a pleasant neighborhood park, is only 5 minutes away by foot. Perhaps the nicest thing about this hotel is the low-key, tasteful atmosphere; there is only one bar in the hotel (in the Hungarian/International restaurant) and there is very little for sale in the establishment. The suites are among the nicest rooms in the city; duplexes all, they have skylights over the upstairs bedrooms and enormous floor-to-ceiling windows, letting in endless sunlight. All rooms in the hotel are spacious, with simple wood furniture and large bathrooms.

Facilities/Services: 24-hour room service, sauna, massage, gift shop, hairdresser.

HOTEL CENTRAL, VI. Munkácsy Mihály u. 5-7, 1063 Budapest. Tel./fax 121-2000. 36 rms, 6 suites (with bath). TV TEL MINIBAR **Metro:** Bajza utca (Yellow line).

$ **Rates** (including breakfast): DM 138 ($86.25) single; DM 156 ($97.50) double; DM 186 ($116.25) triple; DM 200–260 ($125–$162.50) suite for one to four people. Rates 40% lower in low season. AE, MC, V. **Parking:** Free.

It's a bit ugly from the outside, but don't be fooled: The Central is a gem of a hotel. It's located in an exclusive embassy neighborhood just off Andrássy út, a minute's walk from Heroes' Square and City Park. The lobby is small but cozy, with four interior marble columns, and a comfortable lounge on each floor. The suites are absolutely marvelous—enormous and furnished with vintage Hungarian furniture, carpets, and prints. They also have large double beds (a rarity in Hungary) and a bathroom (with windows) the size of most hotel rooms themselves! There is a private safe in each suite. The standard rooms, although quite nice, do not match up to the suites, so you might consider splurging here. All rooms and suites have a terrace.

Dining/Entertainment: The hotel restaurant serves very good Hungarian food on world-famous Herend china. Prices are moderate despite a rather luxurious setting. The hotel also has a bar.

CENTRAL BUDA & THE CASTLE DISTRICT

BUDA CENTER HOTEL, II. Csalogány u. 23, 1027 Budapest. Tel. 201-6333. Fax 201-7843. 34 rms, 3 suites (with shower). TV TEL **Metro:** Red line to Moszkva tér or Battyhány tér.

$ Rates (including breakfast): DM 120 ($75) single; DM 140 ($87.50) double; DM 200 ($125) suite. Rates 40% lower in low season. AE. **Parking:** 500 Ft ($5.55) per day.

Conveniently located halfway between Buda's Moszkva and Battyhány squares, the Buda Center Hotel is a peculiar place, sharing a building with numerous private companies (the hotel is not conspicuously marked from the street, so look carefully for it). A Chinese restaurant, Kínai Shanghai Étterem (open 11am to midnight, main courses 300 to 1,000 Ft/$3.35 to $11.10) has its entrance through the otherwise cozy hotel lobby. The rooms are on the small side, with plenty of ugly furniture, but the twin beds have no gap between them, making them feel like a real double bed. About a third of the rooms have balconies, but there are no views to speak of. This hotel should be chosen on the basis of its location.

Dining/Entertainment: In addition to a breakfast room and a cocktail bar, there is a Chinese restaurant (under different management) on the premises.

HOTEL BUDAPEST, II. Szilágyi Erzsébet fasor 47, 1026 Budapest. Tel. 202-0044. Fax 110-5496. 280 rms (with bath). TV TEL **Tram:** 56 from Moszkva tér to Fogaskerekű Vasút.

$ Rates (including breakfast): DM 140 ($87.50) single; DM 170 ($106.25) double; DM 214 ($133.75) triple. Rates 20% lower in low season. AE, DC, MC, V. **Parking:** Free.

A metallic looking 1960s Socialist cylinder from the outside, the Hotel Budapest, a HungarHotel, is nonetheless rather interesting inside. The lobby is surprisingly large and cheerful, with comfortable armchairs. Circular hallways on the floors have amazingly ugly brown plastic walls. The rooms, though small and modestly furnished, with time-worn carpets, boast a full wall of windows. The hotel soars above the neighborhood, and offers numerous views; your room may overlook the Danube or face up into the hills of Buda. Try to get a room on a high floor (there are 14 in all). The vista over the city from the roof garden is simply breathtaking at night. The hotel is walking distance from Moszkva tér, Buda's central transportation hub, and just across the street from the base of the cogwheel railway, which takes you straight up into the Buda Hills. Hungarians love to hate the Hotel Budapest, and many foreigners find it a blight on the landscape, but it is a fascinating place.

Dining/Entertainment: The hotel has a restaurant, beer cellar, and a nightclub.

Facilities: Roof garden, sauna, solarium.

HOTEL ORION, I. Döbrentei u. 13, 1013 Budapest. Tel.

175-5418 or 156-8933. Telex 22-7112. 33 rms (with bath). TV
TEL MINIBAR A/C **Tram:** 19 from Batthyány tér to Döbrentei tér.

$ Rates (including breakfast): DM 140 ($87.50) single; DM 182
($113.75) double; DM 32 ($20) extra bed. Rates 20%–25% lower
in low season. AE, DC, MC, V. **Parking:** No parking facilities.

Conveniently located between Castle Hill and the Danube, this small
five-story Pannonia hotel is tucked away on a relatively quiet street
near many of the city's best sites. Though the rooms are bright and
cheerful enough, and five have balconies, they unfortunately enjoy
neither castle nor river views. Döbrentei tér, a messy but convenient
transportation hub, is a few minutes away by foot.

Dining/Entertainment: The hotel has a restaurant serving
Hungarian/International cuisine.

Facilities/Services: Room service, sauna, car rental.

THE BUDA HILLS

**HOTEL AGRO, XII. Normafa út 54, 1121 Budapest. Tel./
fax 175-6164.** 150 rms (with bath). TV TEL MINIBAR **Bus:**
Red 21 from Moszkva tér to Normafa út.

$ Rates (including breakfast): DM 110 ($68.75) single; DM 135
($84.40) double; DM 165 ($103.10) suite; DM 19 ($11.90) extra
bed. Rates 40% lower in low season. AE, DC, MC, V. **Parking:**
Free.

Owned by the Hungarian Farmer's Cooperative, the aptly named
Agro is located high up on Buda's Sváb-Hegy (Schwab Hill), not far
from a huge park and close to the bus stop. Every room has a terrace;
the views are pleasant, and the neighborhood quiet. The swimming
pool is tiny and the food in the restaurant mediocre, but the service is
friendly. The Agro is primarily used as a conference center but
welcomes non-group guests.

Dining/Entertainment: Restaurant.

Facilities: Swimming pool, sauna, fitness room, tennis courts.

**HOTEL PANORÁMA, XII. Rege u. 21, 1121 Budapest. Tel.
175-0583.** Fax 175-9727. 36 rms (with bath), 54 bungalows
(with shower). Hotel: TV TEL (local only) MINIBAR; Bungalows:
TV **Cog Railway:** Széchenyi-Hegy.

$ Rates (including breakfast): DM 125 ($78.10) single; DM 165
($103.10) double; DM 148–192 ($92.50–$120) bungalow. Rates
40%–50% lower in low season. AE, DC, MC, V. **Parking:** Free.

Best reached by the cog railway (a standard part of Budapest's
public transit system, with normal running hours), which
practically stops at the front door, the Hotel Panoráma (a
HungarHotel renovated in 1989) stands alone in a serene neighborhood of Freedom Hill (Szabadság-Hegy). The hotel lobby is small,
but the hallways feature comfortable armchairs. The staff is extremely friendly and helpful, and the rooms are very bright and clean, with
spectacular views. The bungalows are darker, decorated in a kind of
hunting lodge style, and each has a private patio. The whole complex

is situated in a shady grove which stays relatively cool even in the hottest weather. The southern terminus of the Children's Railroad (Gyermek Vasút) is a 5-minute walk.

Dining/Entertainment: The hotel features a restaurant and a bar.

Facilities: Restaurant, bar, swimming pool, sauna.

HOTEL QUEEN MARY, XII. Béla király út 47, 1121 Budapest. Tel./fax 156-8377. 20 rms, 2 suites (with shower). TV TEL MINIBAR **Bus:** 28 from Moszkva tér to Béla király út.

$ Rates (including breakfast): $75 single; $80 double; $100 triple; $100 suite for two people; $120 suite for three or four people. Rates 30% lower in low season. AE, MC, V. **Parking:** Free.

Opened in 1992, this hotel is situated high up in the hills in a wealthy neighborhood and is not far from a bus stop. The rooms are very modern and efficient, but lacking in character. Each room has a terrace; those on the ground floor share the terrace with adjacent rooms. Unfortunately, the hotel has very little public space, with no lobby to speak of and less garden space than most Buda pensions. There is, however, a sauna, solarium, and restaurant with outdoor dining in summer. The hotel also has a laundry service.

PETNEHÁZY COUNTRY CLUB, II. Feketefej u. 2-4, 1029 Budapest. Tel. 176-5992 or 176-5982. Fax 176-5738. 45 bungalows (with bath). TV TEL MINIBAR **Directions:** By car only.

$ Rates (with breakfast): DM 185 ($115.65) small bungalow for two; DM 230 ($143.75) large bungalow for four. Weekly rates available. Rates 10% lower in low season. AE, DC, MC, V. **Parking:** Free.

The word "bungalow" does not do justice to the luxurious Scandinavian-style wooden houses of the Petneházy Country Club, opened in 1991. Furnished entirely with well-built wooden furniture, each bungalow has a private sauna, kitchen, and porch. They are spacious, bright and airy, and sparkling clean. Deep in the Cold Valley (Hüvösvölgy) region of the Buda Hills, Petneházy is unfortunately beyond the reach of Budapest's public transportation system. Just down the road is the Petneházy Lovasiskola, where you can go horseback riding in the nearby hills (see "Sports and Recreation" in Chapter 6).

Dining/Entertainment: There is a restaurant and a bar at the hotel.

Facilities: Swimming pool, tennis, solarium, bicycle rental.

SAS CLUB HOTEL, XII. Törökbálinti út 51-53, 1121 Budapest. Tel./fax 166-9899. 95 rms, 13 suites (with shower). TV TEL **Bus:** 8 or 8a from Március 15 tér to Oltvány utca.

$ Rates (including breakfast): DM 132 ($82.50) single; DM 170 ($106.25) double; DM 227 ($141.90) suite; DM 32 ($20) extra bed. Rates 40% lower in low season. AE, DC, MC, V. **Parking:** Free.

The Sas Club Hotel (Eagle Club Hotel) is a sprawling hotel complex set in a quiet residential neighborhood. Modern, comfortable guest rooms are spread out over five separate buildings. Although it is located quite a distance from the center of town, a bus conveniently stops right in front of the hotel. The Sas Club is a sports paradise, and the on-premises brewery makes it the liveliest place in the neighborhood. There is also a restaurant featuring Gypsy/South American music.

Facilities/Services: Bowling, tennis, swimming pool, sauna, solarium, fitness room, massage.

3. MODERATE

THE INNER CITY & CENTRAL PEST

HOTEL MEDOSZ, VI. Jókai tér 9, 1061 Budapest. Tel. 153-1700 or 153-1434. Fax 131-4568. 70 rms (with bath). TV **Metro:** Oktogon (Yellow line).
$ Rates (including breakfast): 3,800 Ft ($42.20) single; 4,100 Ft ($45.50) double; 4,700 Ft ($52.15) triple. Rates are the same all year. No credit cards. **Parking:** Difficult in neighborhood.

The MEDOSZ was formerly a trade-union hotel for agricultural workers. Its location on sleepy Jókai tér, in the heart of Pest's theater district, is as good as it gets off the river in central Pest. Although the hotel has not been renovated since privatization, it remains a great value given its location. The rooms are simple and comfortable, without any frills. There is a restaurant and bar in the hotel. Next door is one of Budapest's special treats for children: a puppet theater (*bábszínház*).

JUST BEYOND CENTRAL PEST

HOTEL DÉLIBÁB, VI. Délibáb u. 35, 1062 Budapest. Tel. 122-8763, 142-8153, or 142-9301. 33 rms (with shower). TEL **Metro:** Hősök tere (Yellow line).
$ Rates (including breakfast): 3,110 Ft ($34.50) single; 4,020 Ft ($44.60) double. No triples possible. Rates 5%–10% lower in low season. No credit cards. **Parking:** Neighborhood difficult.

One of the least expensive establishments in this price category, the Hotel Délibáb enjoys a wonderful location across the street from Heroes' Square and the City Park, in an exclusive Pest neighborhood that is home to most of the city's embassies. There is a small reception desk as you enter, but no lobby to speak of. Rooms are quite spacious and have wood floors; the fixtures are old, but everything works and everything is clean. There are TVs in 12 rooms and refrigerators in 12 rooms; all rooms are the same price.

HOTEL METROPOL, VII. Rákóczi út 58, 1074 Budapest.

Tel. 142-1175, 142-1171, or 142-0922. Telex 22-6209. 102 rms (10 with bath, 24 with shower). **Metro:** Blaha Lujza tér (Red line).

$ Rates (including breakfast): $35 single without bath, $43 single with bath; $46 double without bath, $58 double with shower, $61 double with bath; $62 triple without bath, $73 triple with shower, $85 triple with bath. Rates 30% lower in low season. **Parking:** Available for a fee in neighborhood garage.

The Metropol is housed in a faded, but clearly once grand, turn-of-the-century yellow building. It is one of the relatively few centrally located hotels not to have undergone renovation and the subsequent elevation of prices. The hotel's location on bustling Blaha Lujza Square means that street noise does permeate the rooms, but that is the price you pay for staying in busy central Pest. Everything about the place is a bit shabby and old, but the facilities are clean. A Pannonia Hotel.

HOTEL PARK, VIII. Baross tér 10, 1087 Budapest. Tel. 113-1420 or 113-5619. Telex 22-6274. 151 rms (10 with bath and toilet, 32 with shower and no toilet) TEL **Metro:** Keleti pu. (Red line).

$ Rates (including breakfast): 2,540 Ft ($28.20) single without bath, 3,000 Ft ($33.30) single with shower and no toilet; 3,400 Ft ($37.75) double without bath, 4,120 Ft ($45.75) double with shower and no toilet, 4,480 Ft ($49.70) double with bath and toilet; 930–1,020 Ft ($10.30–$11.30) extra bed. Rates are the same all year. AE, MC, V. **Parking:** Available for a fee in neighborhood garage.

Conveniently located just across the street from Keleti Station, this 1914 hotel, formerly owned by the Pannonia hotel chain, offers unparalleled budget prices for this location. The area around Keleti Station, however, does have a thin veneer of sleaziness to it. The hotel bar and restaurant manage to attract more than their share of unsavory characters. That said, though, the room rates are unbeatable. Rooms, though worn, have nice hard-wood floors with throw rugs, big windows, and high ceilings. Double doors protect you from the noise of late-night hallway activity. Some rooms even have balconies, and the 10 rooms with full bathrooms also have TVs. The public facilities are clean. The atmosphere is definitely pre-1989 Eastern Europe, although there is a certain charm here that you won't find elsewhere.

CENTRAL BUDA & THE CASTLE DISTRICT

HOTEL IFJÚSÁG, II. Zivatar u. 1-3, 1024 Budapest. Tel. 115-4260 or 135-3331. Fax 135-3989. 100 rms (with bath). **Bus:** 91 from Nyugati pu. to Zivatar utca.

$ Rates (including breakfast): DM 75 ($46.90) single; DM 95 ($59.40) double; DM 30 ($18.75) extra bed. Rates 20% lower in low season. DC, MC. **Parking:** Free.

Ⓕ **FROMMER'S COOL FOR KIDS: HOTELS**

Hotel Gellért (*see p. 78*) Children will appreciate both the indoor pool and the outdoor pool with artificial waves at this sprawling art nouveau hotel.

Hotel Liget (*see p. 76*) The Liget has the most kid-friendly location in town: directly across from City Park, site of the zoo, amusement park, and circus.

Mariana Apartman Villa (*see p. 92*) This family-run pension in the Buda Hills rents apartments with full kitchens at very reasonable rates. The owners have three young children of their own and enjoy mixing with guests.

Hotel Ifjúság, in the quiet and dignified Rose Hill (Rózsadomb) section of Buda, is perched in a prime location just minutes by bus from Nyugati station. A somewhat tired old hotel, built in the drab, utilitarian style of the late 1960s and early 1970s, it has a dark, forbidding lobby. The four floors are served by a single elevator. Rooms are clean and spacious; they all have terraces, some have telephones, and half boast a panoramic view over both Pest and Buda, from Gellért Hill all the way to Parliament. There is a restaurant and bar in the hotel.

HOTEL PAPILLON, II. Rózsahegy u. 3/b, 1024 Budapest. Tel. 115-3883 or 135-0321. Fax 115-8437. 20 rms (with shower). TV **Bus:** 91 from Nyugati pu. to Zivatar utca.
$ Rates (including breakfast): 4,000 Ft ($44.40) single; 4,500 Ft ($49.95) double; 5,500 Ft ($61.05) triple. Rates 25% lower in low season. No credit cards. **Parking:** Available on street.

The Hotel Papillon, opened in 1992 as a joint Hungarian-German venture, is a pleasing Mediterranean looking white building on a side street just beneath Hotel Ifjúság. The Mediterranean feeling pervades the interior and spare pink guest rooms as well. The rooms are a bit on the small side, though seven of them have terraces (17 have refrigerators). There is a bar and restaurant on the premises, the latter serving meals on an outdoor terrace in summer. Laundry service is offered. The hotel is owned by the same group which owns the Hotel Bel Ami and the Rózsadomb Panzió

HOTEL RÓZSADOMB, II. Vérhalom u. 17, 1025 Budapest. Tel. 115-0287. Fax 115-5481. 228 rms (with bath). TV TEL **Bus:** 191 from Nyugati pu. to Vérhalom utca.
$ Rates (including breakfast): DM 70 ($43.75) single; DM 100 ($62.50) double; DM 140 ($87.50) triple. Rates 30% lower in low season. AE, DC, MC, V. **Parking:** Free.

A former trade-union hotel, this vintage 1971 hotel is perched dramatically atop a hill overlooking the Danube. It's quite centrally located, in the fashionable Rose Hill (Rózsadomb) neighborhood of Buda, just 10 minutes or so by bus from Nyugati station. Sixty percent of the rooms face the river; they are bright and have balconies to go with the great panoramas. The other rooms have little to boast about, so if you reserve ahead of time, be specific in requesting a river-side room. Rooms are standard, with the addition of a refrigerator. There is a sixth-floor restaurant with a great panorama over the town, a fifth-floor terrace beer bar, and a lobby bar. The hotel also has its own small park and various outdoor decks and terraces.

THE BUDA HILLS

BUDAI HOTEL, XII. Rácz Aladár u. 45-47, 1121 Budapest. Tel. 186-8987 or 181-0141. Fax 186-8987. 31 rms (with shower). TV TEL MINIBAR **Tram:** 59 from Moszkva tér to last stop.

$ Rates (including breakfast): DM 80 ($50) single; DM 100 ($62.50) double; DM 120 ($75) suite; DM 20 ($12.50) extra bed. Rates 20%–25% lower in low season. No credit cards. **Parking:** Free.

A 15-minute winding walk from the tram station, the Budai is high up in a quiet section of the Wolf Meadow (Farkasrét) district of the Buda Hills. The rooms are simply furnished; some have terraces. The rooms on the top floor have the best views of the surrounding hills and all are of different dimensions. There is a restaurant and bar on the premises and extensive terrace-dining space.

CINEGE PANZIÓ, XII. György Aladár u. 35-39, 1125 Budapest. Tel. 155-5122 or 156-8200. Fax 156-8199. 38 apts (with shower). TV TEL MINIBAR **Bus:** 28 from Moszkva tér to György Aladár utca.

$ Rates: 4,000 Ft ($44.40) single; 4,500 Ft ($49.95) double; 800 Ft ($8.90) extra bed. Breakfast 300 Ft ($3.35) extra. AE, MC, V. **Parking:** Free.

The Cinege Panzió offers apartments in a modern, six-building complex located in a residential neighborhood. The apartments are clean and functional; a quarter of them have fully equipped kitchens, while the others have just refrigerators. There are tennis courts and a sauna on the premises (both 300 Ft per hour) and a large lawn area between the buildings, but no garden per se. A drawback to staying here is the intensely steep (but not very long) walk from the bus stop.

HOTEL TANNE, XII. Esze Tamás u. 6, 2092 Budapest. Tel. 176-6144 or 138-6520. Fax 138-6942. 42 rms (with shower). TV TEL MINIBAR **Bus:** 22 Red or Black from Moszkva tér to Szanatórium utca.

$ Rates (with breakfast): DM 80 ($50) single; DM 100 ($62.50) double; DM 20 ($12.50) extra bed. Half board DM 20 ($12.50), full board DM 35 ($21.90). Rates 20% lower in low season. AE, DC, MC, V. **Parking:** Free.

⭐ 💲 Every room is different in the Hotel Tanne, but all are tastefully furnished and the bathrooms are large and airy. Some top-floor rooms feature skylights, and the genuine double beds are a rare find in Hungary, the land of twin beds. The lobby is comfortable and sunny, also with a skylight. The neighborhood, near the Budapest city line, has a village-like feel and is near numerous hiking trails. A very direct bus line makes the hotel quickly accessible from the city center. The hotel restaurant features Hungarian wild game dishes at very reasonable prices.

---

4. INEXPENSIVE

JUST BEYOND CENTRAL PEST

RADIO INN, VI. Benczúr u. 19, 1068 Budapest. Tel. 142-8347 or 122-8284. Fax 122-8284. 30 apts (with bath and toilet). TV TEL **Metro:** Bajza utca (Yellow line).

💲 **Rates:** 3,392 Ft ($37.65) for one person; 3,922 Ft ($43.55) for two people; 6,042 Ft ($67.05) for three or four people; 848 Ft ($9.40) extra bed for fifth person. Breakfast available for 275 Ft ($3.05). Rates 30% lower in low season. No credit cards. **Parking:** Available on street.

⭐ 💲 This may be the best accommodation deal in the city. As the official guesthouse of the Hungarian National Radio, Radio Inn houses many visiting dignitaries as well as offering apartments to individual tourists. Reserve well ahead of your arrival. The inn is in an exclusive embassy neighborhood (next door to the Chinese Embassy), a stone's throw from the City Park, and a block from grand Andrássy út. There is an enormous, private, flower-filled courtyard behind the building. The huge apartments (all with fully equipped, spacious kitchens) are handsomely furnished and painstakingly clean. Note that the WC and the bathroom are separate, European style.

CENTRAL BUDA & THE CASTLE DISTRICT

CHARLES APARTMENTS, I. Hegyalja út 23, 1016 Budapest. Tel. 175-4379 or 175-0255. Fax 175-0255. 26 apts (with bath and toilet). TV TEL **Bus:** 78 from Keleti pu. to Mészáros utca.

💲 **Rates:** 3,000–3,500 Ft ($33.30–$38.85) per apartment for one or two people; 400 Ft ($4.45) for additional bed. Rates 10%–15% lower in low season. No credit cards. **Parking:** 300 Ft ($3.35) per day.

⭐ This is one of the better housing deals in Budapest. Owner Károly Szombati has bought up 22 apartments in a single apartment building in a dull but convenient Buda neighborhood (near the large luxury Hotel Novotel), in addition to four apartments in nearby buildings. All are average Budapest flats in average residential buildings. Furnishings are comfortable and clean, and all apartments have full bathrooms and kitchens. Hegyalja is a very busy street, but only two of the flats face out onto it; the rest are in the interior or side of the building. There is a park nearby with tennis courts and a track and next door is an ABC grocery store. The friendly, English-speaking reception is open 24 hours. Laundry service is offered.

BUDA HILLS & ÓBUDA

HOTEL RÓMAI, III. Szent János u. 16, 1039 Budapest. Tel./fax 188-6167 or 168-7479. 20 rms, 16 suites (with shower and toilet). TV TEL MINIBAR **Metro:** Suburban HÉV line from Batthyány tér to Római Fürdő. Then Bus 34 to Szent János utca.

$ Rates: DM 40 ($25) single; DM 55 ($34.40) double; DM 85 ($53.10) suite for one; DM 97 ($60.60) suite for two; DM 11 ($6.90) additional bed in suite. Breakfast costs DM 6 ($3.75). Rates 20% lower in low season. AE, V. **Parking:** Free.

The $34 double room at the Hotel Római is one of the best deals in Budapest. A former resort for minor Communist party officials, it is a bit off the beaten track, but its location in the Római Fürdő section of Óbuda, on the banks of the Danube, is peaceful. The lobby is spacious and comfortable, with pool tables and a bar. The rooms, with frayed rugs and battered wood furniture, show their age, but the beds are authentic double beds and every room has a balcony. A new wing was added in 1993; these rooms are fresher. There is a restaurant, an outdoor swimming pool, and lots of garden space. There are also 16 bungalows for rent at 30–54 DM ($18.75–$33.75); bungalows have shared bathroom facilities.

5. PENSION ACCOMMODATIONS

Budapest's pensions are often private homes converted into small hotels. Although they generally have fewer facilities than hotels, pensions are none the less comfortable, often very charming, and are a good option for budget travelers. A number of the pensions listed below are in quiet and scenic areas away from the noise and congestion of the city center.

All the pensions listed below are in the "Moderate" or "Inexpensive" price categories.

OUTER PEST

DETTY PANZIÓ, XIV. Gervay u. 23, 1145 Budapest. Tel. 252-0820, 183-2756, or 183-0390. Fax 183-4928. 15 rms (with bath). TV TEL A/C **Bus:** Red 7 from Keleti pu. to last stop; then 5–10 minute walk.

$ Rates (including breakfast): DM 90 ($56.25) single; DM 100 ($62.50) double; DM 110 ($68.75) triple. Rates 10% lower in low season. AE, DC, MC, V. **Parking:** Free.

A pleasant and surprising find, the Detty, opened in 1989, is a Buda-like pension in Pest. Tucked away on a quiet, tree-lined street in the attractive Zugló district, it offers extremely clean and tastefully furnished rooms with big windows. The Detty may well be the only mid-priced establishment in town to offer air conditioning in every room. There is a tiny bar off the cozy reception area, and a small garden features a wading pool.

RICHTER PANZIÓ, XIV. Thököly út 111, 1145 Budapest. Tel. 163-3956, 163-5735, or 163-5761. Fax 163-3956. 24 rms (20 with bath, 4 with shower). TV TEL **Bus:** Black 7 from Keleti Station to Kolumbusz (or Columbus) utca.

$ Rates (including breakfast): 4,000 Ft ($44.40) single; 5,000–6,000 Ft ($55.50–$66.60) double; 6,000–7,000 Ft ($66.60–$77.70) triple. Rates 10%–20% lower in low season. No credit cards. **Parking:** Free.

Across the street from the Honvéd Hotel, the Richter Panzió sits in a busy Zugló neighborhood, just 5 minutes by bus from Keleti Station (on a night bus route). The pension was opened in 1991 by the famous Hungarian circus family of the same name and is manned by a friendly staff. There is a small bar in the cozy lobby, and an outdoor deck off to one side. The guest rooms are delightful, with fine wooden floors and huge windows. Most rooms have double beds; some have bathrooms with a window; six rear rooms have terraces. There is a small pool, a sauna, and a fitness room. Laundry service is available.

BUDA HILLS & ÓBUDA

BEATRIX PANZIÓ, II. Széher út 3, 1021 Budapest. Tel./ fax 176-3730. 12 rms, 2 suites (with shower). **Bus:** 56 from Moszkva tér to Hüvösvölgyi út, then bus 29 to Széher út.

$ Rates (including breakfast): DM 60–90 ($37.50–$56.25) single; DM 70–100 ($43.75–$62.50) double; DM 120 ($75) triple; DM 150 ($93.75) suite. Rates 25% lower in low season. No credit cards. **Parking:** Free.

Beatrix Panzió, opened in 1991, is a tasteful, modern place, with well-appointed and comfortable rooms. Ten of the 12 rooms have TV, and three have private balconies. The breakfast area in the lobby is a bit cramped, but in good weather breakfast is served in the garden. In addition to a sauna, there is a barbecue area where the management occasionally treats guests to a Hungarian barbecue. Széher út is a small but heavily traveled road. An ABC grocery store is conveniently located down the street.

G.G. PANORÁMA PANZIÓ, II. Fullánk u. 7, 1026 Buda- pest. Tel./fax 176-4718. 3 rms (with shower). TV **Bus:** 11 from Batthyány tér to Majális utca.

$ Rates: $50 single or double; $11 extra bed; $3 breakfast. **Parking:** Available on street.

G.G. are the initials of Mrs. Gábor Gubacsi, the friendly English-speaking owner of this small guesthouse. All guest rooms are on the top floor of the Gubacsi home, located on a steep quiet street in the Rose Hill (Rózsadomb) section of the Buda Hills. Several bus lines from different parts of the center converge on the neighborhood, making it a fairly convenient place to stay. The rooms are small, but tastefully furnished; they share a common balcony, which has a great vista of the hills. There are also a common kitchen and dining area for the guests, with full facilities (including minibar), and garden space for eating, reading, and relaxing. It is a casual but classy place, and the Gubacsis take good care of their guests.

GIZELLA PANZIÓ, XII. Arató u. 42/b, 1121 Budapest. Tel./fax 182-0324. 9 rms (with shower). TV TEL **Tram:** 59 from Moszkva tér to last stop.

$ Rates (with breakfast): 4,200 Ft ($46.60) single; 4,500 Ft ($49.95) double. No credit cards. **Parking:** Free.

This charming pension is a 10-minute walk from the nearest tram station. Built on the side of a hill, it has a lovely view and a series of terraced gardens leading down to the swimming pool. The pension also features a sauna, solarium, fitness room, and bar. Guest rooms are all different, quaint, and sunny. Owner Gizella Varga clearly has good taste.

MARIANA APARTMAN VILLA, II. Hidegkúti út 14, 1028 Budapest. Tel. 176-8223. 3 apts (with shower and toilet). TV TEL **Bus:** 56 from Moszkva tér to the last stop.

$ Rates: $35–$70 depending on which apartment and number of people. Rates 10% lower in low season. No credit cards. **Parking:** Free.

Opened in 1990, this small pension is run by István Pogácsás and his wife Marian. The Pogácsás have three young children, and the whole family likes to mix with guests, so the Mariana Villa is especially recommended for families with children. István will organize tours in and around Budapest, recommend restaurants, and take you fishing at his favorite fishing hole. The apartments all have full kitchens and washing machines. Although there is not much garden space here and Hidegkúti is a noisy street, a register full of returning guests shows that the Pogácsás are doing something right.

SAN MARCO GUESTHOUSE, III. San Marco u. 6, 1034 Budapest. Tel. 188-9997. 5 rms (3 with shower and toilet, other 2 with shared shower and toilet). TV **Tram:** 17 from Margit híd (Buda side) to Nagyszombat utca, or Bus 60 from Batthyány tér to Nagyszombat utca.

$ Rates: 2,200 Ft ($24.20) single or double with shared shower and toilet, 2,500 Ft ($27.75) single or double with private shower and toilet; 300 Ft ($3.35) extra cot for child. Continental breakfast

150 Ft ($1.65); full breakfast 250 Ft ($2.80). No credit cards. **Parking:** Available on street.

Paul and Eva Stenczinger run this small pension on the top floor of their house. They speak fluent English and will help guests with restaurant reservations, theater tickets, taxis, train tickets, and other matters. The house is comfortable but unassuming—much like the residential Óbuda neighborhood where it is located. Three rooms face the back, where there is a flower-filled garden (breakfast is served here in summer). All rooms have slanted ceilings and good windows. There is a common refrigerator (with minibar) and a common hotplate in the hallway. Most of the Stenczinger's business consists of returning guests.

SIESTA VILLA, II. Madár u. 8/a, 1025 Budapest. Tel. 142-1404. 3 rms (with shower). TV **Bus:** 11 from Batthyány tér to last stop.

$ Rates (including breakfast): $42 single; $50–$57 double; $74 triple. Rates 10% lower in low season. No credit cards. **Parking:** Free.

Deep in the heart of a fashionable section of the Buda Hills, this lovely little pension's only drawback is that it's a good 15-minute walk from the bus stop. There are three guest rooms, each with a spacious bathroom and large windows. In summer, breakfast is served in the garden, and budget travelers will appreciate that the drinks in the common self-serve minibar are priced at supermarket prices. The owner, Dr. Ágota Borbás, speaks English and lives on the premises.

ST. CHRISTOPH VILLA, II. Galóca u. 20, 1028 Budapest. Tel. 176-8604. 5 rms (with shower). MINIBAR **Bus:** 56 from Moszkva tér to last stop, then bus 64 to Kossuth Lajos utca.

$ Rates (with breakfast): DM 60 ($32.50) single; DM 80 ($50) double; DM 20 ($12.50) extra bed. Rates 15% lower in low season. AE. **Parking:** Free.

Opened in 1991, St. Christoph Villa is a small family-run pension in a pleasant neighborhood of the Buda Hills. The bright rooms have large windows and solid blonde-wood furniture. Each room is different—4 and 5 are the nicest. The common indoor space is unimpressive, but the garden is pretty. Breakfast is served outside in nice weather.

VADVIRÁG PANZIÓ, II. Nagybányai út 18, 1025 Budapest. Tel./fax 176-4292. 9 rms (7 with shower, 1 with bath). TV TEL **Bus:** 5 from Március 15 tér or Moszkva tér to Pasaréti tér (last stop).

$ Rates (including breakfast): 500 Ft ($5.55) single without bath, 3,800 Ft ($42.20) single with shower; 4,600–5,100 Ft ($51.05–$56.60) double with shower or bath. Rates are the same all year. No credit cards. **Parking:** Free.

A 10-minute walk from the bus stop, Vadvirág (its name means wildflower in Hungarian) is in a gorgeous part of the Buda Hills just a few blocks behind the Béla Bartók Memorial House. The pension is surrounded by sloping gardens and terraces. The hallways are decorated with prints by the Hungarian-born op artist Victor Vasarely. The rooms are all different; most are small but tastefully furnished. Half the rooms have balconies, and most have reproductions of well-known Hungarian paintings. Room 2 is the best in the house: the only room with a bath, it is a small suite with a balcony. The tiny single without bath is a great deal at 500 Ft. There is a small restaurant and bar, with plenty of outdoor tables, and a sauna.

6. PRIVATE ROOM ACCOMMODATIONS

Private rooms have long been considered the best option for budget travelers in Hungary. When you book a private room you get a room in someone's apartment; usually you share the bathroom with the hosts or with other guests. Breakfast is not officially included, but the host will often offer it for a small fee. You generally have limited kitchen privileges. Some landlords will greet you when you arrive, give you a key, and seemingly disappear; others will want to befriend you, change money, show you around, cook for you. It is your right to be aloof if you find the landlord too obtrusive; after all, you're on vacation. Most rooms are quite adequate, some are even memorable, but there are any number of reasons which may cause you to dislike your room: Noisy neighborhoods, tiny bathrooms, and bad coffee are among the complaints we've heard from the occasional displeased traveler. The great majority of guests, though, are satisfied.

You can book rooms through accommodation agencies (see information at the beginning of this chapter). Prices vary slightly between agencies, but generally speaking single rooms cost 750–1,500 Ft ($8.30–$16.65), while doubles cost 800–2,000 Ft ($8.90–$22.20). Most agencies add a 30% surcharge (to the first night only) for stays of less than four nights. When booking a room, make sure you know its exact location on a map before leaving. There is scarcely an address in Budapest that cannot be reached by some form of public transportation, so regard with skepticism anyone who tells you that you must take a taxi. In peak season you may need to shop around a bit for the location you want, but you can always find a room somewhere. Arriving at an agency early in the day will afford you the best selection of rooms.

In Keleti Station, where most international trains arrive, you will undoubtedly be approached by people offering you private rooms. Most are honest folks who are trying to drum up some business personally. The more aggressive ones can be annoying, and you may choose to dismiss them out of hand. But keep in mind that when the middleman (the agency) is eliminated, the prices tend to be slightly better, so you might consider taking a room from one of these people, especially if you arrive late at night when the agencies are closed or long lines at the agencies drive you to despair. Trust your judgment and don't let anyone pressure you.

7. YOUTH HOSTEL ACCOMMODATIONS

All official youth hostels in Hungary belong to the Hungarian Youth Hostel Federation (Magyar Ifjúsági Szállások Szövetsége); for a full list of their hostels you can write to 1535 Budapest, Konkoly Thege Miklós út 21, Hungary (tel. 36-1/156-2857). Although **Express,** which formerly ran all official youth hostels, still has a significant role, it is unclear exactly what role it will have in the future. Its main office is at Szabadság tér 16 (tel. 131-7777), and in the meantime this is where you can buy an IYHF card (250 Ft/$2.75).

There is now intense competition between youth hostels as the transition from state management to private management is made. This may eventually lead to improvements in facilities and services, but the main impact thus far is to make your quest for a hostel bed in Budapest very confusing. It is best to book a bed in advance at a recommended hostel; if you haven't, you can make phone calls on your arrival and try to secure one or book one through an accommodation agency (see information on agencies at the beginning of this chapter). You can also try the "hawkers" who will undoubtedly approach you at the train stations. Hawkers make a commission on every customer they bring in and have a reputation for being pushy and saying whatever they think you want to hear about their hostel. So use your judgment, shop around, and don't let yourself be pressured. Most hostels that send hawkers to the station also have a van parked outside. The ride to the hostel is free, but you may have to wait a while until the van is full.

We have listed below a number of Budapest's year-round hostels. In the summer, dozens of other youth hostels open in university dormitories and other empty student housing. Their locations change from year to year, as do their management. Because of these factors we cannot review them in this guide, but you might want to keep in mind the following centrally located dormitories expected to remain in use as summer hostels: **Strawberry I,** IX. Ráday u. 43-45 (tel. 138-4766); **Strawberry II,** IX. Kinizsi u. 2-6 (tel. 117-3033); **Universitas,** XI. Irinyi J. u. 9-11 (tel. 181-2313); and **Zoltán Schönherz,** XI. Irinyi J. u. 42 (tel. 166-5460 or 166-5422).

The youth hostels and budget lodgings listed below are all open year-round.

ANANDA YOUTH HOSTEL, XIV. Bonyhádi út 18/b, 1141 Budapest. Tel./fax 163-3735. 38 beds (two 10-bed rms, two

6-bed rms, one 2-bed rm, 4 addtl beds). **Trolleybus:** 80 from Keleti pu. to Nagy Lajos király útja.

$ Rates: 380 Ft ($4.20) per bed for IYHF members; 420 Ft ($4.65) per bed for non-IYHF members; 560 Ft ($6.20) per person (one or two people, IYHF members) for the double room; 600 Ft ($6.65) per person (one or two people, non-IYHF members) for the double room; breakfast costs 80 Ft (90¢). Rates 10% lower in low season. No credit cards. **Parking:** Free.

The Ananda Youth Hostel, opened in 1992, is almost too good to be true. Located on a quiet tree-lined street in Zugló, a neighborhood in Outer Pest, it offers some of the cheapest accommodations in Budapest. It's a 10-minute trolleybus ride from Keleti Station, and the line has night service. The rooms are bright and clean, with sturdy wooden bunkbeds; bathrooms, too, are admirably clean. The friendly manager, Jairo Bustos, is a Colombian yoga instructor who gives free instruction to interested guests. Free English-language sightseeing tours and free evening cultural entertainment (lectures, films, slide shows) are offered as well. Guests (and nonguests) may order full dinners from the vegetarian kitchen for only 280 Ft ($3.10); order your meal at least two hours in advance. The kitchen may also be used by guests when not in use by management. There is no curfew, all ages are welcome, and the management will try to find space for you even if the hostel is full. The Ananda is a member of the Hungarian Youth Hostel Federation.

CSILLEBÉRCI GYERMEK ÉS IFJÚSÁGI KÖZPONT, XII.
Konkoly Thege u. 21, 1535 Budapest. Tel. 156-5772.
Fax 175-9327. 32 bungalows, 4 suites, private youth hostel rooms. (Suites and bungalows with shower and toilet) TV MINIBAR (Suites and bungalows only) **Bus:** Red 21 from Moszkva tér to last stop; switch to 90, two stops to complex.

$ Rates: DM 15 ($9.40) single youth hostel room, DM 21 ($15.10) double youth hostel room, DM 25 ($15.65) triple youth hostel room; DM 63 ($39.40) for suite or bungalow, up to four people. Rates 30%–40% lower in low season. No credit cards. **Parking:** Free.

Although it's a long ride from downtown, great prices for simple accommodations are found in this sprawling youth complex in the Buda Hills. There is a large cafeteria which offers three meals daily for DM 2–8 ($1.25–$5). Sports facilities include tennis, handball, volleyball, soccer, and a swimming pool. The hostel is a member of the Hungarian Youth Hostel Federation; hostel cards are not required and all ages are welcome.

DONÁTI, I. Donáti u. 46, 1015 Budapest. Tel. 201-1971.
Fax 120-7135. 72 beds, in 6 to 20-bed rooms. **Metro:** Batthyány tér (Red line).

$ Rates: 460 Ft ($5.10) per bed. Rates are the same all year. IYHF or ISIC card required. **Parking:** Available on street.

One of a number of youth hostels managed by a company called

"More than Ways," Donáti, just behind Batthyány tér in the quiet Watertown neighborhood of Buda, is the best located of Budapest's year-round hostels (note, however, that only one 20-bed room is open September to June). The bathrooms are passably maintained, and each bed comes with an accompanying locker to store gear safely. There are no kitchen facilities and no breakfast offered, but sheets and the use of (primitive) washing machines are free. There is no curfew; checkout is at 9am. The hostel is a member of the Hungarian Youth Hostel Federation.

HOTEL CITADELLA, XI. Citadella sétány, 1118 Budapest. Tel. 166-5794. Telex 22-7648. 5 dorm rms (without shower or toilet), 15 quad rms (8 with shower and no toilet). **Bus:** 27 from Móricz Zsigmond tér to the Citadella.

$ Rates: 320 Ft ($3.55) bed in dorm room; 1,800 Ft ($20) double without shower; 2,000 Ft ($22.20) double with shower; 2,170 Ft ($24.10) triple without shower, 2,370 Ft ($26.30) triple with shower; 2,540 Ft ($28.20) quad without shower, 2,740 Ft ($30.40) quad with shower. Breakfast costs an additional 300 Ft ($3.35). Rates are the same all year. No credit cards. **Parking:** Free.

Budapest's most celebrated budget hotel, this tired old establishment is located inside the Citadella, the 19th-century Habsburg garrison which commands a panoramic view over the city from the top of Gellért Hill. Unfortunately, plans are afoot to convert it into a luxury hotel, but that conversion should not get under way until 1995 or later. In the meantime, beds remain very cheap. The rooms, luxuriously big, are well-worn but clean, with high ceilings and remarkable views. The public bathrooms are passable. Nearby you'll find an expensive restaurant, a nightclub, and a casino.

HOTEL EXPRESS, XII. Beethoven u. 7-9, 1126 Budapest. Tel./fax 175-3082. 30 rms (without bath) **Tram:** 59 from Moszkva tér or Déli pu. to Ugocsa utca.

$ Rates: 1,500 Ft ($16.65) single or double; 1,880 Ft ($20.85) triple; 2,260 Ft ($25.10) quad; 2,640 Ft ($29.30) five-bed rm. ISIC or IYHF cardholders are given 10% discount. Rates are the same all year. No credit cards. **Parking:** Available on street.

One of the best located of the budget establishments in Budapest, the Express is in a quiet central Buda neighborhood, just three tram stops from Déli Station. Although it calls itself a "hotel," the atmosphere at Express says "youth hostel." Rooms and facilities are standard East European youth hostel: clean, but tired and worn and with no frills. Plenty of tourist information is available at the reception desk; they actually have a better stash of free pamphlets than most luxury hotels.

CHAPTER 5

WHERE TO EAT IN BUDAPEST

- **FROMMER'S SMART TRAVELER: RESTAURANTS**
- **1. VERY EXPENSIVE**
- **2. EXPENSIVE**
- **3. MODERATE**
- **4. INEXPENSIVE**
- **5. SPECIALTY DINING**
- **FROMMER'S COOL FOR KIDS: RESTAURANTS**

Budapest is awash in newly opened private restaurants and many of the older, formerly state-owned eateries are getting a new lease on life after privatization—together with an aggressive facelift. Ethnic restaurants have also proliferated in the last few years; you'll find Chinese, Japanese, Korean, Middle Eastern, Turkish, Greek, Mexican, and Polynesian restaurants throughout the city. Of course, most tourists want Hungarian food while in Budapest. In this city, traditional fare runs the gamut from greasy to gourmet. There are few palates that can't find happiness here and few pocketbooks that will be much worse for the wear. Budapest is quickly gaining a reputation for fine dining at reasonable prices, so live it up.

TYPES OF EATING ESTABLISHMENTS *Étterem* is the most common Hungarian word for restaurant and is applied to everything from cafeteria-style eateries to first-class restaurants. A *vendéglő*, or guesthouse, is a smaller, more intimate restaurant, often with a Hungarian folk motif; a *csárda* is a country-side *vendéglő*. An *étkezde* is basically a lunchroom cafeteria, serving mostly locals and open only in the daytime. Stand-up *bufés* are often found in bus stations and near busy transportation hubs. A *cukrászda* or *kávéház* is a classic Central European coffeehouse, where lingering has developed into an art form.

TRICKS OF THE TRADE There are a few "menu tricks" visitors should be aware of when dining out in Budapest. Sometimes there is an English-language menu without prices written in. As long as the waiter offers you a Hungarian menu for the sake of comparison, this won't be a problem but occasionally, everything is listed in a different order; sometimes the English menu is twice as long, or only half as long. In such situations there is no way of matching up the dishes with the prices.

Sometimes waiters will mention "specials" which do not appear on the menu. It is customary to ask the price before ordering such a special. Also, some restaurants do not list drinks on the menu, while others list them but omit the prices. Again, inquire about the price before ordering.

If you think the bill is mistaken, don't be embarrased to call it into question. Waiters will admit their "mistake" and readily correct the bill when challenged.

PAYING THE BILL　The customer has to initiate the paying ritual. You may find that your waiter has disappeared by the time you are ready to settle up. Call over any restaurant employee and ask to pay. The bill is usually written out on the spot. After handing over the bill, the waiter will wait for payment. Hungarians never leave tips on the table, so payment should include the tip (generally about 10%). Occasionally a service charge may already be added, in which case a tip is unnecessary.

MUSIC　Live Gypsy music is a feature in many Hungarian restaurants, although primarily in the ones catering to tourists. Many Hungarians wouldn't go near a place with a Gypsy band, since generally speaking, this type of music is not authentic Gypsy music, but a pop variety. If a member of the band plays a piece at your table, good manners dictate that you give a tip (100 Ft is an appropriate amount). You may, however, politely decline his or her offer to play for you.

RESTAURANT REVIEWS　*Budapest Week* published a book of restaurant reviews called ***Good Food Guide to Budapest*** in 1992. At press time, they had yet to come out with a revision. *Budapest Week* and the *Budapest Sun* regularly review new restaurants in town.

PRICE CATEGORIES　"Expensive" and "inexpensive" are relative terms; an expensive meal in Budapest might not be considered so in most other European capitals, so Budapest may well be the place for you to splurge.

 **FROMMER'S SMART TRAVELER:
RESTAURANTS**

VALUE-CONSCIOUS TRAVELERS SHOULD CONSIDER THE FOLLOWING:

1. Drink draft beer rather than bottled. Most restaurants now offer German or Austrian beer from the tap.
2. Look for fixed price "menu" meals, which usually include soup, salad, and dessert.
3. Avoid the tourist traps in central Pest and Buda's Castle District. You can get the same quality for far less at neighborhood establishments.

In the listings below, restaurants are rated **"Very Expensive"** if the majority of the main courses cost over 1,000 Ft ($11.10); **"Expensive"** if the cost is between 600 and 1,000 Ft ($6.65–$11.10); **"Moderate"** if the cost is between 300 and 600 Ft ($3.35–$6.65); and **"Inexpensive"** if they are under 300 Ft ($3.35).

Few restaurants outside the very expensive and expensive categories accept credit cards, and some in these two categories do not even accept them. You can assume that English-language menus are available in all very expensive and expensive restaurants. For all others, availability is noted in the listing.

1. VERY EXPENSIVE

THE INNER CITY & CENTRAL PEST

FRUTTA DI MARE, VI. Bajcsy-Zsilinszky út 21. Tel. 112-1039.
   Cuisine: ITALIAN/SEAFOOD. **Reservations:** Recommended.
   Metro: Arany János utca (Blue line).
   $ Prices: Appetizers 260–550 Ft ($2.90–$6.10); main courses 550–1,600 Ft ($6.10–$17.80). AE, DC, MC, V.
   Open: Daily noon–1am.
Opened in 1992, Frutta di Mare has already established itself as Budapest's premier seafood restaurant. The interior features marble floors, stucco walls, soft candlelight, and mauve tablecloths. Service is attentive but not overbearing. The fish is all imported from Italy, and the presentation is impeccable. For starters, try the Marseilles salad, a delicious blend of chopped apple, celery, nuts, and lemon. The salmon entree is perfectly prepared in a butter-dill dressing. Non-seafood dishes have recently been added to the menu.

LEGRADI TESTVÉREK, V. Magyar u. 23. Tel. 118-6804.
   Cuisine: HUNGARIAN. **Reservations:** Required. **Metro:** Kalvin tér (Blue line).
   $ Prices: Soups 200–300 Ft ($2.20–$3.30); main courses 850–1,500 Ft ($9.45–$16.65). No credit cards.
   Open: Weekdays 6pm–1am. **Closed:** Weekends.
A very small (nine tables) and inconspicuously marked restaurant on a sleepy side street in the northern part of the Inner City, Legradi Brothers is one of Budapest's most elegant and formal eateries. Food is served on world-famous Herend china, and an excellent string trio livens the atmosphere with its repertoire of Hungarian classics. If you're on a budget, pass on the initial, pre-menu offer of hors d'oeuvres which cost 800 Ft ($8.90). If you're inclined to try a soup, the cream of asparagus is a fine interpretation of a Hungarian favorite. The chicken paprika will surpass any you've tried elsewhere, and the

veal *cavellier*, smothered in a cauliflower cheese sauce, is equally sumptuous.

JUST BEYOND CENTRAL PEST

GUNDEL, XIV. Állatkerti út 2. Tel. 121-3550.
   Cuisine: HUNGARIAN/INTERNATIONAL. **Reservations:** Required. **Metro:** Hősök tere (Yellow line).
$ Prices: Soups 210–470 Ft ($2.35–$5.20); main courses 1,300 Ft ($14.45) and up. AE, DC, MC, V.
   Open: Restaurant: Daily noon–4pm and 7pm–midnight; terrace: Daily 10am–midnight.

Budapest's fanciest and most famous restaurant, Gundel was reopened in 1992 by the well-known restaurateur George Lang, owner of New York's Café des Artistes. The Hungarian born Lang, author of *The Cuisine of Hungary*, along with his partner Ronald Lauder, son of Estee Lauder, has spared no effort in attempting to re-create the original splendor for which Gundel, founded in 1894, achieved its international reputation. Located in the City Park, Gundel has an opulent dining room and a large, carefully groomed garden. The restaurant prides itself on preparing traditional dishes in an innovative fashion. Lamb and wild game entrees are house specialties. The menu also tends to highlight fruits and vegetables in season. In late spring, for instance, don't miss out on the asparagus served in hollandaise with grilled salmon. Gundel has perhaps the most extensive wine list in town; waiters are well versed in its offerings. The homemade fruit ice cream served in the shape of the fruit makes for a delectable dessert, as does the famous Gundel torta, a decadently rich chocolate layer cake. Budget-minded travelers should consider eating at Bagolyvár, the less fancy "home style" restaurant next door also owned by George Lang (see "Moderate," below).

CASTLE DISTRICT

ALABÁRDOS, I. Országház u. 2. Tel. 156-0851.
   Cuisine: HUNGARIAN **Reservations:** Required. **Bus:** Várbusz from Moszkva tér, bus 16 from Deák tér, bus 116 from Március 15 tér, or funicular from Clark Adam tér, to Castle Hill.
$ Prices: Soups 200–450 Ft ($2.20–$5); main courses 900–1,700 Ft ($10–$18.85). AE, DC, MC, V.
   Open: Mon–Sat noon–4pm and 7pm–midnight.

Alabárdos offers nouvelle cuisine Hungarian style in a small, posh setting. The historic building in which it is housed has several medieval details; 15th-century arches can be seen in the courtyard. The atmosphere inside is hushed and elegant, with a touch of pretentiousness. The walls are judiciously decorated with a medieval motif. A guitarist performs unobtrusively. Meals are served on Zsolnay porcelain, from Pécs. Outdoor dining is available in the courtyard.

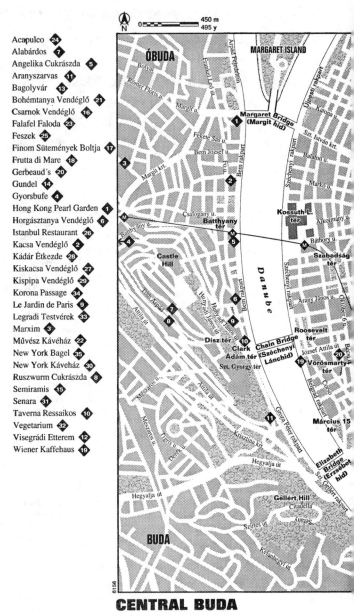
CENTRAL BUDA

KACSA VENDÉGLŐ, I. Fő u. 75. Tel. 201-9992.
   Cuisine: HUNGARIAN. **Reservations:** Recommended.
   Metro: Batthyány tér (Red line).
$ Prices: Soups 200 Ft ($2.25); main courses 800–1,700 Ft ($8.90–$18.90). AE, DC, MC, V.
   Open: Daily 6pm–1am.

CENTRAL BUDAPEST DINING

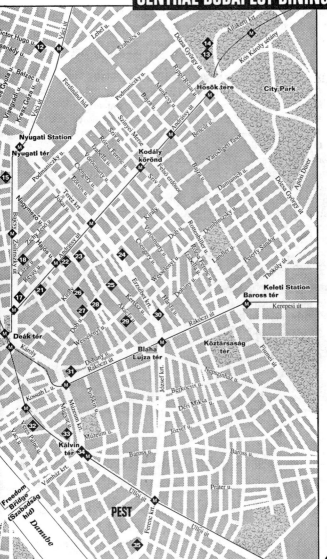

 Kacsa (which means "duck") is located on the main street of Watertown, the Buda neighborhood which lies between Castle Hill and the Danube. Here you'll find an intimate dining atmosphere, complete with attentive waiters and a concert-quality pianist. The understated elegance will appeal to diners who appreciate getting their money's worth. Enticing main courses include roast duck with sour cherries, haunch of venison with grapes, and pike perch Russian style. For dessert, sample the assorted strudels, prepared with fruits in season.

NORTHERN BUDA & ÓBUDA

KÉHLI VENDÉGLŐ, III. Mókus u. 22. Tel. 188-6938.
   Cuisine: HUNGARIAN. **Reservations:** Recommended.
   Metro: HÉV suburban railway from Batthyány tér to Árpád híd.
$ Prices: Soups 150–200 Ft ($1.65–$2.25); main courses 500–1,500 Ft ($5.55–$16.65). AE.
   Open: Daily 6pm–midnight.

Housed in a historic Óbuda building, Kéhli is an upscale traditional Hungarian restaurant with a cozy dining room and an enclosed garden. Located behind the Thermal Hotel Aquincum in Óbuda's old city, the restaurant can be difficult to find. Szinbad's Favorite, named for the famous pirate introduced to Hungary by author Gyula Krúdy, is one of the house specialties: pork stuffed with chicken liver rolled in bacon and served in a paprika-and-mushroom sauce. Another dish which is certainly worth sampling is the roast goose liver with garlic. Dinner is accompanied by live music.

KIS BUDA GYÖNGYE, III. Kenyeres u. 34. Tel. 168-6402.
   Cuisine: HUNGARIAN. **Reservations:** Highly recommended.
   Tram: 17 from Margit híd (Buda side).
$ Prices: Soups 120–180 Ft ($1.35–$2); main courses 480–1,200 Ft ($5.30–$13.30); fish dishes to 2,400 Ft ($26.65). AE.
   Open: Daily noon–midnight.

On a quiet side street in a residential Óbuda neighborhood, Kis Buda Gyöngye, which means the "Little Pearl of Buda," is a favorite of Hungarians and tourists alike. A lively, cheerful establishment, its interior garden sits in the shade of a wonderful old gnarly tree. Inside, an eccentric violin player entertains diners. The food, standard Hungarian fare, is prepared with great care. Try the goose plate, a rich combination platter including roast goose leg, goose cracklings, and goose liver. Various bottled import beers are available. The service is slow.

2. EXPENSIVE

THE INNER CITY & CENTRAL PEST

ACAPULCO, VII. Erzsébet körút 39. Tel. 122-6014.
   Cuisine: MEXICAN. **Reservations:** Accepted. **Tram:** 4 or 6 to Király utca.
$ Prices: Main courses 475–800 Ft ($5.30–$8.90). No credit cards.

Open: Daily noon–midnight.

Acapulco offers the only authentic Mexican food in Budapest, in a somewhat cliché Mexican atmosphere. Acapulco's homemade tortilla chips are terrific; unlimited chips and salsa come without charge. The enormous and sumptuous burrito is the best buy for hungry diners. Vegetarians simply need to request any dish from the menu prepared to order without meat. The beer, including Corona, is overpriced—starting at 210 Ft ($2.35). Margaritas are 300 Ft ($3.35). There is a happy hour Monday to Thursday from 7 to 9pm, and all-you-can-eat Sunday brunch from noon to 4pm. The restaurant's owner is George Hemingway, the Hungarian-American who brought Dunkin' Donuts, Kentucky Fried Chicken, Pizza Hut, and the ubiquitous Bon Bon Hemingway to Hungary.

ISTANBUL RESTAURANT, VII. Király u. 17. Tel. 122-1466.
   Cuisine: TURKISH. **Reservations:** Recommended for dinner.
   Metro: Oktogon (Yellow line).
   $ Prices: Main courses 500–700 Ft ($5.55–$7.75). No credit cards.
   Open: Mon–Sat noon–11pm; Sun 6–11pm.

A 5-minute walk from Oktogon, the Istanbul is a dark, sober looking place with a varied, authentic Turkish menu. During the day, they sell delicious doner kebab sandwiches from a window (140 Ft/$1.55 each); unfortunately, they're only available from the street. An English-language menu is available.

SENARA, VII. Dohány u. 5. Tel. 142-6313.
   Cuisine: KOREAN. **Reservations:** Recommended. **Metro:** Astoria (Red line).
   $ Prices: Main courses 410–1,900 Ft ($4.55–$21.10); menu meals 830–890 Ft ($9.20–$9.90). 10% service charge added to bill. AE, DC, MC, V.
   Open: Daily 11:30am–2:30pm and 6–10:30pm.

Senara offers top-flight Korean fare in air-conditioned comfort in the heart of Pest. Tables have considerable privacy, with tasteful wood-lattice work dividing them. Korean music plays softly in the background. Many of the meat meals are cooked on a grill sunk into the middle of each table. The menu, though in English, is complicated and arcane. Your best bet is to select one of the special menu meals, which come with soup, salad, rice, *kimshi* (fiery hot Korean cabbage), and a main course. The Pulkogi menu is a beef and chicken combination: You cook the thin strips of meat at your table, dip them in soy sauce, and eat them with rice—a delicious meal!

CENTRAL BUDA

ARANYSZARVAS, I. Szarvas tér 1. Tel. 175-8424.
   Cuisine: HUNGARIAN. **Reservations:** Recommended. **Bus:**

A number of buses serve Döbrentei tér, including the 8 from Március 15 tér.

$ Prices: Soups 120 Ft ($1.35); main courses 450–790 Ft ($5–$8.75). AE, DC, MC, V.

Open: Mon–Sat noon–2am, Sun noon–midnight.

⑤ "The Golden Stag" is located in a historic building in central Buda's Tabán district, just beneath and to the south of Castle Hill. There is indoor seating in a dining room with a restrained wild game motif, but on pleasant nights customers dine on the outdoor terrace, where they are serenaded by a string trio. As the name and decor suggest, this is a wild game restaurant: The English-language menu lists a variety of reasonably priced dishes, such as hunter's saddle of hare, Serbian wild boar, and venison stew. Elsa Furst (from New York City) tried the pheasant with mustard sauce, which turned out to be a risotto: "First I was disappointed, but then I was pleasantly surprised." German beer (Warsteiner) is on draft. The desserts are worth sampling as well, particularly the mixed strudel, prepared with seasonal fruit.

HONG KONG PEARL GARDEN, II. Margit körút 2. Tel. 115-3606.

Cuisine: SZECHUAN. **Reservations:** Recommended. **Tram:** 4 or 6 to Buda side of Margaret Bridge.

$ Prices: Soups 180–250 Ft ($2–$2.75); main courses 480–2,000 Ft ($5.30–$22.20). No credit cards.

Open: Mon–Sat noon–2:30pm and 6:30–11:30pm, Sun noon–10pm.

⑤ In a prime location just over the Margaret Bridge on Buda's Margit körút, the Hong Kong Pearl Garden opened in 1993. Though Budapest is saturated with Chinese restaurants, this one was well received and immediately became popular. The atmosphere is luxurious, but not suffocating. Tables are well spread out and the lighting is restrained, homage to the natural brightness of the many-windowed establishment. Service is on the slow side, but the wait staff is uniformly friendly, and all speak some English. There is a variety of duck dishes—including Peking Duck (order in advance)—on the English-language menu.

LE JARDIN DE PARIS, I. Fő u. 20. Tel. 201-0047.

Cuisine: FRENCH. **Reservations:** Recommended. **Metro:** Batthyány tér (Red line).

$ Prices: Main courses 450–1,100 Ft ($5–$12.20). AE, DC, V.

Open: Daily 11am–midnight.

In the heart of Buda's Watertown (Vízíváros), directly across the street from the monstrous Institut Francais, Le Jardin de Paris is Budapest's closest approximation of a French bistro. It is a cozy cellar restaurant, with an eclectic collection of graphic arts on the walls. A jazz trio often accompanies the dining. The menu, in French as well as English, contains a variety of nouvelle French specialties, including bouillabaisse and pâte foie gras. Presentation is impeccable, and the wine list features a variety of both French and Hungarian vintages.

THE BUDA HILLS

UDVARHÁZ A HÁRMASHATÁRHEGYEN, I. Hármashatár-hegyi út 2. Tel. 188-8780.

    Cuisine: HUNGARIAN. **Reservations:** Recommended. **Bus:** 65 from Kolosy tér in Óbuda.

$ Prices: Soups 110–170 Ft ($1.25–$1.90); main courses 550–1,100 Ft ($6.10–$12.20). AE, DC, MC, V.

    Open: Daily Nov–Apr 6–11pm; May–Oct 11am–11pm.

This lovely restaurant high in the Buda Hills boasts several elegant dining rooms, in addition to tables on the terrace with a great panoramic view of the city. Dinner here is a full evening; in the courtyard there is a folklore show, with music and dance. The menu features a large variety of Hungarian specialties, particularly fish and game specialties. Other than by taxi, the only way to get here is by taking the 65 bus to the last stop (the last bus heads back at 10pm).

3. MODERATE

THE INNER CITY & CENTRAL PEST

FÉSZEK, VII. Kertész u. 36. Tel. 122-6043.

    Cuisine: HUNGARIAN. **Reservations:** Recommended. **Tram:** 4 or 6 to Király utca.

$ Prices: Main courses 260–590 Ft ($2.90–$6.55); special menu 370–420 Ft ($4.10–$4.65). No credit cards.

    Open: Daily noon–1am.

This restaurant is owned by the same people who own the better-known Kispipa Vendéglő (see below). Just as at Kispipa, wild game dishes are the specialty of the house, and the best deal is to be had with a special menu meal. At Fészek you'll find a lovely, quiet interior garden, offering an outdoor dining experience without equal in the busy center of Pest. Be sure to reserve ahead of time since Fészek is always crowded. An English-language menu is available.

KISPIPA VENDÉGLŐ, VII. Akácfa u. 38. Tel. 142-2587.

    Cuisine: HUNGARIAN. **Reservations:** Recommended. **Metro:** Oktogon (Yellow line).

$ Prices: Main courses 260–590 Ft ($2.90–$6.55); special menu 370–420 Ft ($4.10–$4.65).

    Open: Mon–Sat noon–1am.

Unobtrusively located on a residential street in Erzsébetváros, behind the old Jewish district, Kispipa (Little Pipe) is a well-lit, medium-sized establishment. The cream-colored walls are lined with vintage Hungarian poster advertisements, and piano music contributes to the relaxed atmosphere. The menu is extensive; wild game dishes are the house specialty. Five "complete menu" deals offer soup, main course, and dessert for a very reasonable price. Kispipa, at one time one of

Budapest's only private restaurants, is popular among Hungarians, who constitute at least half of its daily clientele. There is an English menu translation.

VEGETARIUM, V. Cukor u. 3. Tel. 138-3710.
   Cuisine: VEGETARIAN. **Reservations:** Recommended for dinner. **Metro:** Ferenciek tere (Blue line).
$ Prices: Main courses 300–500 Ft ($3.35–$5.55).
   Open: Noon–10pm daily.

Vegetarium, one of Budapest's few strictly vegetarian restaurants, is unusually fancy and a touch pretentious, with waiters in black tie. The prices, however, are moderate, with most main courses costing around 400 Ft ($4.45). The menu, heavy on macrobiotic dishes, is translated into English. Alcoholic drinks are available. The cream of broccoli soup, a rare find in Hungary, is a treat.

JUST BEYOND CENTRAL PEST

BAGOLYVÁR, XIV. Állatkerti út 2. Tel. 121-3550.
   Cuisine: HUNGARIAN. **Reservations:** Recommended.
   Metro: Hősök tere (Yellow line).
$ Prices: Soups 60–75 Ft (65¢–80¢); main courses 200–420 Ft ($2.20–$4.65). AE.
   Open: Daily 11am–10pm.

S Bagolyvár (Owl Palace) offers something unique to the budget traveler—a taste of Gundel, Budapest's most famous (and most expensive) restaurant, at budget prices. George Lang, the well-known owner of Gundel, wanted to offer Hungarian "home-style" cooking to the general public at a reasonable price, and thus was born his second Budapest eatery, located just next door to Gundel in the City Park. The Bagolyvár menu is limited to a half dozen main courses (supplemented by daily specials), which include roast veal with green beans as well as layered savoy cabbage. Delicious desserts include chocolate poppyseed cake and fresh fruit salad. The food is carefully prepared and presented. The decor and ambience are pleasant and unpretentious. Outdoor dining is available in the restaurant's garden.

CENTRAL BUDA

HORGÁSZTANYA VENDÉGLŐ, I. Fő u. 29. Tel. 201-0683.
   Cuisine: HUNGARIAN. **Reservations:** Accepted. **Metro:** Battyhány tér (Red line).

IMPRESSIONS

The cafes are never empty here . . . Everyone loiters on the Corso, for no one is in a hurry in Budapest. If a cool breeze comes up, the waiters bring small steamer rugs for their patrons.
—GRACE HUMPHREY, AMERICAN MEMOIRIST, 1936

$ Prices: Soups 80–105 Ft (90¢–$1.15); main courses 235–630 Ft ($2.60–$7). AE.

Open: Daily noon–midnight.

Just a short block from the Danube, in Buda's Watertown (Víziváros), the Horgásztanya Vendéglő is a family-style fish restaurant. Although the restaurant specializes in fish dishes, non-fish eaters can dine here too; the extensive menu (in English) lists a variety of Hungarian specialties. The decor is traditional Hungarian and unpretentious.

TAVERNA RESSAIKOS, I. Apor Péter u. 1. Tel. 135-0361.

Cuisine: GREEK. **Reservations:** Recommended. **Bus or tram:** Any to Clark Ádám tér, including bus 16 from Deák tér.

$ Prices: Appetizers 100–250 Ft ($1.10–$2.75); main courses 450–650 Ft ($5–$7.20). No credit cards.

Open: Daily noon–midnight.

This new Greek restaurant is located in the heart of Buda's Watertown (Víziváros), just next door to the Hotel Alba Budapest. The chef is Greek, and the food is both savory and well priced. The live guitar music is wonderful, but a tad too loud: Conversation can be difficult. The menu (in English) offers standard Greek fare. Try the delicious calamari, or the sumptuous lamb in wine. The menu also features a number of goat dishes and Amstel beer on tap at reasonable prices. Service is attentive, but on the slow side.

THE BUDA HILLS

NANCSI NÉNI VENDÉGLŐJE, II. Ördögárok út 80. Tel. 176-5809.

Cuisine: HUNGARIAN. **Reservations:** Recommended for dinner. **Tram:** 56 from Moszkva tér to last stop, switch to bus 63 to Széchenyi utca.

$ Prices: Main courses 400–700 Ft ($4.45–$7.80). No credit cards.

Open: Daily noon–10pm.

Decorated with photographs of turn-of-the-century Budapest (including a copy of the coffee shop picture which appears on the cover of John Lukacs' sentimental *Budapest, 1900*), this restaurant is located high in the hills. There is outdoor garden dining in the summer, with live accordion music at night. The menu (available in English) features typical Hungarian dishes, which are prepared with care. Avoid the table located too close to the men's room. The restaurant is near Mariana Villa, St. Christoph Villa, and the Petneházy Country Club.

SZÉP ILONA, II. Budakeszi út 1-3. Tel. 155-2851.

Cuisine: HUNGARIAN. **Bus:** 158 from Moszkva tér (departs from Csaba u., at the top of the stairs, by the little Várbusz.)

$ Prices: Soups 80–170 Ft (90¢–$1.90); main courses 260–500 Ft ($2.90–$5.55). No credit cards.

Open: Daily 11:30am–10pm.

This cheerful, unassuming restaurant serves a mostly local clientele. There is a good selection of Hungarian specialties on the English-language menu; try the veal paprika (*borjúpaprikás galuskaval*) served with *knockerl* (a typical central European–style of dumpling). There is a small sidewalk-side garden for summer dining. Szép Ilona is located in a pleasant Buda neighborhood; after your meal take a walk through the tree-lined streets.

NORTHERN BUDA & ÓBUDA

MALOMTÓ ÉTTEREM, II. Frankel Leo u. 48. Tel. 135-0315.
   Cuisine: HUNGARIAN. **Reservations:** Recommended for dinner. **Tram:** 17 from Margit híd (Buda side) to Lukács Baths (Lukács Fürdő).
$ Prices: Soups 90–150 Ft ($1–$1.65); main courses 295–580 Ft ($3.30–$6.45). AE, DC, MC, V.
   Open: Daily 11am–11pm.

Right across the street from the Lukács Baths, the Malomtó (named for the Mill Pond nearby) is built at the base of a hill. There is an outdoor terrace, and piano music nightly. The menu is well-translated and features a good variety of Hungarian specialties. Salads are quite good, but since the main course portions are themselves huge, you may want to bypass soup and salad. The *Kolozsvári töltött kaposzta* (stuffed cabbage, Kolozsvár style) is one of the best available in Budapest restaurants of this price category.

SIPOS HALÁSZKERT, III. Fő tér 6. Tel. 188-8745.
   Cuisine: HUNGARIAN/SEAFOOD. **Reservations:** Recommended. **Metro:** Suburban HÉV line to Árpád híd.
$ Prices: Main courses 300–1,000 Ft ($3.35–$11.10). 10% service charge added to the bill. MC, V.
   Open: Daily noon–midnight.

   In its own handsome building on Óbuda's dignified main square, the restaurant consists of several rooms with a comfortable air of worn elegance. The menu, specializing in Hungarian seafood dishes, is translated into English. The experienced musicians in the string trio enhance the atmosphere.

4. INEXPENSIVE

THE INNER CITY & CENTRAL PEST

BOHÉMTANYA VENDÉGLŐ, VI. Paulay Ede u. 6. Tel. 122-1453.
   Cuisine: HUNGARIAN. **Reservations:** Recommended. **Metro:** Deák tér (all lines).

$ Prices: Soups 70–130 Ft (75¢–$1.45); main courses 180–480 Ft ($2–$5.30). No credit cards.
Open: Daily 11am–11pm.

Its location on a narrow side street, just minutes from the bustle of Deák tér, makes the Bohémtanya a perfectly placed pit stop for the weary tourist. A famous old Pest establishment, now often included in Western tour guides, this vendéglő retains its local flavor. The *bableves* (bean soup) may be the best in the city; a giant bowl, for 130 Ft ($1.45), can constitute a meal in itself. A beerhall atmosphere reigns, with wooden tables and booths beneath bare white walls. Indeed, everyone here seems to be drinking half-liter draft beers. The service is a bit sketchy, so don't go if you're in a hurry. The menu has been recently translated into English.

CSARNOK VENDÉGLŐ, V. Hold u. 11. Tel. 112-2016.

Cuisine: HUNGARIAN. **Metro:** Arany János (Blue line).
$ Prices: Soups 35–52 Ft (40¢–60¢); main courses 150–270 Ft ($1.65–$3). MC.
Open: Daily 9am–midnight.

On the Inner City's quiet Hold utca (Moon Street), the Csarnok Vendéglő is located between Szabadság tér and Bajcsy-Zsilinszky út. Its name comes from the wonderful turn-of-the-century market hall (*csarnok*) next door. One of the few restaurants in this part of the Inner City, it is even more notable for its uniformly low prices. The menu (in English translation) features typical Hungarian vendéglő fare, heavy as usual on meat dishes. Outdoor seating is available on the sidewalk, but sit inside for the full effect.

FALAFEL FALODA, VI. Paulay Ede u. 53. No tel.

Cuisine: MIDDLE EASTERN. **Metro:** Oktogon or Opera (Yellow line).
$ Prices: Felafel 95 Ft ($1.05); large salad 110 Ft ($1.20).
Open: Weekdays 10am–8pm. Erratic hours in summer.

Falafel Faloda is a small, fast-paced, cafeteria-style eatery, with informal dining in a loft. The loft has surprisingly good air circulation and is usually cooler than the street. Order a large salad with a slice of pita bread. Build yourself a towering felafel salad from the salad bar. The restaurant is on the corner of Nagymező utca, halfway between Oktogon and the Opera House.

KÁDÁR ÉTKEZDE, VII. Klauzál tér 9. Tel. 121-3622.

Cuisine: HUNGARIAN. **Metro:** Astoria (Red line) or Deák tér (all lines).
$ Prices: Soups 60–70 Ft (65¢–80¢); main courses 120–250 Ft ($1.35–$2.80). No credit cards.
Open: Tues–Sat 11:30am–3:30pm.

By 11:45, Uncle Kádár's, in the heart of the historic Jewish district, is filled with a steady stream of lunchtime regulars— from paint-spattered workers to elderly Jewish couples. Uncle

Kádár, a neighborhood legend, personally greets them as they file in. It's no more than a lunchroom, but it has a great atmosphere: high ceilings, wood-paneled walls with photographs (many autographed) of actors and athletes, and old-fashioned seltzer bottles on every table. The food is simple, but hearty. The service is fast and friendly. The menu is only in Hungarian, but if you see something you like on someone else's plate you can always employ the pointing technique. Try the *hideg gyümölcsleves* (cold fruit soup), followed by the *töltött paprika* (stuffed peppers). Table sharing is the norm here.

KISKACSA VENDÉGLŐ, VII. Dob u. 26. Tel. 122-6208.

Cuisine: HUNGARIAN. **Metro:** Deák tér (all lines).
$ Prices: Main courses 150–300 Ft ($1.65–$3.35). No credit cards.
Open: Daily 10am–midnight.

"The Little Duck" offers very cheap Hungarian fare on Dob utca, in the heart of Pest's historic Jewish district. At lunchtime local residents fill their lunch pails at the kitchen window. The pasta is homemade—try the *túró csúsza,* a kind of macaroni-and-cheese dish. Vegetarians should ask for it *tepertő nélkül* (without bacon). Salads are on the small side. The menu is only in Hungarian and German, and no one here speaks English. It's a clean, bright place, with red tablecloths. There is live music nightly.

KORONA PASSAGE, V. Kecskeméti u. 14. Tel. 117-4111.

Cuisine: CRÊPERIE/SALAD BAR. **Metro:** Kálvin tér (Blue line).
$ Prices: Crêpes 120–220 Ft ($1.35–$2.45); salad bar 140–200 Ft ($1.55–$2.20). No credit cards.
Open: Daily 10am–10pm.

This is a great place for lunch in central Pest. The prices here are incredibly low, especially considering that it's in the Korona luxury hotel. Giant crêpes are made to order; fillings range from cheese to chopped walnut. The self-serve salad bar is one of only a handful in Budapest. A long arcade-style restaurant, with a skylight and a tree in the middle, the atmosphere is bright and clean. The Hotel Korona was built at the spot where the original medieval Pest city wall once stood, and a piece of it remains in the restaurant.

SEMIRAMIS, V. Alkotmány u. 20. Tel. 111-7627.

Cuisine: MIDDLE EASTERN. **Metro:** Kossuth tér (Red line).
$ Prices: Appetizers 80–130 Ft (90¢–$1.45); main courses 170–340 Ft ($1.90–$3.80). No credit cards.
Open: Mon–Sat noon–9pm, closed Sun.

Located just a block from Parliament and a few blocks from Nyugati Station, this little restaurant is best suited for lunch since they tend to run out of the more popular dishes by evening. Seating is upstairs in a small room, decorated with tapestries and colorful straw trivets. The atmosphere is casual.

The waiters are uniformly friendly, and all speak a little English (though the menu is only in Hungarian and Arabic). Everything is delicious, including the house specialty, chicken breast with spinach (*spenótos csirkemell*). Vegetarians can easily build a meal out of several appetizers; try the yogurt-cucumber salad (*yogurtos salata*) and the *fül* (a zesty garlic and bean dish).

JUST BEYOND CENTRAL PEST

VISEGRÁDI ÉTTEREM, XIII. Visegrádi u. 50/a. Tel. 140-3316.
    Cuisine: VEGETARIAN. **Metro:** Lehel tér (Blue line).
$ Prices: Soups 85–95 Ft (95¢–$1.05); main courses 160–270 Ft ($1.80–$3); half-liter draft beer 120 Ft ($1.35). No credit cards.
    Open: Daily noon–midnight.

North of Pest's city center, this vegetarian restaurant occupies the former space of a slightly somber and wanna-be-elegant state restaurant. Given the amount of energy most new private Budapest restaurants are putting into decor—too often at the expense of quality—it is refreshing to find one which seems content to occupy a room so clearly designed for a different, now almost vanished kind of eatery. Of the two connected rooms, one has been designated non-smoking, a rarity in this town. Visegrádi's menu (with English translation) mixes ethnic specialties with innocent abandon: You'll find tzatziki (*cacika*) and cold cherry soup (both delicious), soy bean roast and chopped millet of Djajpora, pizza and falafel. Indulge: It's all tasty, and it all has a slight Hungarian overtone. Friday and Saturday nights there's music and dancing from 8pm.

CENTRAL BUDA

MARXIM, II. Kisrókus u. 23. Tel. 115-5036.
    Cuisine: PIZZA. **Metro:** Moszkva tér (Red line).
$ Prices: Pizza 120–220 Ft ($1.35–$2.45); pasta 130–190 Ft ($1.45–$2.10). No credit cards.
    Open: Mon–Thurs noon–1am, Fri–Sat noon–2am, Sun 6pm–1am.

On a gritty industrial street near Moszkva tér, Marxim's appeal lies not in its cuisine, but in its decor. The motif is Marxist nostalgia. The cellar space is decorated with barbed wire, red flags, banners, posters, and photographs recalling Hungary's dark past. Amazingly, this is one of the few places in Budapest where you can actually see this kind of stuff, so thorough has been the erasure of the symbols of the Communist period. Marxim is actually operating in violation of a controversial new law banning the display of the symbols of "hateful" political organizations. There is an English-language menu of pizza and pasta; Amstel beer is on draft.

THE BUDA HILLS

MAKKHETES VENDÉGLŐ, XII. Németvölgyi út 56. No tel.
    Cuisine: HUNGARIAN. **Bus:** 105 from Deák tér.
$ Prices: Soups 60–90 Ft (65¢–$1); main courses 180–350 Ft ($2–$3.90). No credit cards.

Open: Daily noon–11pm.

In the lower part of the Buda Hills, Makkhetes ("7 of Acorns," a Hungarian playing card) is an unassuming neighborhood eatery. The food is good, the portions large. The menu, though fairly extensive, is unavailable in English translation. You won't go wrong with the *paprika csirke galuskaval* (chicken paprika with dumplings). Outdoor dining is available.

5. SPECIALTY DINING

COFFEEHOUSES

Imperial Budapest, like Vienna, was famous for its coffeehouse culture. Literary movements and political circles alike were identified in large part by which coffeehouse they met in. Sandor Petöfi, the revolutionary poet of 1848 fame, is said to have instructed his friend János Arany, another leading Hungarian poet of the day, to write to him in care of the Pilvax Coffee House; he spent more time there than at home. Communism managed to dull this cherished institution, but a few classic coffeehouses have miraculously survived the tangled tragedies of the 20th century.

All the classic coffeehouses offer delicious pastries and coffee in an atmosphere of luxurious splendor. Many offer small sandwiches, some serve ice cream, and some feature bar drinks. Pastries are displayed in a glass case and generally cost between 50 and 100 Ft (55¢–$1.10); coffee costs between 50 and 75 Ft (55¢–85¢). Table

---

**Ⓕ FROMMER'S COOL FOR KIDS:
RESTAURANTS**

Bagolyvár *(see p. 108)* This is the place to go if your visit to the child-oriented sights in City Park takes you to the lunch or dinner hour. Under the same management and right next door to the famous (and pricey) Gundel, Bagolyvár offers excellent home-style cooking at very moderate prices.

Gerbeaud's *(see p. 115)* Be sure to make a stop at Budapest's most famous coffeehouse for a special dessert. It's an elegant place, but in good weather you can get a table outside on bustling Vörösmarty tér and watch the kids play around (and on) the square's fountain.

Marxim *(see p. 113)* Come to this cellar restaurant for good ol' pizza and pasta; teenagers will appreciate what may be Budapest's most bizarre restaurant decor.

sharing is customary. Lingering for hours over a single cup of coffee or pastry is perfectly acceptable in Budapest.

THE INNER CITY & CENTRAL PEST

GERBEAUD'S, V. Vörösmarty tér 7. Tel. 118-1311.

Gerbeaud's is probably the city's most famous coffeehouse. Founded in 1858, it has stood on its current spot since 1870. Whether you sit inside amidst the splendor of the turn-of-the-century furnishings or outside on one of Pest's liveliest squares, you will be sure to enjoy the fine pastries which have made the name Gerbeaud famous. Its reputation and location assure that it is filled to capacity throughout the year; good luck getting a table in the late afternoon. **Metro:** Vörösmarty tér (Yellow line). **Open:** Daily 9am–9pm.

MŰVÉSZ KÁVÉHÁZ, VI. Andrássy út 29. Tel. 112-4606.

Just across Andrássy út from the Opera House, Művész, which means *Artist*, is one of the finest traditional coffeehouses in Budapest. The lush interior includes marble table tops, crystal chandeliers, and mirrored walls. Despite its grandeur, Művész retains a casual atmosphere. There are tables on the street, but sit inside for the full coffeehouse effect. Decaffeinated cappuccino is available, a rarity in Budapest. **Metro:** Opera (Yellow line). **Open:** Daily 9am–midnight.

NEW YORK KÁVÉHÁZ, VII. Erzsébet körút 9-11. Tel. 122-3849.

In the ground floor of a spectacular art nouveau palace built at the end of the 19th century, the New York Coffeehouse has a history as rich as the ornate decoration of its interior. In the early 20th century it was perhaps the city's best-known meeting place for artists, poets, writers, and actors, and portraits of famous regulars line the walls upstairs. From 1954 to 1989 it was known as the Hungaria. In spite of the presence of the seemingly permanent scaffolding outside, the interior has been carefully restored. Expensive but mediocre meals (800–1,000 Ft) are served in a sunken room in the center, but this establishment is best suited for coffee and pastries. **Metro:** Blaha Lujza tér (Red line). **Open:** Daily 9am–10pm.

WIENER KAFFEEHAUS, V. Hotel Forum, Apáczai Csere János u. 12-14. Tel. 117-9111.

A faithful reproduction of a Viennese coffeehouse, located inside one of Budapest's finer luxury hotels, the Wiener Kávéház serves up delicious pastry. The bon bons are particularly popular, and are available in variously sized gift packages. **Metro:** Deák tér (all lines). **Open:** Daily 9am–10pm.

CENTRAL BUDA

ANGELIKA CUKRÁSZDA, I. Batthyány tér 7. Tel. 115-5233.

The Angelika Cukrászda is housed in a historic building next to St. Anne's Church in Buda's Batthyány tér. The sunken rooms of this cavernous cafe provide the perfect retreat on a hot summer day. Stained-glass windows, marble floors, and emerald green upholstery contribute to the quiet old-world atmosphere, and there are excellent pastries. **Metro:** Batthyány tér (Red line). **Open:** Daily 10am–10pm.

CASTLE DISTRICT

RUSZWURM CUKRÁSZDA, I. Szentháromság u. 7. Tel. 175-5284.

The only authentic coffeehouse in the Castle District, the Ruszwurm is over 100 years old. It is an utterly charming little place, with tiny tables and chairs, and wall shelves lined with antiques. It can be very difficult to find a free table. **Bus:** Várbusz from Moszkva tér, bus 16 from Deák tér, bus 116 from Március 15 tér, or funicular from Clark Ádám tér, to Castle Hill. **Open:** Daily 10am–10pm.

SNACKS & FAST FOOD

Western fast-food joints like McDonalds, Burger King, Kentucky Fried Chicken, Dairy Queen, and Dunkin' Donuts have arrived in Budapest. But why not sample the local fare? Below are some of the best places in Budapest to grab a snack on the run.

The **Finom Sütemények Boltja** (Shop of Delicious Pastries), at VI. Révay u. 2, is located on Bajcsy-Zsilinszky út, near the rear of St. Stephen's Basilica. It's no more than a bakery, though limited seating is available. Try the quintessentially Hungarian *pogácsa* (15–20 Ft/17¢–22¢), a flaky flat-topped biscuit that comes in many varieties. Three types are offered here—*vajas* (butter), *burgonyas* (potato), and *tepertős* (prepared with bacon fat). Also try the *rétes* (25 Ft/28¢), or strudel. Offerings here include *túró* (a cottage cheese–like filling) and *meggy* (sour cherry). It's open weekdays 8am to 6:30pm, Saturday 8am to 3:30pm. Metro: Deák tér (all lines).

Hungarian-style fast-food sandwiches are available 24 hours a day from the **Gyorsbufe** (Fast Buffet) kiosk in Moszkva tér. As you emerge from the metro (Red line), it's to the left of the clock; look for the line of people. The menu changes daily, but usually two or three types of hot sandwiches are available: *húsos meleg szendvics* is meat sauce and melted cheese on half a baguette; *gomba meleg szendvics* is the same, but with a mushroom rather than meat sauce; and *hamburger* is a Hungarian variant on the tradition (*sajtos* is with cheese). *Hamburger hús nélkül,* a bun stuffed with fixings, is the best choice for vegetarians. All sandwiches cost 50–70 Ft (55¢–80¢). Sodas and ice cream are also for sale.

Bagels were born in Eastern Europe, and though they haven't been seen here for some half century or more, three New Yorkers (actually they're from New Jersey!) have decided to reintroduce them to Budapest. The happy result is **New York Bagel,** at Ferenc Körút 20 (tel. 215-7880) (Metro: Ferenc körút-Blue line). Not the best bagel to ever come down the pike, but definitely passable. They cost 32–36

Ft (35¢–40¢), with added cost for spreads and toppings, which include cream cheese and lox, both unavailable elsewhere in Budapest. Try the mixed bagel (*vegyes*), baked with Hungarian paprika. There is free delivery on orders of 400 Ft ($4.45) or more—and that's a good thing since New York Bagel is rather inconveniently located at the far southern end of Pest's Outer Ring boulevard.

CHAPTER 6

WHAT TO SEE & DO IN BUDAPEST

Historic Budapest is surprisingly small, and many of the sights listed in the following pages can be reached by foot from the center of the city. Take the time to stroll from one attraction to the next; you'll find yourself passing magnificent, if faded, examples of the various types of architecture.

SUGGESTED ITINERARIES

IF YOU HAVE 1 DAY

Day 1: Spend a few hours in the morning exploring the Inner City and central Pest. Walk the length of Váci utca, the city's trendiest shopping street, to Vörösmarty tér. Stop for cappuccino and a slice of apple strudel (almás rétes) at the sumptuous Gerbeaud coffeehouse. Walk along the Danube as far as the Neo-Gothic Parliament building, noting along the way the Chain Bridge and the Gresham Palace. Lunch with the locals at Bohémtanya Vendéglő on Paulay Ede utca. Save the whole afternoon for the major sites of Castle Hill and to explore the cobblestoned streets of the Castle District. Splurge for dinner at Alabardos, one of the district's fancier restaurants.

IF YOU HAVE 2 DAYS

Day 1: See Pest, as above, saving the Castle District for tomorrow. Walk the Outer Ring boulevard noting Nyugati Railway Station and the New York Palace, grand examples of turn-of-the-century architecture. Stop for coffee and a slice of *dobos torta* (layer cake) at the exquisite New York Cafe, inside the Palace. Later, head to Buda's Gellért Hotel and unwind in its medicinal spa waters. Refreshed, hike the stairs of Gellért Hill to see the Liberation Monument and an unparalleled panorama of the city.

Day 2: Devote most of the day to the Castle District, as above. Visit some of the smaller museums as well, like the Music History Museum (check for a recital) or the Military History Museum. Head back to Pest later to see Heroes' Square and City Park. Splurge on dinner at Gundel, where visiting royalty dined in turn-of-the-century Budapest. Afterwards, stroll the length of grand Andrássy út back towards the center of Pest.

IF YOU HAVE 3 DAYS

Days 1–2: Spend days 1–2 as above. Spend one evening attending a concert at the Ferenc Liszt Music Academy, Budapest's finest hall.

Day 3: Take a boat up the Danube to Szentendre, a charming riverside town, home to a flourishing artist's colony. Don't miss the Margit Kovács Museum, where the work of Hungary's most innovative ceramic artist can be seen. Return in time for a final dinner at elegant Kacsa Vendéglő in Budapest's Watertown.

IF YOU HAVE 5 DAYS

Days 1–3: Spend days 1–3 as above.

Day 4: In the morning, visit some of the central Pest sights you may have missed, like the Opera House or St. Stephen's Basilica. After lunch, cross the Chain Bridge to Watertown, Buda's historic riverside neighborhood. See St. Anne's Church, the Capuchin Church, and the Király Baths, one of the only remaining examples of Turkish architecture in Budapest. Later, take a ride through the scenic Buda Hills on the Children's Railroad.

Day 5: First thing in the morning, visit one of Pest's authentic indoor market halls and sample Hungary's scrumptious fruit in season.

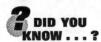

DID YOU KNOW . . . ?

- Budapest's Jewish population (about 80,000) is the largest of any European city outside Russia.
- Budapest was the site of the European continent's first underground metro line, which is still running today (the Yellow line).
- All of Budapest's bridges were blown up by the retreating Nazis in the final days of World War II.
- Before he became Roman emperor, Hadrian served as Governor of Pannonia, the Roman province which had Aquincum, in Óbuda, as its capital. Ovid lived in Aquincum.
- Budapest is home to the northernmost Islamic shrine in Europe, the tomb of Gül Baba.

Head to the Ethnographical Museum or the Applied Arts Museum, treasure troves of the rich Hungarian culture. After lunch, get away from the hustle and bustle of the city on Margaret Island. Stroll through the rose gardens, rent a bike, or just sunbathe in this peaceful setting. Later, as the sun is setting, return to the Castle District for a final look.

1. THE TOP ATTRACTIONS

PEST

MUSEUMS

ETHNOGRAPHICAL MUSEUM [NÉPRAJZI MÚZEUM], V. Kossuth tér 12. Tel. 132-6340.

Directly across Kossuth tér from the House of Parliament, the vast Ethnographical Museum is located in the stately Neo-Renaissance/eclectic former Hungarian Supreme Court building. The ornate interior rivals that of the Opera House, the lobby dominated by a ceiling fresco of Justitia, the goddess of justice, by the well-known artist Károly Lotz. Although a third of the museum's holdings are from outside Hungary, concentrate on the items from Hungarian ethnography. The fascinating permanent exhibition, "From Ancient Times to Civilization," features everything from drinking jugs to razor cases to chairs to clothing.

Admission: 40 Ft (45¢).

Open: Tues–Sun 10am–6pm. **Metro:** Kossuth tér (Red line).

MUSEUM OF FINE ARTS [SZÉPMŰVÉSZETI MÚZEUM], XIV. Hősök tere. Tel. 142-9759.

Planned at the time of the 1896 millennial celebration of the Magyar Conquest, the Museum of Fine Arts opened 10 years later in this neoclassical behemoth on Heroes' Square, at the edge of the City Park. The museum is the main repository in Hungary of foreign art; as such, it ranks among Central Europe's major collections. A significant part of the collection was acquired in 1871 from the

FROMMER'S FAVORITE BUDAPEST EXPERIENCES

A Night at the Opera The Opera House is one of Budapest's most spectacular buildings. For the price of a mediocre opera ticket back home, you can sit in the royal box, once the preserve of Habsburg monarchs.

A Walk in the Buda Hills It's hard to believe that such an expanse of hilly forest land is right here within the capital city. There are trails aplenty; every Budapest native has a favorite hiking trail.

The Market Halls Built at the turn of the century, Budapest's vintage market halls continue to be home to lively commerce in fruits and vegetables. Even if the vendors seem oblivious of the great halls they work in, you'll marvel at their size and dignity.

Coffee and Pastry at the New York Coffeehouse One of the city's finest art nouveau interiors, the New York has been serving coffee and pastries since the turn of the century, when it was *the* place for artists, writers, and actors.

Thermal Bath at the Hotel Gellért No Central European could imagine a trip to Budapest without at least one session in the city's fabled thermal waters. The Hotel Gellért is the most glorious of the many bath houses.

Dinner at Gundel Although this is Budapest's most expensive and fanciest restaurant, you can get a meal here for the price of a casual lunch in Vienna. The new owner is George Lang, whose book *The Cuisine of Hungary* is the authoritative source on the subject.

A Boat Ride on the Danube The wide stretch of the Danube divides Buda from Pest; a boat ride affords you a view of most of the city's great buildings. Even on the hottest day, a breeze blows on the river.

A Walk in the Jewish District Budapest has the largest Jewish population of any city on the European continent (outside Russia). Pest's historic Jewish neighborhood, run-down but relatively unchanged, resonates with the magic and tragedy of the past.

Esterházys, an enormously wealthy family who had spent centuries amassing great art. There are eight departments: Egyptian Art, Antiquities, Antique Sculpture, Old Masters, Drawings and Prints,

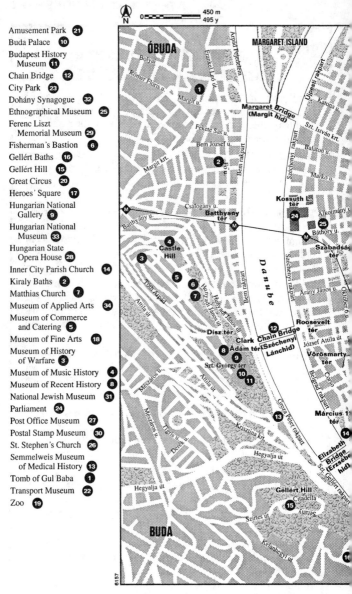
19th- and 20th-century masters, and Modern Sculpture. Most of the great names associated with the Old Masters—Tiepolo, Tintoretto, Veronese, Titian, Raphael, Van Dyck, Brueghel, Rembrandt, Rubens, Hals, Hogarth, Dürer, Cranach, Holbein, Goya, Velasquez, El Greco, and others—are represented here. Of 19th-century French artists, the museum is best represented by Delacroix, Corot, and Manet. It has been said, though, that while the museum suffers no shortage of

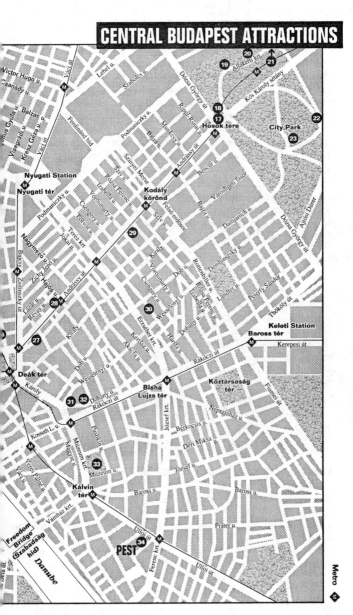

CENTRAL BUDAPEST ATTRACTIONS

works by the Old Masters, it can boast precious few outright masterpieces.

Admission: 40 Ft (45¢); students free.

Open: Tues–Sun 10am–6pm. **Metro:** Hősök tere (Yellow line).

HUNGARIAN NATIONAL MUSEUM (NEMZETI MÚZE-UM), VIII. Múzeum körút 14. Tel. 138-2122.

The Hungarian National Museum, an enormous neoclassical structure built in 1837–47, was one of the great projects of the early 19th-century Age of Reform, a period which also saw the construction of the Chain Bridge and the National Theater (no longer standing), as well as the development of the modern Hungarian identity. The museum played a major role in the beginning of the Hungarian Revolution of 1848–49; it was on its wide steps on March 15, 1848, that the poet Sándor Petőfi and other young radicals are said to have exhorted the people of Pest to revolt against the Habsburgs. The very presence of such an imposing structure in the capital, and its exhibits proudly detailing the accomplishments of the Magyars, played a significant role in the development of 19th-century Hungarian nationalism. The main attraction in the museum is the crown of St. Stephen (King Stephen ruled from 1000–1038), ceremoniously returned by Secretary of State Cyrus Vance to Hungary in 1978 from the United States, where it had been stored since the end of World War II. Few Hungarians would assert that the two-tiered crown on display ever actually rested on Stephen's head, its lower part having been, evidently, a gift to King Géza I (1074–1077), and its upper part built for Stephen V, almost 250 years after the first Stephen's death. Out of respect, visitors must put slippers on over their shoes when entering the room where the crown is displayed. The two main exhibits in the museum are "The History of the Peoples of Hungary from the Paleolithic Age to the Magyar Conquest" and "The History of the Hungarian People from the Magyar Conquest to 1849."

Admission: 40 Ft (45¢).

Open: Tues–Sun 10am–6pm. **Metro:** Kálvin tér (Blue line).

HISTORIC BUILDINGS & SQUARES

HEROES' SQUARE (HŐSÖK TERE), XIV.

Situated at the end of Pest's great boulevard, Andrássy út, and at the entrance to its most famous park, City Park (Városliget), the wide open plaza of Heroes' Square is one of the symbols of the city. Socialist holidays were invariably celebrated with huge military reviews in the square during the country's communist era. In 1989, a rally here on the day of the reburial of Imre Nagy (executed after the 1956 revolution) attracted 300,000 people to the square.

The square, like the park beyond it, was laid out for the 1896 Magyar Conquest millennial celebration. In its center stands the 36-meter-high Millennial Column; arrayed around the base of the column are equestrian statues of Árpád and the six other Magyar tribal leaders who led the conquest. Behind the column, arrayed along a colonnade, are 14 heroes of Hungarian history, including King Stephen I, the country's first Christian king (first on left); King Matthias Corvinus, who presided over Buda's Golden Age (sixth from right); and Lajos Kossuth, leader of the 1848–49 War of

Independence (first on right). Flanking Heroes' Square are two of Budapest's major museums, the Museum of Fine Arts and the Exhibition Hall. (Note that Városligeti Étterem, a restaurant across the street from the square, is not recommended.)

Metro: Hősök tere (Yellow line).

HUNGARIAN STATE OPERA HOUSE [MAGYAR ÁLLAMI OPERAHÁZ], VI. Andrássy út 22. Tel. 153-0170.

Completed in 1884, the Opera House, on Pest's elegant Andrássy út, is the crowning achievment of the famous Hungarian architect Miklós Ybl's career. Budapest's most celebrated performance hall, it boasts a fantastically ornate interior featuring frescoes by two of the best-known Hungarian artists of the day, Bertalan Székely and Károly Lotz. There are dozens of statues, both exterior and interior, of such greats as Beethoven, Mozart, Verdi, Wagner, Smetana, Tchaikovsky, and Monteverdi. Home to both the State Opera and the State Ballet, the Opera House has a rich and evocative history. A political scandal marked the first opening performance in 1884. Ferenc Liszt had written a piece to be performed especially for the event, but when it was discovered he had incorporated elements of the "Rákóczi March," a patriotic (and anti-Habsburg) Hungarian melody, he was prevented from playing it. Well known directors of the Opera House include Gustav Mahler and Ferenc Erkel. See "The Performing Arts," in Chapter 9 for information on performances.

Admission: Tour is 250 Ft ($2.75); 120 Ft ($1.35) for students.

Open: Entry only by guided tours; daily at 3 and 4pm, all year. No need to preregister. **Metro:** Opera (Yellow line).

PARLIAMENT, V. Kossuth tér. Tel. 112-0600.

Budapest's great Parliament building, an Eclectic design by Imre Steindl which mixes the predominant Neo-Gothic style with a Neo-Renaissance dome, was completed in 1902. Standing proudly on the Danube bank, visible from almost any riverside vantage point, it has from the outset been one of the very symbols of Budapest, though until 1989 a democratically elected government had convened here exactly once (just after World War II, before the Communist takeover). It was built at a time of extreme optimism and national purpose, and was self-consciously intended to be one of the

IMPRESSIONS

When I got tired of the noisy streets of Pest and the artificial gay life there, I loved to wander about quaint silent Buda, where everything and everybody seemed to have stood still a couple of centuries ago.
—ELIZABETH KEITH MORRIS, ENGLISH MEMOIRIST, 1931

world's great houses of Parliament. There are 691 rooms inside and 88 statues decorating the exterior. The interior decor is predominantly Neo-Gothic. The ceiling frescoes are by Károly Lotz, Hungary's best known artist of that genre; Mihály Munkácsy's epic painting of the Magyar Conquest is also prominently displayed.

Admission: 45-minute Ibusz tours, 900 Ft ($10).

Open: By guided tour only, and only when Parliament is not in session (see "Organized Tours," later in this chapter); starting times are Wed and Fri 2pm, May–Oct. Meet at Gate XII. It's best to reserve a space ahead of time, but you may be able to join a tour if you show up at the meeting point. **Metro:** Kossuth tér (Red line).

CHURCHES & SYNAGOGUES

DOHÁNY SYNAGOGUE, VII. Dohány u. 2-8. Tel. 142-8949.

Built in 1859, this is the largest synagogue in Europe and the world's second-largest. It is still used by Budapest's Jewish community. There are striking Moorish elements to the architecture; the interior is vast and ornate, with two balconies, and the unusual presence of an organ. The synagogue has a rich but tragic history. Adolf Eichmann arrived with the occupying Nazi forces in March 1944 to supervise the establishment of the Jewish ghetto and the subsequent deportations. He set up his headquarters inside the synagogue itself. Up to 20,000 Jews took refuge inside the synagogue complex, of whom 7,000 did not survive the bleak winter of 1944–45. They are buried in the courtyard, where you can also see a transported piece of the original brick ghetto wall. An ambitious restoration is currently in progress, funded in large part by a foundation set up by the American actor Tony Curtis, who is of Hungarian-Jewish descent. Completion of the restoration is scheduled for 1996, but as work progresses you can see the original splendor of the building begin to shine through decades of soot and neglect. The National Jewish Museum is inside the Synagogue complex (see "More Attractions," below).

Admission: By donation.

Open: Erratic hours during restoration. **Closed:** Nov–Apr. **Metro:** Astoria (Red line) or Deák tér (all lines).

INNER CITY PARISH CHURCH [BELVÁROSI PLÉBÁNI-ATEMPLOM], V. Március 15 tér. Tel. 118-3108.

The Inner City Parish Church, standing flush against the Erzsébet Bridge in Pest, is one of the city's great architectural monuments. The 12th-century Romanesque church first built on this spot was constructed inside the remains of the walls of the Roman fortress of Contra-Aquincum. In the early 14th century, a Gothic church was built; it is this medieval church, with numerous additions and reconstructions reflecting the architectural trends of the time, which stands today. Both Gothic and baroque elements can be observed on the exterior. Inside are niches built in both styles, as

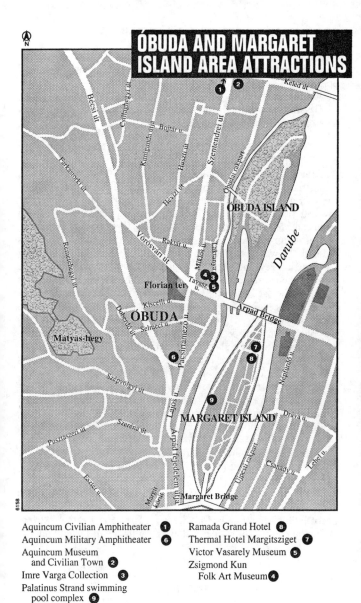

ÓBUDA AND MARGARET ISLAND AREA ATTRACTIONS

ÓBUDA ISLAND

Danube

Florian tér

ÓBUDA

Mátyás-hegy

MARGARET ISLAND

Margaret Bridge

6158

Aquincum Civilian Amphitheater **1**
Aquincum Military Amphitheater **6**
Aquincum Museum
  and Civilian Town **2**
Imre Varga Collection **3**
Palatinus Strand swimming
  pool complex **9**

Ramada Grand Hotel **8**
Thermal Hotel Margitsziget **7**
Victor Vasarely Museum **5**
Zsigmond Kun
  Folk Art Museum **4**

well as a *mihrab* (prayer niche) dating from the Turkish occupation, evidence of its conversion in those years to a mosque. The painting on the altar is the work of 20th-century artist Pál Molnár (his work can also be seen in St. Anne's Church). The church was almost torn down when the Erzsébet Bridge was built in the late 19th century. Fortunately, an alternative plan won out, calling for the new bridge to wind around the church in a serpentine fashion (this interesting construction is best viewed from Gellért Hill). Daily mass 6:30am, 8am, and 6pm; Sunday mass 7am, 9am, 10am, 11:30am, noon, and 6pm.

Admission: Free.

Open: Officially Fri–Sat 6:30am–7pm; in reality more often. **Metro:** Ferenciek tere (Blue line).

ST. STEPHEN'S CHURCH (BAZILIKA), V. Szent István tér 33. Tel. 117-2859.

Although not a basilica in the technical sense of the word, Hungarians like to call St. Stephen's "The Basilica" in honor of its sheer size: It is the largest church in the country. The Basilica took over 50 years to build (the collapse of the dome in 1868 caused significant delay) and was presided over by three leading architects, two of whom (József Hild and Miklós Ybl) died before work was finished. It was finally completed in 1906, but during its long construction Pest had undergone radical growth; strangely, while the front of the church dominates sleepy Szent István tér, the rear faces out onto the far busier Inner Ring boulevard. The bust above the main entrance is of King Stephen, Hungary's first Christian king. Inside the church, in the Chapel of the Holy Right (*Szent Jobb Kápolna*), you can see Hungarian Catholicism's most cherished— and bizarre—relic: Stephen's preserved right hand. The church was considered so sturdy that it was used to store important documents and art works during the bombing of Budapest in World War II. There are great views from the tower, but the climb is not recommended for the weak-kneed. Organ concerts are held here on Monday evenings (7pm) during the summer. Daily mass 7am, 8am, 5:30pm, and 6pm; Sunday mass 7:30am, 8am, 9am, 10am, noon, 6pm, and 7:30pm.

Admission: Church and treasury 30 Ft (35¢), 10 Ft (10¢) for students; tower 100 Ft ($1.10), 50 Ft (55¢) for students; Szent Jobb Chapel 20 Ft (20¢).

Open: Church open Mon–Sat 6am–7pm, Sun 6am–8:30pm; tower open daily 10am–5:30pm; treasury open daily 9am–5pm; Szent Jobb Chapel open Mon–Sat 9am–5pm, Sun 1–5pm. **Metro:** Arany János utca (Blue line) or Bajcsy-Zsilinszky út (Yellow line).

BUDA

MUSEUMS

BUDAPEST HISTORY MUSEUM (BUDAPESTI TÖRTÉNETI MÚZEUM), I. Buda Palace, wing E. Tel. 175-7533.

The Budapest History Museum, also known as the Castle Museum, has two permanent exhibitions: "The Medieval Royal Palace and its Gothic Statues" and "2,000 Years of Budapest." The former consists almost entirely of rooms and artifacts uncovered during the post–World War II excavation and rebuilding of the palace. A visit here is more notable perhaps for the rooms and halls themselves than for the fragments and occasional undamaged pieces of statues, stone carvings, earthenware, and the like which are displayed in them. The "2,000 Years of Budapest" exhibit is most notable for its photographs and other art depicting Budapest over the years.

It's probably worth splurging for a guided tour (250 Ft); even though the descriptions are written in English, the history of the palace's repeated construction and destruction is so confusing and arcane that it is difficult to understand what you are really seeing. Nonetheless, this museum is the best place to get a sense of the once-great medieval Buda.

Admission: 40 Ft (45¢); 20 Ft (20¢) students; temporary exhibits up to 100 Ft ($1.10) each; Wednesday free.

Open: Mar–Oct, Wed–Mon 10am–6pm; Nov–Feb, Wed–Mon 10am–4pm. **Directions:** Várbusz from Moszkva tér, bus 106 from Deák tér, bus 116 from Március 15 tér, or funicular from Clark Ádám tér.

HUNGARIAN NATIONAL GALLERY [NEMZETI GALÉRIA], I. Buda Palace, wings B, C, and D. Tel. 175-7533.

A repository of Hungarian art from medieval times to the 20th century, the Hungarian National Gallery is an enormous museum whose entire collection you couldn't possibly view during a single visit. The museum dates its founding to the great reform period of the mid-19th century, moving to its present location in the Buda Palace in 1975. Few people outside Hungary are familiar with even the country's best-known artists. Nevertheless, Hungary has produced some fine artists, particularly in the late 19th century, and this is *the place* to view their work. The giants of the time are the brilliant Mihály Munkácsy, whose masterpieces include *The Lint-makers, Condemned Cell,* and *Woman Carrying Wood;* László Paál, a painter of village scenes, among whose best pictures are *Village Road in Berzova, Path in the Forest at Fontainbleau,* and *Depth of the Forest;* Károly Ferenczy, whose mastery of light is seen in *Morning Sunshine* and *Evening in March;* and Pál Szinyei Merse, the *plein-air* artist, whose own development paralleled that of the early French Impressionists (see *Picnic in May*). Some other artists to look for are: Gyula Benczúr, who painted grand historical scenes; Károly Lotz, best known as a fresco painter (Opera House, Matthias Church), here represented by a number of nudes and several fine thunderstorm paintings; and Bertalan Székely, a painter of historical scenes and landscapes. József Rippl-Rónai's canvasses represent the premier examples of Hungarian Post-Impressionism and art nouveau (see *Father and Uncle Piacsek Drinking Red Wine* and *Grandmother*), while Tivadar Csontváry Kosztka, the "Rousseau of the Danube," is considered by some critics to be a genius of early modern art. See "Architecture, Art, Literature and Music" in Chapter 1 for more information on Hungary's artists.

Admission: 40 Ft (45¢); students free; Saturday free.

Open: Mar–Oct, Tues–Sun 10am–6pm; Nov–Feb, Tues–Sun

10am–4pm. **Directions:** Várbusz from Moszkva tér, bus 106 from Deák tér, bus 116 from Március 15 tér, or funicular from Clark Ádám tér.

A CHURCH

MATTHIAS CHURCH [MÁTYÁS TEMPLOM], I. Szentháromság tér 2. Tel. 116-1543.

Officially named the Church of Our Lady, the symbol of Buda's Castle District is popularly known as Matthias Church after the much-loved 15th-century king who was twice married here. Although the structure dates to the mid-13th century, like other old churches in Budapest it has an interesting history of destruction and reconstruction, always being refashioned in the architectural style of the time. The last two Hungarian kings (Habsburgs) were crowned in the church; Franz Joseph in 1867 (Liszt wrote and performed his Coronation Mass) and Charles IV in 1916. The interior of the church is decorated with works of two outstanding 19th-century Hungarian painters, Károly Lotz and Bertalan Székely. Organ concerts are held here on most Friday evenings from June through September. Daily mass 7am, 8am, and 6pm; Sunday mass 7:30am, 8am, 9am, 10am, noon, 6pm, and 7:30pm.

Admission: 25 Ft (25¢).

Open: Daily 9am–7pm. **Directions:** Várbusz from Moszkva tér, bus 106 from Deák tér, bus 116 from Matthias 15 tér, or funicular from Clark Ádám tér.

PANORAMAS

FISHERMAN'S BASTION [HALÁSZBÁSTYA], I.

The Neo-Romanesque Fisherman's Bastion, perched on the edge of Buda's Castle District near Matthias Church and the Hilton Hotel, affords a marvelous panorama of Pest. It was built at the turn of the last century and, despite its military appearance, was intended mainly for decorative purposes. Looking out over the Danube to Pest, you can see (from left to right): Margaret Island and the Margaret Bridge, Parliament, St. Stephen's Basilica, the Chain Bridge with the Hungarian Academy of Sciences and the Gresham Palace behind it, the Vigadó Concert Hall, the Inner City Parish Church, the Erzsébet Bridge, and the Szabadság Bridge.

Admission: Free.

Open: Always. **Directions:** Várbusz from Moszkva tér, bus 106 from Deák tér, bus 116 from Március 15 tér, or funicular from Clark Ádám tér.

GELLÉRT HILL [GELLÉRT HEGY], XI.

Gellért Hill, towering 230 meters above the Danube, offers the single best panorama of the city. The hill is named after the Italian Bishop Gellért who assisted Hungary's first Christian king, Stephen I, in converting the Magyars. Gellért became a martyr when he was rolled in a barrel to his death from the side of the hill on which his enormous statue now stands, defiantly holding a cross in his outstretched hand. On top of Gellért Hill you'll find the **Liberation Monument,** built in 1947 to commemorate the Red Army's liberation of Budapest from Nazi occupation. A mammoth statue, it's one of the last Socialist Realist memorials you'll find in Hungary. The statue's centerpiece, a giant female figure holding a leaf aloft, is affectionately known as *Kiflis Zsuzsa* (*kifli* is a crescent-shaped roll eaten daily by many Hungarians, while Zsuzsa, or Susie, is a common girl's name). Hungarian children like to call the smaller flame-holding figure on her side *Fagylaltos fiú* (the boy with the ice cream cone). Also atop Gellért Hill is the **Citadella,** a symbol of power built by the Austrians in 1851, shortly after they crushed the Hungarian War of Independence of 1848–49.

Admission: Free; 20 Ft (20¢) to enter the Citadella.

Bus: 27 from Móricz Zsigmond körtér.

ÓBUDA

ROMAN RUINS OF AQUINCUM, III.

The ruins of Aquincum, the once bustling capital of the Roman province of Pannónia, are spread throughout the southern part of Óbuda. The various sites are far enough away from each other, and the layout of modern Óbuda sufficiently anti-pedestrian, that it is difficult to see everything. Fortunately, two of the major sites are right across the street from each other, near the Aquincum station of the suburban HÉV railroad. The ruined **Amphitheater of the Civilian Town** is directly beside the HÉV station. It's open all the time, and you are free to wander through (you should know, though, that homeless people now live inside its walls). The main Budapest–Szentendre highway cuts through Óbuda, causing no small amount of pedestrian frustration. Across it stand the ruins of the **Civilian Town.** Everything is visible from the roadside, except for the collection of the **Aquincum Museum** (III. Szentendrei út 139; tel. 180-4650), a neoclassical structure built at the end of the 19th century in harmony with its surroundings. The museum exhibits coins, utensils, jewelry, and pottery from Roman times. It's open from mid-April through October, Tuesday to Sunday from 9am to 6pm (in October closing at 5pm). Entry is 20 Ft (20¢); 10 Ft (10¢) for children and students. Take the HÉV suburban railroad from Batthyány tér to Aquincum.

A BRIDGE BETWEEN PEST & BUDA

THE CHAIN BRIDGE (SZÉCHENYI LÁNCHÍD)

The Chain Bridge is perhaps the dominant symbol of Budapest. As the first permanent bridge across the Danube (1849), it paved the way for the union of Buda, Óbuda, and Pest into a single city. Prior to 1849, people relied on a pontoon bridge which had to be dismantled when ships passed and could be swept away in stormy weather. The initiative for the Chain Bridge came from the indefatigable Count István Széchenyi, the leading figure of Hungarian society during the mid-19th-century Age of Reform. The Scotsman Adam Clark, for whom the square on the Buda side of the bridge is named, came to Budapest to supervise the massive project; he remained in the city until his death many years later. The bridge was blown up by the retreating Nazis in World War II, but was rebuilt immediately after the war. Located in the heart of the city, it's best admired at night, when it's lit up like a chandelier.

2. MORE ATTRACTIONS

PEST

MUSEUMS

MUSEUM OF APPLIED ARTS (IPARMŰVÉSZETI MÚZE-UM), IX. Üllői út 33-37. Tel. 117-5222.

It's worth making a trip to the Museum of Applied Arts just to see the marvelous building in which it's housed, designed by Ödön Lechner in the 1890s. Lechner, whose most famous creation is the Town Hall in the Great Plain city of Kecskemét, is the architect who was most adventurous in combining traditional Hungarian folk elements with the art nouveau style of his time. The building's ceramic decoration comes from the famous Zsolnay factory in Pécs. If you are impressed by this structure, pay a visit to the former Post Office Savings Bank on Hold utca, another fine example of Lechner's work (see "Walking Tour 3—Leopold Town & Theresa Town," in Chapter 7). The permanent exhibits of the museum are divided into five sections: furniture; textiles; metalwork; ceramics, porcelain, and glass; and an eclectic display of books, leather, and ivory. Much of the museum's space is given to temporary exhibitions.

Admission: 40 Ft (45¢).
Open: Tues–Sun 10am–6pm. **Metro:** Ferenc körút (Blue line).

NATIONAL JEWISH MUSEUM (NEMZETI ZSIDÓ MÚZE-UM), Dohány u. 2-8. Tel. 142-8949.

This fascinating museum is located in the Dohány Synagogue complex; a tablet outside informs that Theodor Herzl, the founder of

IMPRESSIONS

How much beauty there is in the Chain Bridge, what elegant silence, haughty humility, charming lightness, and archaic melancholy!
—ANTAL SZERB, 20TH-CENTURY HUNGARIAN WRITER

Zionism, was born on this spot. The four-room museum is devoted to the long history of Jews in Hungary. Displays include Sabbath and holiday items (including some gorgeous examples of Herend passover plates) and ritual and everyday artifacts. The last room has a moving exhibit on the Holocaust in Hungary.

Admission: By donation.

Open: May–Oct only, Mon and Thurs 2–6pm; Tues, Wed, Fri, and Sun 10am–1pm. **Closed:** Sat and Nov–Apr. **Metro:** Astoria (Red line) or Deák tér (all lines).

POST OFFICE MUSEUM (POSTAMÚZEUM), VI. Andrássy út 3. Tel. 142-7938.

The exhibits in the Post Office Museum are of limited interest, but the building itself and the apartment in which the museum is situated—the opulently furnished former Sexlehner family flat—is simply dazzling. Chandeliers dangle from the frescoed ceilings and intricately carved wood moldings trim the walls.

Admission: 20 Ft (20¢).

Open: Tues–Sun 10am–6pm. **Metro:** Bajcsy-Zsilinszky út (Yellow line) or Deák tér (all lines).

POSTAL STAMP MUSEUM (BÉLYEGMÚZEUM), VII. Hársfa u. 47.

Generations of philatelists the world over have admired the artistic creations of Magyar Posta. This wonderful little museum has rack after rack of the country's finest stamps. The mistakenly printed upside down "Madonna with Child" in rack 49 is Hungary's most valuable stamp, worth around 400,000 Ft ($4,444). The stamps of rack 65 abjectly demonstrate how the worst inflation the world has ever seen devastated Hungary in the 1940s. Variations on Lenin and Stalin can be seen in racks 68–77, and racks 70–80 contain numerous brilliant examples of socialist realism. You don't have to be a stamp collector to enjoy a visit to the Postal Stamp Museum.

Admission: 20 Ft (20¢); students free.

Open: Tues–Sun 10am–6pm. **Tram:** 4 or 6 to Wesselényi utca.

A CEMETERY

KOZMA CEMETERY, X. Kozma u. 6.

The city's main Jewish cemetery is in the eastern end of the Kőbánya district. An estimated half-million people are buried here. A vast, peaceful place, it is still in use today. Ornate art deco tombs stand proudly near the main entrance, their faded grandeur a testament both to the status of those buried beneath them and to the steady passage of time. The cemetery is also the site of Hungary's most moving Holocaust memorial, a set of nine walls with the names of victims etched in. About 6,500 names appear, of the 600,000 Hungarian Jews estimated to have perished in the war. Survivors and relatives have pencilled in hundreds of additional names. It's a long, slow tram ride from the center.

Open: Mon–Thurs 7am–4pm, Fri and Sun 7am–3pm. **Tram:** 37 from Blaha Lujza tér to second to last stop.

BUDA

MUSEUMS

MUSEUM OF COMMERCE AND CATERING [KERES-KEDELMI ÉS VENDÉGLÁTÓIPARI MÚZEUM], I. Fortuna u. 4. Tel. 175-6249.

These are two separate but related exhibits located on opposite sides of a courtyard in the Castle District; a single ticket entitles you to entry to both. The prime attraction of the catering exhibit is the antique baking equipment: pie tins, cookie molds, and utensils. The commerce exhibit has a wider appeal, with assorted (somewhat randomly assembled) vintage items: cigar boxes, advertisments, liquor bottles, fountain pens, sewing equipment, ration books. A "Gyula Meinl" display shows that the ubiquitous Austrian grocery chain had an early presence in Hungary. Two fascinating photos (why they're here is inexplicable) show the World War II destruction of the Chain Bridge and the Erzsébet Bridge.

Admission: 30 Ft (35¢); students free; Friday free.

Open: Tues–Sun 10am–6pm. **Directions:** Várbusz from Moszkva tér, bus 106 from Deák tér, bus 116 from Március 15 tér, or funicular from Clark Ádám tér.

MUSEUM OF THE HISTORY OF WARFARE [HADTÖR-TÉNETI MÚZEUM], I. Tóth Árpád sétány 40. Tel. 156-9522.

Housed in a former barracks in the northwestern corner of the Castle District, this museum has exhibits from the time of the Turkish occupation to the 20th century. Uniforms, decorations, models, weapons, maps, and photographs are unfortunately accompanied only by Hungarian text. The display of Turkish weaponry is particularly interesting, but the highlight is undoubtedly the room devoted to the 1956 Hungarian uprising. Here the 10 chaotic days are detailed by consecutive panels of large, mounted photographs. Artifacts round out the display, in particular a Soviet flag with the center cut out (where hammer and sickle were), and the legendary hand of Stalin, the only surviving piece of the giant statue of the Soviet dictator whose public destruction was one of the dramatic moments of the failed uprising. Toy soldiers are available in the gift shop.

Admission: 20 Ft (20¢); students free.

Open: Tues–Sat 9am–5pm, Sun 10am–6pm. **Directions:** Várbusz from Moszkva tér, bus 106 from Deák tér, bus 116 from Március 15 tér, or funicular from Clark Ádám tér.

MUSEUM OF RECENT HISTORY [LEGÚJABBKORI MÚZEUM], I. Buda Palace, wing A. Tel. 175-7533.

In the northern end of the Buda Palace, this was formerly the Museum of the Hungarian Worker's Movement. Now converted to a more politically correct purpose, it houses changing exhibitions. Critically successful recent showings included "Sztálin-Rákosi," a stunning portrayal of the cult of personality in Hungary in the early 1950s; and "World Press Photo," an exhibit of poster-size blow-ups of the best press photography of 1992. The Ludwig Museum upstairs has a less-than-inspiring permanent exhibition of contemporary Hungarian and international art.

Admission: 80 Ft (90¢); 20 Ft (20¢) students. Admission price entitles you to entry to the adjoining Ludwig Museum.

Open: Tues–Sun 10am–5pm. **Directions:** Várbusz from Moszkva tér, bus 106 from Deák tér, bus 116 from Március 15 tér, or funicular from Clark Ádám tér.

SEMMELWEIS MUSEUM OF MEDICAL HISTORY (SEMMELWEIS ORVOSTÖRTÉNETI MÚZEUM), I. Apród u. 1-3. Tel. 175-3533.

This museum, which traces the history of medicine from ancient times to the modern era, is located in the former home of Ignác Semmelweis, Hungary's leading 19th-century physician. Semmelweis is hailed as the "saviour of mothers" for his role in identifying the cause of puerperal (childbed) fever and preventing it by advocating that physicians wash their hands between patients. The museum is spread over four rooms and displays everything from early medical instruments to anatomical models to old medical textbooks. There is also a faithfully reconstructed 19th-century pharmacy. Descriptions are only in Hungarian, but many of the exhibits are self-explanatory. The Semmelweis Memorial Room has two bookcases displaying the eminent scholar's collection of medical texts. Keen eyes might notice the seven volumes of Osler's Modern Medicine, written long after Semmelweis' death; they were a gift from George Bush to Hungarian Prime Minister József Antall, formerly the director of the museum.

Admission: 50 Ft (55¢); Wed free.

Open: Tues–Sun 10:30am–5:30pm. **Directions:** Any bus or tram to Döbrentei tér (for example, bus 8 from Március 15 tér).

TOMB OF GUL BABA (GÜL BABA TURBÉJE), II. Mecset u. 14. Tel. 155-8849.

⭐ The unfortunate Turkish dervish Gül Baba died at dinner; it was no ordinary meal, rather a 1541 gala in Matthias Church celebrating the conquest of Buda. Today his simple tomb, located in a wonderfully steep, twisting neighborhood at the beginning of the Hill of Roses (Rózsadomb) district, is maintained as a Muslim shrine by the Turkish government. The descriptions are in Hungarian and Turkish, but an English-language pamphlet is available on request. The tomb is set in a tiny sunken park, surrounded by lovely rose gardens.

Admission: 20 Ft (20¢); 10 Ft (10¢) students.

Open: Tues–Sun 10am–6pm. **Tram:** 4 or 6 to Buda side of

Margaret Bridge; the most direct route to Gül Baba tér is via Mecset utca, off Margaret utca.

A BATHHOUSE

KIRÁLY BATHS, I. Fő u. 84.

The Király Baths are one of Budapest's most important architectural monuments to Turkish rule, and a place where Hungarian culture meets the eastern culture which has so profoundly influenced it. The bath itself, built in the late 16th century, is housed under an octagonal domed roof through whose windows sunlight is filtered. In addition to the thermal bath, there are also sauna and steam bath facilities here. Even if you are not going to bathe (which you should do!), you are welcome to take a peek at the interior. (See "Sports and Recreation" later in this chapter for more information on spa bathing.)

Admission: 150 Ft to baths.

Open: For men: Mon, Wed, and Fri 6:30am–6pm. For women: Tues and Thurs 6:30am–6pm, Sat 6:30am–noon. **Metro:** Batthyány tér (Red line).

ÓBUDA

MUSEUMS

ZSIGMOND KUN FOLK ART MUSEUM (LAKÁSMÚZE-UM), III. Fő tér 4.

Here in Zsigmond Kun's former apartment you can admire his wonderful collection of Hungarian folk art. For almost a century he traveled around Hungary collecting and documenting folk art. On display are ceramics and brandy flasks, tapestries and chairs, sheep bells, shepherds' hats, and hundreds of other examples of Hungarian folk art. One-hundred-year-old Kun is presently writing his memoirs. The museum staff speaks fondly of "Zsigmond Bácsi" (Uncle Zsigmond).

Admission: 30 Ft (35¢); students free; English-language guidebook 35 Ft (40¢).

Open: Tues–Fri 2–6pm, Sat–Sun 10am–6pm. **Metro:** HÉV suburban railroad from Batthyány tér to Árpád híd.

IMRE VARGA COLLECTION (VARGA IMRE GYŰJTE-MÉNY), III. Laktanya u. 7.

Imre Varga is Hungary's best-known contemporary sculptor. This small museum, just off Óbuda's Fő tér, shows a good cross section of his sensitive, piercing work. Historical subjects on display inside the museum range from the pudgy, balding figure of Imre Nagy, reluctant hero of the 1956 Hungarian uprising, to the dapper, capped Béla Bartók. The museum also has a garden where Varga's sad, broken figures stand forlornly or sit on benches resting their weary feet; cats also live in the garden, enhancing the atmosphere.

Admission: 30 Ft (35¢); 15 Ft (15¢) students; Wed free.
Open: Tues–Sun 10am–6pm. **Metro:** HÉV suburban railroad from Batthyány tér to Árpád híd.

PARKS & GARDENS

Hungarians love a stroll in the park, and on weekends and summer afternoons, it seems as if the whole of Budapest is out enjoying what Hungarians lovingly refer to as "the nature." Popular **Margaret Island** (Margit-sziget) has been a public park since 1908. The long, narrow island, connected to both Buda and Pest via the Margaret and Árpád bridges, is barred to most vehicular traffic. In addition to three important ruins (the Dominican Convent, a 13th–14th century Franciscan Church, and a 12th-century Premonstratensian Chapel), facilities on the island include the Palatinus Strand open-air baths (see "Sports and Recreation," below), which draw upon the famous thermal waters under Margaret Island; the Alfréd Hajós Sport Pool; and the Open Air Theater. Sunbathers line the steep embankments along the river, and bicycles are available for rent. There are also several snack bars and open-air restaurants. Despite all this, Margaret Island is a quiet, tranquil place. In any direction off the main road you can find well-tended gardens or a patch of grass under the shade of a willow tree for a private picnic. Margaret Island is best reached by bus 26 from Nyugati tér, which runs the length of the island, or tram 4 or 6, which stop at the entrance to the island midway across the Margaret Bridge.

City Park (Városliget) is an equally popular place to spend a summer day, and families are everywhere in evidence. Heroes' Square, at the end of Andrássy út, is the most logical starting point for a walk in City Park. Built in 1896 as part of the Hungarian millennial celebrations, it has been the sight of some important moments of Hungarian history. The lake behind the square is used for boating in the summer and ice skating in the winter. The Vajdahunyad Castle was built as a temporary structure in 1896 for the millennial celebration to demonstrate the different architectural styles in Hungary; it was so popular that a permanent structure was eventually designed to replace it. The park's Animal Garden Boulevard (Állatkerti körút), the favorite street of generations of Hungarian children, is where the zoo, the circus, and the amusement park are all

---

IMPRESSIONS

The last time we were here we happened to see the breaking of the winter's ice, and it was a wondrous sight to behold the great blocks borne down by the swift current, heave and struggle and beat against each other, and then clash headlong against the massive stonework of the Chain Bridge, with a crash like that of a volley of musketry.
—NINA ELIZABETH MAZUCHALLI, ENGLISH TRAVELER, 1881

found (see "Cool for Kids," below). Gundel, Budapest's most famous restaurant, is also here, as are the Széchenyi Baths. The southern end of City Park is considerably less crowded, with fewer buildings. The Transport Museum is among the few sites here, while the nearby Petőfi Csarnok is the venue for a variety of cultural events.

The Yellow metro line makes stops at Hősök tere (Heroes' Square), at the edge of the park, and Széchenyi Fürdő, in the middle of it.

There are numerous parks and nature reserves in the **Buda Hills.** You can ride the Children's Railroad through the hills or the János Hill Chairlift to its highest point (see "Cool for Kids," below). The Buda Hills are a great place to explore on your own; you'll hardly ever stray too far from a bus or tram line, and yet you'll feel like you're in the countryside, far from a bustling capital city. Moszkva tér is the best place to start an excursion into the hills. Pick up tram 56 or bus 21, 22, or 28; get off when you see an area you like.

For a very different kind of park experience, you may want to check out the planned **Socialist Statue Park.** Only a few short years ago Budapest was filled with memorials to Lenin, Marx and Engels, the Red Army, and to the many lesser-known figures of Hungarian and international Communism. Boldly torn from their pedestals, they sat for a few years in warehouses gathering dust, until a controversial plan to gather them all together in a giant statue park was finally realized. To be located somewhere in the XXII district in extreme southern Buda, it will be a memorial to an era and to despotism, but more than anything else, perhaps, to bad taste. The park is due to open in late 1993. Ask about its location and hours at Tourinform when you arrive in Budapest.

3. COOL FOR KIDS

The following attractions are definitely not just for kids; everyone loves a train ride in the hills, a Ferris wheel, or a good puppet show. Three of the attractions here—the zoo, the amusement park, and the circus—are located in the City Park (Városliget), along the famed Animal Garden Boulevard (Állatkerti körút). You could easily spend a whole children-oriented day here.

See also "Sports and Recreation," later in this chapter for information on the Palatinus Strand outdoor swimming pool complex and horse and pony riding in the Buda Hills.

ATTRACTIONS IN CITY PARK

AMUSEMENT PARK (VIDÁM PARK), XIV. Állatkerti körút 14-16. Tel. 142-0996.

Budapest's amusement park is a marvelous example of the city's faded splendor. The Vidám Park (literally "Happy Park") is much frequented by Hungarian families and, unlike Disneyland or Copenhagen's Tivoli, it is eminently affordable. There are two rides in particular not to be missed. The delightfully rickety old **Merry-Go-Round** (*Körhinta*), constructed almost entirely of wood, was clearly once a thing of great beauty. The ornate horses face out from the center, like the spokes of a wheel. The rider must actively pump to keep the horse rocking. There is no music, but as the apparatus spins round and round it creaks mightily. The whole experience is just charming. The **Ferris Wheel** (*Óriáskerék*) is another must. It has little in common with the rambunctious Ferris wheels of the modern age. A gangly, pale yellow structure, it rotates at a liltingly slow pace, gently lifting you high into the sky for a remarkable view of the surrounding area.

There is a toddlers' amusement park next door (Kis Vidám Park), although there are numerous rides in the Vidám Park suitable for toddlers.

Admission: 20 Ft (20¢); pay for rides individually, most in 25–50 Ft (30¢–55¢) range.

Open: Weekdays 9:45am–6:15pm, weekends 9:45am–6:30pm. Many rides closed in winter. **Metro:** Széchenyi fürdő (Yellow line).

TRANSPORT MUSEUM [KÖZLEKEDÉSI MÚZEUM], XIV.
Városligeti körút 11. Tel. 142-0565.

Located near Petőfi Csarnok in the little touristed southeastern corner of the City Park, this wonderful museum features large-scale working models of various kinds of historic transportation mechanisms, especially trains. On Sundays at 11am a film is shown on the history of aviation. The aviation exhibit is housed in the Petőfi Csarnok, an all-purpose community center nearby.

Admission: 30 Ft (35¢); students free.

Open: Tues–Sun 10am–6pm. **Trolleybus:** 74 from Károly körút (pick it up on Dohány utca, across the street from Dohány Synagogue).

ZOO [ÁLLATKERT], XIV. Állatkerti körút 6-12. Tel. 118-6429.

Opened in 1866, the zoo is located near the circus and the amusement park on the City Park's famous Animal Garden Boulevard, a favorite spot for Hungarian youngsters for over a century. The zoo has been modernized several times but still retains the sad flavor of an old-style, fairly inhumane zoo. Nice attractions here are the pony rides and two important examples of art nouveau architecture: the main entrance gate and the elephant house. Directly across the street from the zoo is a playground with trampolines; privately run, the tramps cost 40 Ft (45¢) for 5 minutes' use.

Admission: Adults 75 Ft (85¢); children 35 Ft (40¢).

Open: Daily 9am–6pm, closed Mon in winter. **Metro:** Hősök tere or Széchenyi fürdő (Yellow line).

OTHER ATTRACTIONS

CHILDREN'S RAILROAD [GYERMEK VASÚT].

This scenic narrow-gauge railway is run by children (under adult supervision), making it especially exciting for youngsters. The youthful engineers are dressed in miniature versions of the official MÁV (Hungarian State Railways) uniforms, with all the appropriate paraphernalia. The railway was built in the late 1940s, and was formerly run by the Young Pioneers, the youth movement of the Communist Party, although these days it has no political affiliation. The train winds its way slowly through the Buda Hills, providing numerous panoramas along the way. One-way travel time is 45 minutes; call Tourinform (tel. 117-9800) for more information.

Admission: Round trip 60 Ft (65¢); half price for children under 14.

Open: June–July, 8am–4pm: Tues–Fri, on the hour; weekends, every 45 minutes; Apr–May and Aug–Sept, same as above except not on Tues; Oct–Mar, 8am–4pm: Wed–Fri, every second hour, Sat–Sun, on the hour. **Directions:** To the Széchenyi-hegy terminus: cogwheel railway (fogaskerekű vasút) from Városmajor (across the street from the Hotel Budapest, on Szilágyi Erzsébet fasor in Buda) to the last stop. To the Hűvösvölgy terminus: tram 56 from Moszkva tér to the last stop.

JÁNOS HILL CHAIRLIFT [JÁNOS-HEGY LIBEGŐ], XII. Zugligeti út 93.

⭐ This somewhat primitive chairlift takes you up János Hill to within a steep 10-minute walk of the highest point in Budapest. At the top is the Neo-Romanesque Erzsébet Lookout Tower (Kilátó), built in 1910. It costs 15 Ft/15¢ (10Ft/10¢ for children) to climb the tower, and is well worth it for the glorious view of the forested hills and valleys around. There's a snack bar at the lookout tower. You can ride the chair back down; hike back down to the 158 bus; or, if you have a map of the Buda Hills, hike out to any number of other bus connections. Call Tourinform (tel. 117-9800) for more information.

Admission: One way 60 Ft (65¢) for adults, 50 Ft (55¢) for children; round trip 100 Ft ($1.10) for all.

Open: The chairlift runs non-stop mid-May to mid-Sept, Tues–Sun 9am–5pm; mid-Sept to mid-May, Tues–Sun 9:30am–4pm. **Bus:** 158 from Moszkva tér to the last stop.

ENTERTAINMENT

GREAT CIRCUS [NAGY CIRKUSZ], XIV. Állatkerti körút 7. Tel. 122-9630 or 142-8300.

It's not the Big Apple Circus or the Cirque de Soleil, but kids love it anyway. Actually, Budapest has a long circus tradition, though most Hungarian circus stars opt for the more glamorous and financially rewarding circus life abroad. When buying tickets it's helpful to know that *porond* means ring level and *erkély* means balcony.

Tickets: 100–250 Ft ($1.10–$2.80).

Open: Box office open weekdays 10am–6pm, weekends 9am–

6pm. Performances year round Wed–Sun, though schedule may be abbreviated in winter. **Metro:** Hősök tere or Széchenyi Fürdő (Yellow line).

PUPPET THEATERS [BÁBSZÍNHÁZAK]

⭐ Kids from all countries love Hungarian puppet theater. The shows are all in Hungarian, but with such standard fare as *Cinderella, Peter and the Wolf,* and *Snow White,* no one has trouble following the plot. The audience is an important part of the show: Hungarian children shriek *"Rossz farkas!"* ("Bad wolf!"), for instance, at every appearance of the villainous wolf in *Peter and the Wolf.* There are two puppet theaters in Budapest, with the season running from September to mid-June. Tickets are extremely cheap, usually in the 50- to 150-Ft (55¢–$1.65) range. The **Budapest Puppet Theater** (Budapesti Bábszínház) is at VI. Andrássy út 69 (tel. 142-2702 or 122-5051); the nearest metro station is Oktogon (Yellow line). The **Kolibri Puppet Theater** (Kolibri Bábszínház) is at VI. Jókai tér. 10. (tel. 153-4633); Jókai tér is halfway between the Oktogon and Opera stations of the Yellow metro line. Shows start at various times throughout the day, and tickets are available all day at the box offices.

4. SPECIAL-INTEREST SIGHTSEEING

FOR THE MUSIC ENTHUSIAST

BÉLA BARTÓK MEMORIAL HOUSE [BARTÓK BÉLA EMLÉKHÁZ], II. Csalán u. 29. Tel. 116-4123.

High in the Buda Hills, this little museum is housed in Béla Bartók's last Hungarian home. The country's most celebrated 20th-century musician, Bartók died in the United States, a refugee from fascism. The museum is best visited for a Friday-evening (6pm) concert of the Bartók String Quartet, a prolific group founded in 1957. Concerts are given occasionally on other days as well. For complete schedule information check Budapest's free bimonthly *Koncert Kalendárium,* available at the Central Philharmonic Ticket Office in Vörösmarty tér.

Admission: 30 Ft (35¢) to museum; 200–300 Ft ($2.20–$3.35) for concert.

Open: Tues–Sun 10am–6pm. **Bus:** 5 from Március 15. tér or Moszkva tér to Pasaréti tér (last stop).

FERENC LISZT MEMORIAL MUSEUM [LISZT FERENC EMLÉKMÚZEUM], VI.Vörösmarty u. 35. Tel. 122-9804.

Located in the apartment in which Liszt spent his last years, this modest museum features several of the composer's pianos, including a child's Bachmann and two Chickering & Sons grand pianos. Also interesting are the many portraits of Liszt done by the leading Austrian and Hungarian artists of his time, including two busts by the Hungarian sculptor Alajos Stróbl. Free concerts are given here Saturdays at 11am (no concerts in August).

Admission: 20 Ft (20¢); students free.

Open: Weekdays 10am–6pm, Sat 9am–5pm. **Metro:** Vörösmarty utca (Yellow line).

MUSEUM OF MUSIC HISTORY (ZENETÖRTÉNETI MÚZEUM), I. Táncsics M. u. 7. Tel. 175-9011.

Various instruments and manuscripts are on display in this museum, housed in a historic building in Buda's Castle District. There is also a reproduction of Béla Bartók's workshop, and the Bartók Archives are housed in the building. Concerts are given here as often as twice weekly; check Budapest's bimonthly *Koncert Kalendárium,* available for free at the Central Philharmonic Ticket Office in Vörösmarty tér.

Admission: 40 Ft (45¢); 20 Ft (20¢) students.

Open: Wed–Sun 10am–6pm, Mon 4–9pm. **Closed:** Tues. **Directions:** Várbusz from Moszkva tér, bus 106 from Deák tér, bus 116 from Március 15. tér, or funicular from Clark Ádám tér.

---

5. ORGANIZED TOURS

BOAT & BUS TOURS Ibusz, with decades of experience, sets the standards with organized tours in terms of both quality and quantity. Ibusz offers 18 different boat and bus tours, ranging from basic city tours to special folklore-oriented tours. Ibusz tours operate all year, with an abbreviated schedule in the off season. All buses are air conditioned, and all guides speak English. Some sample offerings: 3-hour Budapest City Tour (1,500 Ft/$16.65); 3-hour Hidden Treasures of the Buda Castle (2,900 Ft/$32.20); 45-minute Parliament tour (900 Ft/$10) (Parliament can only be visited on an organized tour); 3-hour Folklore Evening on the Danube tour (4,500 Ft/$49.95). All bus tours leave from the Erzsébet tér bus station, near Deák tér (all metro lines); all boat tours leave from the Vigadó tér landing. There is also a free hotel pick-up service 30 minutes before departure time. For a full list of tours pick up the Ibusz "Budapest Sightseeing" catalog, available at all Ibusz offices and most hotels. Tours can be booked at any Ibusz office and at most major hotels, or by calling Ibusz directly at 118-1139 or 118-1043.

Legenda, a private company founded in 1990, offers three boat tours on the Danube. A boat tour is a great way to get your measure of the scope and scale of the Hungarian capital, and a majority of the city's grand sights can be seen from the river. Tours run from mid-April through mid-October; all boats leave from the Vigadó tér port, Pier 6 or 7. Tickets are available through most major hotels, at the dock, or through the Legenda office (Fraknó utca 4, tel. 117-2203).

SPECIAL-INTEREST TOURS   **Chosen Tours** (tel. 122-6527, fax 268-0498) is a company which specializes in tours related to Jewish life and heritage in Budapest. The 1½- to 2-hour Guided Walking Tour of Pest's historic Jewish Quarter is a good introduction to that fascinating neighborhood. The tour starts in front of the Dohány Synagogue, on Dohány utca. It costs 1,000 Ft ($11.10); tours are Tuesday and Friday at 10am. Reserve a place or just show up. Chosen Tours also offers a 3-hour air-conditioned bus tour of Jewish sights throughout the city. Called Budapest through Jewish Eyes, it costs 1,450 Ft ($16.10). Starting times are Monday and Thursday at 2pm and Sunday at 10:30am. It's best to reserve a place beforehand. The meeting point is also the Dohány Synagogue. Other tours, available on the basis of private booking, include Tour of Jewish Art and Szentendre.

6. SPORTS & RECREATION

SPA BATHING & SWIMMING

Hungarians are great believers in the medicinal powers of thermal bathing, and few can deny that time spent in thermal baths is enjoyable and relaxing. The baths of Budapest have a long and proud history, stretching back to Roman times. Under Turkish occupation the culture of the baths flourished, and several still-functioning bath houses (Király, Rudas, and Rac) are among the architectural relics of the Turkish period. In the late 19th and early 20th centuries, Budapest's Golden Age, several fabulous bath houses were built: the extravagant eclectic Széchenyi Baths in City Park, the splendid art nouveau Gellért Baths, the solid neo-classical Lukács Baths. All are still in use and are worth a look even for non-bathers.

Thermal bathing is an activity shaped by ritual. For this reason, and because the employees of the bath houses tend to be relics of the old system, many foreigners find a trip to the baths stressful at first. As with any ritualistic activity, it helps to spend some time observing before joining in. The most confusing step may well be the ticket window with its endless list of prices, often without English transla-

IMPRESSIONS

There is no other town of the land of the faithful, and perhaps in all the world which gushes forth in such wonderful abundance its springs to cure all ills, as Buda.
—EVLIA CHELEBI, TURKISH TRAVELER, 16th century.

tions. Chances are you are coming to use one of these facilities: *uszoda,* pool; *termál,* thermal pool; *fürdő,* bath; *gőzfürdő,* steam bath; massage; and sauna. Towel rental is *törülköző* or *lepedő.* An entry ticket generally entitles you to a free locker in the locker room (*öltöző*); you can usually opt to pay an additional fee for a private cabin (*kabin*).

The Most Popular Thermal Baths in Budapest

GELLÉRT BATHS, XI. Kelenhegyi út 4. Tel. 166-6166.

The most spectacular bath house in Budapest, the Gellért Baths are located in Buda's Hotel Gellért (enter baths through the side entrance), the oldest Hungarian spa hotel and an art nouveau jewel. The exterior is in need of restoration, but once inside the lobby you'll be delighted by the details. The mixed-sex indoor pool is without question one of the finest in Europe, with marble columns, majolica tiles, and stone lion-head spouts. The segregated Turkish-style thermal baths, one off to each side of the pool through badly marked doors, are also glorious though in need of restoration. The outdoor roof pool attracts great attention for 10 minutes every hour on the hour when the artificial wave machine is turned on. There are separate nude sunbathing decks for men and women, but you'll have to figure out where they are. In general, you need patience here.

Admission: Thermal bath 140 Ft ($1.55); pools 200 Ft ($2.20) adults, 100 Ft ($1.10) children under 18; pools and thermal baths 300 Ft ($3.35); 30-minute massage 350 Ft ($3.90) plus tip; cabin 100 Ft ($1.10); locker free. Prices posted in English.

Open: Thermal baths, all year, weekdays 6:30am–7pm, weekends 6:30am–1pm; indoor pool, Oct–Apr, weekdays 6am–7pm, weekends 6am–4pm; indoor pool and outdoor pool, May–Sept, daily 6am–7pm. Last entrance one hour before closing. **Tram:** 47 or 49 from Deák tér to Szent Gellért tér.

Outdoor Pool Complex

PALATINUS STRAND, XIII. Margitsziget. Tel. 112-3069.

In the middle of Margaret Island, this is without question Budapest's best located *strand* (literally "beach," but better translated as "outdoor pool complex.") It's a fantastic place, fed by the Margaret Island thermal springs. There are three thermal pools, a vast swimming pool, a smaller artificial wave pool, a water slide, segregated nude sunbathing decks, and large, grassy grounds. The waters of the thermal pools are as relaxing as any of the bath houses, but the experience here is not as memorable as it is at the older bath houses. Facilities include Ping Pong tables, pool tables, trampoline, and dozens of snack bars: in other words, a typical Hungarian *strand.*

Admission: 100 Ft ($1.10); children under 18, 50 Ft (55¢). After 4pm (weekdays only), 50 Ft (55¢) for everyone. Single admission price for all pools.

Open: May and Sept, daily 8am–7pm; June–Aug, daily 7:30am–7pm. Last entry 6pm. **Closed:** Oct–Apr. **Bus:** 26 from Nyugati pu. Beware of pickpockets on bus, especially when crowded!

OTHER SPORTS

HORSEBACK RIDING   Riding is a popular activity in Hungary, and a good place to mount up is the **Petneházy Lovasiskola** (Riding School), at II. Feketefej u. 2 (tel. 176-5937). As far out in the Buda Hills as you can go without leaving the city limits, the school is located in open country, with trails in the hills. The hourly prices are great: Free riding on the track is 300 Ft ($3.35) for children, 350 Ft ($3.90) for adults; open riding with a guide is 550 Ft ($6.10) for children, 650 Ft ($7.20) for adults. There are also ponies for children. The Petneházy Country Club is down the road. There is a great little *csárda* at the stable; plan to have lunch here. Hours are Tuesday to Friday 9am to 5pm (closed noon to 2pm), and weekends 9am to 1pm. **Bus:** 56 (56E is fastest) from Moszkva tér to the last stop, then bus 63 to Feketefej utca, followed by a 10-minute walk.

SQUASH   City Squash Courts, at II. Marczibányi tér. 13. (tel. 135-2518), has four courts. An east walk from Moszkva tér (Red metro line), their hourly rates are, *per person:* 500 Ft ($5.55) weekdays 7am to 5pm, 10pm to midnight, and weekends; 800 Ft ($8.90) weekdays 5 to 10pm.

TENNIS   If you plan to play tennis in Budapest, bring your own racket along since most courts do not rent equipment. Many of Budapest's luxury hotels, particularly those removed from the city center, have tennis courts which can be rented by non-guests. **Hotel Flamenco,** in Buda at XI. Bartók Béla út 63, boasts two indoor courts (tel. 166-5699) and 15 outdoor courts (tel. 161-1001). The indoor courts cost 500 Ft ($5.55) per hour, while the outdoor courts cost 300 Ft ($3.35) per hour. Equipment is not available. Móricz Zsigmond körtér, a transportation hub served by countless buses and trams, is only 5 minutes away.

   Irén Teniszpark, on Irén utca, in the II. district (141-7131), has the most bucolic setting of any tennis club in Budapest. Deep in the Buda Hills, it is situated in a kind of valley which is completely hidden from the nearest road. There are four courts, for 400 Ft ($4.45) per hour. It's open mid-April to mid-October, from 7am to dusk. There are also a playground and picnic tables at the club. Bus 22 (black) from Moszkva tér takes you to Irén utca. It's a tiny, poorly marked street; ask someone to let you know when you arrive.

CHAPTER 7

STROLLING AROUND BUDAPEST

Budapest is best seen on foot, and the following walking tours are intended to introduce you to the texture and color of the city. Many of the city's top attractions—the Buda Palace and Parliament, the National Gallery and the National Museum—are visited on these tours, but dozens of minor sites—vintage pharmacies and quiet courtyards, market halls and medieval walls—are visited as well. On these walking tours special attention is paid to the hidden Budapest, the glorious details that taken together make this the memorable city that it is.

WALKING TOUR 1 —— THE INNER CITY

Start: Deák tér.
Finish: Danube Promenade.
Time: 3 to 4 hours, not including museum stops.
Best Times: Any time except Monday, when museums are closed, or Sunday, when stores are closed.

The medieval city of Pest, like most medieval cities, was surrounded by a protective wall. The wall is long gone, though some remnants remain, which we shall see on this tour. The historic part of the city, inside the walled area, is still known as the *Belváros*, or Inner City. The Erzsébet Bridge divides the Inner City into two parts: the busier, northern half features luxury hotels along the Danube Promenade (*Dunakorzó*) and the boutiques and shops of Váci utca; the quieter southern half, meanwhile, is largely residential, but is also home to the main buildings of Eötvös Loránd University and a number of lovely churches. Pest's Inner Ring boulevard (*Kiskörút*) wraps around both halves, tracing the line of the former medieval city wall. This walking tour spends equal time in each of the two halves of the Inner City, visiting museums, churches, stores, courtyards, and a great market hall en route. We'll end with a leisurely stroll down the Danube Promenade.

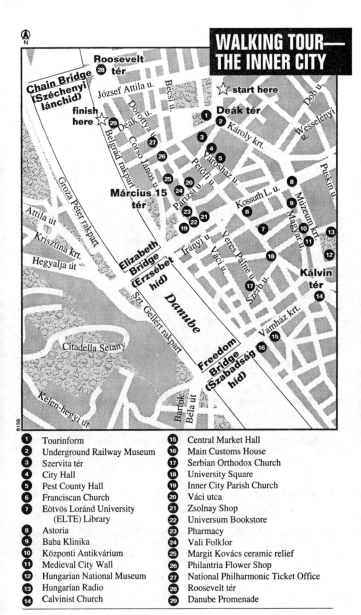

WALKING TOUR— THE INNER CITY

N

Roosevelt tér 28

Chain Bridge (Széchenyi lánchid)

finish here 29

József Attila u.

Bécsi u.

☆ start here

Dob u.

Deák tér

Dorottya u.

Deák u.

Belgrád rakpart

Corso Janos u.

1

27

26

25

2

3

4

5

20

24

Petőfi u.

Váciutca u.

Károly krt.

Wesselenyi u.

Március 15 tér

Pánzsi u.

23 22 21

19

Kossuth L. u.

6

7

Magyar u.

8

9

10

11

Múzeum krt.

Puskin u.

13

12

Attila út

Groza Péter rakpart

Krisztína krt.

Hegyalja út

Elizabeth Bridge (Erzsébet híd)

Trányi u.

Veres Pálne u.

Váci u.

18

Kálvin tér

14

Szent Gellért rakpart

17

Szerb u.

Danube

Citadella Setany

Freedom Bridge (Szabadság híd)

Vámház krt.

15

16

Kelen-hegyi út

Bártók Béla út

6159

❶ Tourinform	⓯ Central Market Hall
❷ Underground Railway Museum	⓰ Main Customs House
❸ Szervita tér	⓱ Serbian Orthodox Church
❹ City Hall	⓲ University Square
❺ Pest County Hall	⓳ Inner City Parish Church
❻ Franciscan Church	⓴ Váci utca
❼ Eötvös Loránd University (ELTE) Library	㉑ Zsolnay Shop
❽ Astoria	㉒ Universum Bookstore
❾ Baba Klinika	㉓ Pharmacy
❿ Központi Antikvárium	㉔ Vali Folklor
⓫ Medieval City Wall	㉕ Margit Kovács ceramic relief
⓬ Hungarian National Museum	㉖ Philantria Flower Shop
⓭ Hungarian Radio	㉗ National Philharmonic Ticket Office
⓮ Calvinist Church	㉘ Roosevelt tér
	㉙ Danube Promenade

Begin at Deák tér, where all three metro lines converge. If you have any questions about theater tickets, activities, or excursions, now would be a good time to pop into:

1. **Tourinform,** Budapest's main tourist information bureau, at Sütő utca 4. Alternatively, you could start with a visit to the:

2. **Underground Railway Museum,** located in the underground passage beneath Deák tér. Here you can see a beautifully

preserved original train from the European continent's first underground system, built in Budapest in 1896. From nearby Szomory Dezső tér, head down Fehérhajó utca towards Szervita tér, formerly Martinelli tér. Ahead of you, you'll notice Váci utca, the crowded pedestrian street. The tour will return there later; for now turn left into:

3. **Szervita tér,** site of the early 18th-century baroque Servite Church; the column of the Virgin Mary; and the former Török Banking House with its colorful Secessionist mosaic. Continue now on Városház utca (City Hall Street) which begins to the left of the church. Dominating this street is the 18th-century:

4. **City Hall,** the largest baroque edifice in Budapest. The lime-green neoclassical building at Városház u. 7 is the 19th-century:

5. **Pest County Hall.** Here, you can visit the inner courtyards. Emerging now onto busy Kossuth Lajos utca, you can see the Erzsébet Bridge to your right, with the northern slope of Gellért Hill behind it. Directly across the street (reached via the underpass) is the:

6. **Franciscan Church.** A church stood here as early as the 13th century, but the present church dates from the 18th. The relief on the side of the building depicts Miklós Wesselényi's heroic rescue effort during the awful Danube flood of 1838. Next door is a shop selling religious artifacts, including hand-painted icons from Bulgaria, Ukraine, and Russia. Continuing south on Ferenciek tere, the striking neoclassical building with the colorful dome is the:

7. **Eötvös Loránd University (ELTE) Library.** Return to Kossuth Lajos utca, and turn right, away from the Danube. The next big intersection,

8. **Astoria,** is on the Inner Ring boulevard (Kiskörút), on whose near side we will see several remnants of the medieval city wall. Turn right onto Múzeum körút. At Múzeum körút 5 you'll find the:

9. **Baba Klinika,** a tiny workshop where dolls are made and repaired. Some are available for purchase. At Múzeum körút 13-15 you'll find the:

10. **Központi Antikvárium,** a shop selling used and rare books, in addition to maps and prints. Another antikvárium, called Honterus, is ahead at Múzeum körút 35. But first check out the courtyard of Múzeum körút 21, where an impressive piece of the:

11. **medieval city wall** can be seen. Across the street is the massive neoclassical:

12. **Hungarian National Museum.** Legend has it that the fiery poet Sándor Petőfi recited his incendiary "National Song" on the museum steps on the first day of the 1848 anti-Habsburg Hungarian Revolution. The museum's most famous exhibit is the legendary Hungarian crown jewels of King Stephen; in reality, Stephen never saw these jewels since they postdate him by several centuries. There is an astonishing history behind the

jewels nonetheless, complex tales of theft, subterfuge, and rescue. Spirited out of Hungary before the Soviet liberation of 1945, they ended up in U.S. government hands. President Carter ceremoniously returned them to the Hungarian government in 1978. You can spend 10 minutes in the National Museum, or 10 hours. Behind the museum on Bródy Sándor utca is the headquarters of:

13. Hungarian Radio, site of a pitched battle in the 1956 uprising. The building is now being restored; presumably the bullet-scarred facade, long a tourist attraction, will be mended.

REFUELING STOPS Choose between the **Múzeum Kávéház,** Múzeum körút 12 (tel. 138-4221), suitable either for a Hungarian lunch or just for coffee and pastries, or **Korona Passage,** an airy crêperie/salad bar in the Korona Hotel at nearby Kálvin tér.

Kálvin tér is named for the 19th-century:

14. Calvinist Church which graces it. Medieval Pest's Kecskeméti Gate stood in Kálvin tér, on the site of the bridge passage between the two buildings of the Hotel Korona. You're now on the Vámház (Customs House) körút section of the Inner Ring. Rounding the bend, you'll see ahead of you the green span of the Szabadság (Freedom) Bridge, with the Gellért Hotel towering beyond in Buda. Head down Vámház körút, and at Veres Pálné utca make a short detour off the körút. At the first corner, Bástya utca, at the rear of a playground, is the single best surviving section of the medieval town wall. Amazingly, children are free to climb all over it. Back on Vámház körút, proceed to the:

15. Central Market Hall (Központi Vásárcsarnok), the largest and most spectacular of the city's late-19th–century market halls. It's presently closed for reconstruction, but the market itself is temporarily set up behind the market hall, between Közraktár utca and the Danube, in a series of old warehouses. If the reconstruction is not finished, just get a glimpse of the fantastic interior through one of the iron gates. Next door to the market is the eclectic-style former:

16. Main Customs House, now a university building, sprawled on the Danube. Admire the graceful span of the Szabadság Bridge, our personal favorite of Budapest's six bridges. Now take Molnár utca back into the Inner City (it's parallel to the Danube, one block in). Turn right on narrow Pintér utca, and right again on Váci utca. Váci utca, whose northern end we'll soon visit, is the famed pedestrian street of Pest. Take an immediate left onto Szerb utca, named for the lovely 18th-century:

17. Serbian Orthodox Church. Continue along Szerb utca, noting the small waist-level monument on the corner of Király Pál utca; its map shows the extent of the terrible Danube flood of 1838. Notice that the entire Inner City was under water! Now enter:

18. University Square (Egyetem tér), site of the ELTE Law School; the baroque University Church, with a copy of the *Black Madonna* of Czestochowa above the altar; and the Sándor Petőfi Literary Museum, a veritable shrine to the literary heroes of a country which adores literature (almost all are largely unknown outside of Hungary). Take Papnovelde utca down to Veres Pálné; turn right. At Irányi utca, you can turn right and in half a block you'll find the next:

REFUELING STOP   Cabar, at Irányi u. 25, is a tiny Israeli-style felafel shop. It has no seating, but delicious felafel and *soarma* (a kind of meat sandwich) are available for a song.

Follow Irányi utca down to the Danube. Passing under the Erzsébet Bridge, you are now back in the northern, more crowded half of the Inner City. Towering above you is the:

19. Inner City Parish Church, built and rebuilt numerous times since the 12th century. Gothic and baroque elements can be detected from the outside; inside, there are niches built in both those styles, as well as a *mihrab* (prayer niche) dating from the Turkish occupation. Passing under the archways of the ELTE Arts Faculty building (walking away from the river) the next street is:

20. Váci utca, Pest's pedestrian-only shopping street. At Kígyó utca 4 (Snake Street), you'll find the:

21. Zsolnay Shop, with Budapest's widest selection of delightfully gaudy Zsolnay porcelain, from the southern city of Pécs. Even if you don't intend to buy, come just to see some fabulous examples of this internationally known china. Nearby, at Váci utca 31-33, is the:

22. Universum Bookstore. Here you'll find the best selection of English-language books about Hungary, both colorful coffee-table books, and more serious literary and historical titles. At Váci utca 34, on the corner of Kígyó utca, is a wonderful old:

23. pharmacy, furnished with antique wooden cabinets and drawers. Proceed down Váci utca now. You'll probably make numerous stops along your way, but one of them should definitely be at:

24. Vali Folklor, in the courtyard of Váci utca 23. In this tiny shop, you'll find a fine assortment of authentic second-hand Hungarian folk costumes, as well as tapestries, ceramics, and figurines. Just down Régiposta utca, across the street from McDonald's, above the door of Régiposta utca 13, is a lovely, but faded:

25. Margit Kovács ceramic relief of a horse and coach. Kovács was Hungary's greatest ceramic artist. A superb museum dedicated to her work can be visited in Szentendre, on the Danube

Bend (See "Szentendre," in Chapter 10). The art nouveau interior of the:

26. **Philantria Flower Shop,** at Váci utca 9, consists of whimsical carved moldings, as well as wall murals recalling the style of Toulouse-Lautrec. Váci utca ends in Vörösmarty tér, one of Pest's loveliest squares, which has a number of attractions in addition to the monumental statue of the great Romantic poet Mihály Vörösmarty, author of "The Appeal," Hungary's "second national anthem." The:

27. **National Philharmonic Ticket Office** (Nemzeti Filharmónia Jegypénztár) is at Vörösmarty tér 1. Here you can buy advance tickets for most Budapest performances. There is no commission. In the same building, you'll find the Hungaroton Record Store, with an excellent selection of both classical and folk music. Across the square, half a block away, at Deák Ferenc utca 10, is Budapest's American Express office. But certainly the best known feature of Vörösmarty tér is Gerbeaud's, the legendary coffeehouse, where you should have a:

REFUELING STOP **Gerbeaud's,** Vörösmarty tér 7. Founded in 1858, Gerbeaud's has been on this site since 1870. The decor and the furnishings are classic turn-of-the-century. The pastries are among the best in Budapest. In summertime, try any of the fresh fruit strudels (*gyümölcs rétes*).

Your next stop is:

28. **Roosevelt tér** (described in "Walking Tour 3—Leopold Town and Theresa Town," below). The Buda Palace looms on Castle Hill directly across the river, which is spanned here by the Széchenyi Chain Bridge. Here, where the statue of the great 19th-century educator József Eötvös stands, is the beginning of the fabled:

29. **Danube Promenade** (Dunakorzó). Gone are the traditional coffeehouses which once lined its turn-of-the-century length between the Chain Bridge and the Erzsébet Bridge. In their place rise luxury hotels, the most monstrous of which is the cement behemoth called Duna Intercontinental. Nevertheless, Budapest still comes to stroll here: join the throngs, equal parts native and tourist. Unobstructed, the glorious view of Buda across the river remains as it ever was. Castle Hill towers above the Watertown, whose many steeples pierce the sky. Along the promenade, you'll find artists, musicians, vendors, and craftspeople.

WALKING TOUR 2 — THE CASTLE DISTRICT

Start: Roosevelt tér, Pest side of Chain Bridge.
Finish: Tóth Árpád sétány, Castle District.

Time: 3 to 4 hours, not including museum stops.
Best Times: Any time except Monday, when museums are closed.

A limestone-capped plateau rising impressively above the Danube, Castle Hill was first settled in the 13th century and remains today the spiritual capital of Hungary. The district has been levelled periodically, most recently by the 1945 Soviet shelling of Nazi forces. Always, it was painstakingly rebuilt in the prevailing style of the day: from Gothic to baroque to Renaissance. After World War II, an attempt was made to incorporate into the general restoration various elements of the district's historic appearance. Castle Hill, which was recently added to UNESCO's world cultural heritage list, consists of two parts: the Royal Palace itself and the so-called Castle District, a mostly reconstructed medieval city. The Royal Palace is now home to a number of museums, first among them the Hungarian National Gallery. The adjoining Castle District is a compact, narrow neighborhood of cobbled lanes and twisting alleys; restrictions on vehicular traffic enhance the feeling of tranquility. Prime examples of every type of Hungarian architecture from early Gothic to Neo-Romanesque can be seen. A walk in the Castle District will be a warmly remembered experience.

To get an accurate picture of the dimensions and grandeur of Castle Hill, start the walking tour in Pest's Roosevelt tér, on the:

1. **Széchenyi Chain Bridge,** one of the outstanding symbols of Budapest. The first permanent bridge across the Danube, originally built in 1849, it was destroyed by Nazi dynamite during World War II. The 1949 opening ceremony of the reconstructed bridge was coincidently held 100 years to the day after its original inauguration. Arriving in Buda, you are now in:

2. **Clark Ádám tér,** a square named for the Scottish engineer who supervised the building of the bridge and afterwards made Budapest his home. From Clark Ádám tér, the:

3. **Funicular** (*sikló*) takes you up to the Royal Palace in a minute or two. Dating from 1870, it too was destroyed in World War II; it was not rebuilt until 1986. Alternately, you can walk up the steep stairs to Castle Hill. Whichever method of ascent you choose, the first thing you'll see at the top is the statue of the:

4. **Turul,** the mythical eagle said to have guided the ancient Magyars in their westward migration. The main courtyard of the palace, from where the museums are entered, is around the back, but first go down the stairs to see the:

5. **Equestrian Statue of Prince Eugene of Savoy.** Prince Eugene was one of the leaders of the united Christian armies which ousted the Turks from Hungary in the late 17th century. Inside the palace are a number of museums. You might want to visit them now, or return after the walking tour to explore them. The first is the:

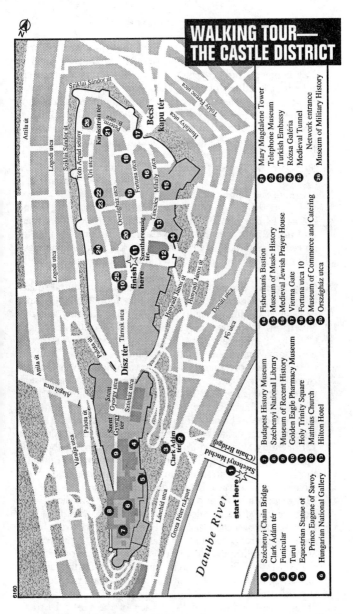

WALKING TOUR— THE CASTLE DISTRICT

N

Sziklai Sándor út

Toldy Ferenc utca

Bécsi kapu tér

Attila út

Logodi utca

Sziklai Sándor út

Petermann bíró utca

Kapisztrán tér

Hunyadi utca

Tóth Árpád sétány

Úri utca

Mihály utca

Petermann

Országház utca

Fortuna utca

Táncsics Mihály utca

Szentháromság tér

finish here

Szentháromság tér

Logodi utca

Disz tér

Tárnok utca

Hunyadi János út

Donáti utca

Fő utca

Attila út

Alagút utca

Szent György utca

Palota út

Szinház utca

Szent György tér

Clark Ádám tér

Váraija utca

Palota út

Lánchíd utca

Groza Péter rkpart

Danube River

start here

Széchenyi lánchíd (Chain Bridge)

- ① Széchenyi Chain Bridge
- ② Clark Ádám tér
- ③ Funicular
- ④ Turul
- ⑤ Equestrian Statue of Prince Eugene of Savoy
- ⑥ Hungarian National Gallery
- ⑦ Budapest History Museum
- ⑧ Széchenyi National Library
- ⑨ Museum of Recent History
- ⑩ Golden Eagle Pharmacy Museum
- ⑪ Holy Trinity Square
- ⑫ Matthias Church
- ⑬ Hilton Hotel
- ⑭ Fisherman's Bastion
- ⑮ Museum of Music History
- ⑯ Medieval Jewish Prayer House
- ⑰ Vienna Gate
- ⑱ Fortuna utca 10
- ⑲ Museum of Commerce and Catering
- ⑳ Országház utca
- ㉑ Mary Magdalene Tower
- ㉒ Telephone Museum
- ㉓ Turkish Embassy
- ㉔ Rózsa Galéria
- ㉕ Medieval Tunnel
- Network entrance
- ㉖ Museum of Military History

6160

---

6. **Hungarian National Gallery,** the vast repository of much of the greatest art ever produced by Hungarians. Don't miss the works of 19th-century artists Mihály Munkácsy, László Paál, Károly Ferenczy, Pál Szinyei Merse, Gyula Benczúr, and Károly Lotz. Nor should you overlook József Rippl-Rónai, the great art nouveau painter of the turn-of-the-century period. The:

7. **Budapest History Museum's** highlights are the Gothic

rooms and statues uncovered during the post–World War II excavation and rebuilding of the Royal Palace. The rooms and all their contents, dating back as far as the 14th century, were buried for hundreds of years. The:

8. **Széchenyi National Library** is named after Ferenc Széchenyi (not his more famous son István, after whom the Chain Bridge is named), who founded it in 1802. It now houses the world's greatest collection of "Hungarica" with some 4 million holdings. And the:

9. **Museum of Recent History** is in Buda Palace wing A. Formerly the Museum of the Hungarian Worker's Movement, it now houses temporary exhibitions.

Exiting the palace, pass through Dísz tér (where bus 16 and 116 can be caught later) to Tárnok utca, where you'll see the:

10. **Golden Eagle Pharmacy Museum** (Arany Sas Patika-múzeum), at Tárnok u. 49. Renaissance and baroque pharmacy relics are displayed in this cavernous little museum. Straight ahead is:

11. **Holy Trinity Square** (Szentháromság tér), the central square of the Castle District. Here you'll find the Holy Trinity Column, or Plague Column, dating from the early 18th century, and the:

12. **Matthias Church** (Mátyás templom). Officially called the Church of Our Lady, this symbol of the Castle District is universally known as Matthias Church because Matthias Corvinus, one of Hungary's most revered kings, was married twice inside it. There is a collection of ecclesiastical art inside. Organ concerts are held Friday evenings in the summer. Next door to the church is the:

13. **Hilton Hotel.** The only hotel in the Castle District, the Hilton tastefully incorporates two ruins into its award-winning design: a 13th-century Dominican Church, with a tower rising above the hotel, and the baroque facade of a 17th-century Jesuit college, the hotel's main entrance. Summer concerts are held in the Dominican Courtyard. Behind the Hilton is the:

14. **Fisherman's Bastion** (Halászbástya), a sprawling Neo-Romanesque structure affording a marvelous panorama of Pest. Looking out over the Danube to Pest, you can see (from left to right): Margaret Island and the Margaret Bridge, Parliament, St. Stephen's Basilica, the Chain Bridge, the Vigadó Concert Hall, the Inner City Parish Church, the Erzsébet Bridge, and the Szabadság Bridge. Avoid the overpriced restaurant housed inside the Fisherman's Bastion.

Because the entire length of each of the Castle District's north–south streets is worth seeing, the tour will now take you back and forth between the immediate area of Szentháromság tér and the northern end of the district. First head down Táncsics Mihály utca, to the:

15. **Museum of Music History,** at Táncsics M. u. 7. Beethoven stayed here for a spell in 1800, when it was a private home. The

Bartók Archives are housed in the museum. The building next door, Táncsics M. u. 9, served for many years as a prison. Among those incarcerated here were Mihály Táncsics, a 19th-century champion of land reform, and Lajos Kossuth, the leader of the 1848–49 anti-Habsburg revolution. Táncsics utca was the center of the medieval Jewish community of Buda. During general post-war reconstruction work in the 1960s the remains of several synagogues were uncovered. The:

16. **Medieval Jewish Prayer House,** at Táncsics Mihály u. 26, dates from the 14th century. In the 15th and 16th centuries the Jews of Buda thrived under Turkish rule. The 1686 Christian reconquest of Buda was soon followed by a massacre of Jews. Many of the survivors fled Buda; this tiny Sephardic synagogue was turned into an apartment. Turn right on Babits Mihály köz; and left onto Babits Mihály sétány. This path will take you onto the top of the:

17. **Vienna Gate** (Bécsi kapu), one of the main entrances to the Castle District. From the top of the gate, you can look out into the fashionable Rose Hill (Rózsadomb) neighborhood in the Buda Hills. The enormous Neo-Romanesque building towering above Bécsi kapu tér houses the National Archives. Bécsi kapu tér is also home to a lovely row of houses (numbers 5–8). From here, head up Fortuna utca to:

18. **Fortuna utca 10,** one of the most photographed houses in the district, which dates originally from the 13th century. Now restored to Louis XVI style, medieval details have been incorporated into the facade. At Fortuna u. 5 you'll find the charming, unassuming:

19. **Museum of Commerce and Catering,** where mostly food-related artifacts from the turn of the century are lovingly displayed. Return to Szentháromság tér, and start down:

20. **Országház utca,** one of two Castle District streets best suited for viewing a mysterious Hungarian contribution to Gothic architecture. Niches of unknown function were built into the entryways of medieval buildings. When uncovered during reconstruction, niches were either preserved or incorporated into the designs of new, modern structures. Niches can be seen in Országház u. 9 and 20. Number 28 has wooden doors of enormous proportions. Incidentally, Országház utca is also the most commercial of the Castle District through streets.

REFUELING STOP Régi Országház Vendéglő, Országház u. 17 (tel. 175-1767), is perhaps the only reasonably priced restaurant in the Castle District. Good Hungarian meals are available; portions are generous and you dine in either the courtyard or the wine cellar.

Országház utca ends in Kapisztrán tér, site of the:

21. Mary Magdalene Tower. Once part of a large 13th-century church, only the tower survived World War II. Now take Úri utca back in the direction of the Royal Palace. In a corner of the courtyard of Úri u. 49, a vast former cloister, stands the small:

22. Telephone Museum. The prime attraction of this museum is the actual telephone exchange (7A1-type rotary system), in use from 1928 to 1985, which is housed in it. In the courtyard is a lovely grassy area where you can take a load off your feet. Úri u. 45 houses the:

23. Turkish Embassy, ironically the only embassy in the Castle District, which was from 1541 to 1686 the seat of Turkish rule in Hungary. Also on Úri utca are Gothic niches galore, seen in the entryways of numbers 40, 38, 36, 34, 32, and 31. No doubt you've noticed the presence in the Castle District of a large number of art galleries. Hungarian naive and primitive art is on display in:

24. Rózsa Galéria, at Szentháromság u. 13. Prices are reasonable, with the cheapest paintings in the 15,000 Ft ($167) range. Uri u. 9 is the entrance to the:

25. Medieval Tunnel Network which weaves its way through the almost 15 kilometers of rock beneath the Castle District. The only part of this network you can actually see is home to the Buda Wax Works (guided tour required), an unimpressive, tacky exhibit on the "legends" of early Hungarian history. Úri utca ends back in Dísz tér. Take tiny Móra Ferenc utca to Tóth Árpád sétány, the promenade which runs the length of the western rampart of the Castle District. At its northern end, housed in the former barracks at Tóth Árpád sétány 40, is the:

26. Museum of Military History. The highlight of this expansive museum is the room devoted to the 1956 Hungarian uprising, one of the few violent episodes of Budapest's history in which the Castle District was not a primary venue. The 10 chaotic days of the uprising are detailed by consecutive panels of large mounted photographs. The legendary hand of Stalin is here too, the only piece known to remain from the giant statue whose public destruction was one of the dramatic moments of the failed uprising.

The walking tour ends back near Szentháromság tér with a final:

REFUELING STOP Ruszwurm Cukrászda, Szentháromság u. 7. This little coffeehouse has been here since 1827. It's only classic one in the Castle District. The pastries are among the best in the city.

From nearby Szentháromság tér, you can catch the Várbusz down to Moszkva tér, or from Dísz tér you can get bus 16 to Deák tér or bus 116 to Március 15 tér.

WALKING TOUR 3 — LEOPOLD TOWN & THERESA TOWN

Start: Kossuth tér, site of Parliament.
Finish: Müvész Coffeehouse, near the Opera House.
Time: About 3 hours (excluding museum visits and Opera House tour).
Best Times: Any day except Monday, when museums are closed.
Note: If you want to visit the Parliament building, you should book a tour *in advance* with Ibusz or Budapest Tourist.

In 1790 the new region developing just to the north of the medieval town walls of Pest was dubbed Leopold Town (Lipótváros) in honor of the emperor Leopold II. Over the next 100 years or so, the neighborhood developed into an integral part of Pest, housing numerous governmental and commercial buildings; Parliament, government ministries, courthouses, the Stock Exchange, and the National Bank were all built here. This tour will take you through the main squares of Leopold Town. You'll also walk briefly along the Danube and visit a historic market hall. Along the way, you'll stop to admire some of Pest's most fabulous examples of art nouveau architecture, as well as the city's largest church. Then you'll cross Pest's Inner Ring boulevard leaving the Inner City and head up elegant Andrássy út, on the edge of Theresa Town (Terézváros). There you'll explore some wonderful inner courtyards and finish the tour after visiting the dazzling State Opera House (try to arrive here at 3 or 4pm if you would like to tour the Opera House).

Exiting the Kossuth tér metro (Red line), you'll find yourself on the southern end of:

1. **Kossuth tér.** Walk towards Parliament, passing the equestrian statue of the Transylvanian Prince Ferenc Rákóczi II, hero of an early 18th-century anti-Habsburg revolt. Exiled after the failure of his revolt, Rákóczi wandered from Poland to France and then to Turkey, where he remained until his death. The Neo-Gothic:

2. **House of Parliament,** designed by Imre Steindl and completed in 1902, is on your left. Unfortunately you can only enter by pre-arranged tour (book through Ibusz or Budapest Tourist). The eclectic-style building on your right, the former Supreme Court, now houses the:

3. **Ethnographical Museum.** The museum boasts 150,000 objects in its collection. The permanent exhibition entitled "From Ancient Times to Civilization" contains many fascinating relics of Hungarian life. Walk past the statue of 1848 revolutionary hero Lajos Kossuth; after 45 years in exile, the stubborn Kossuth died in Torino, but received a hero's burial in Budapest. Now enter the small park by the Danube at the northern end of Kossuth tér. Admire the sensitive Imre Varga statue of Mihály

Károlyi, first president of the post–World War I Hungarian Republic. Károlyi, too, died in exile. In 1962, seven years after his death, his ashes were brought back to his homeland. Across the Danube, to your left, you can see Castle Hill and the church steeples of Watertown (Víziváros) beneath it. The bridge visible to your right is the Margaret Bridge. Now turn left, go down the stairs and walk south along the river embankment. After completing this circumnavigation of Parliament come back up the next set of stairs. There you'll find a small statue of Attila József, the much loved inter-war working-class poet, whose tragic suicide (by jumping under a train at Lake Balaton) is imitated from time to time in Hungary. Cross the tram tracks and walk two blocks on Akadémia utca, turning left onto Zoltán utca. As you cross Nádor utca, the massive yellow late eclectic–art nouveau building on your right is the Former Stock Exchange, now headquarters of Hungarian Television. It's front is on:

4. **Freedom Square** (Szabadság tér). Directly in front of you is the Soviet Army Memorial, built in 1945. It is topped by one of the few Red Stars remaining in post-Communist Budapest. The American Embassy is at Szabadság tér 12. Paying careful attention to traffic here, walk diagonally through the square, aiming for its southeast corner, site of the eclectic:

5. **Hungarian National Bank** (Magyar Nemzeti Bank). Leaving Szabadság tér via Bank utca, you can enter the National Bank through a side entrance. Its well-preserved ornate lobby reminds one more of an opera house than a bank; its air-conditioned skylit main hall has rows of soft, comfortable chairs where you might rest your feet. Continue on Bank utca, making the first left onto Hold utca (Moon Street), formerly known as Rosenberg házaspár utca, for Ethel and Julius Rosenberg. Next door to the rear of the National Bank, connected to it by a bridge, is the newly restored:

6. **former Post Office Savings Bank** (Posta Takarékpénztár), built in 1901, to the design of Ödön Lechner, the architect who endeavored to fuse Hungarian folk elements with the art nouveau style of his time. On the corner of Hold utca and Nagysándor József utca is the first:

REFUELING STOP Csarnok Vendéglő, Hold utca 11 (tel. 112-2016). An unassuming little vendéglő visited mainly by neighborhood residents, it is suitable for a typical Hungarian lunch. The restaurant's name comes from the nearby:

7. **Inner City Market Hall** (Belvárosi Vásárcsarnok). One of several vast train station–like market halls in Budapest (built 1897), this is one of the liveliest. One section of the hall is still used by peasants selling their produce. Pick up some fruit in

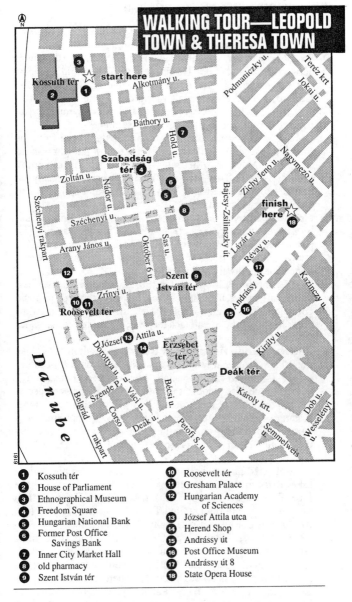

WALKING TOUR—LEOPOLD TOWN & THERESA TOWN

1. Kossuth tér
2. House of Parliament
3. Ethnographical Museum
4. Freedom Square
5. Hungarian National Bank
6. Former Post Office Savings Bank
7. Inner City Market Hall
8. old pharmacy
9. Szent István tér
10. Roosevelt tér
11. Gresham Palace
12. Hungarian Academy of Sciences
13. József Attila utca
14. Herend Shop
15. Andrássy út
16. Post Office Museum
17. Andrássy út 8
18. State Opera House

season. Emerge from the Market Hall onto Vadász utca; turn right. Passing Nagysándor József utca, look to your right for a great view of the colorful tiled roof of the former Post Office Savings Bank you recently passed. Turn right on Bank utca, and left on Hercegprímás utca. On the corner, at Hercegprímás u. 21, is a lovely:

8. old pharmacy, with traditional wooden cabinets and drawers. After a few blocks, you'll find yourself in:

9. Szent István tér, site of the famous St. Stephen's Basilica, built between 1851 and 1905. This is the largest church in Budapest and a stop inside is well worth your while. In the Szent Jobb Kápolna, behind the main altar, you can see an extraordinary holy relic: Stephen's preserved right hand. Monday night organ concerts are held in the church in the summer.

Head down Zrínyi utca, straight across the square from the church entrance. As you pass Október 6 utca you might want to make a slight detour to Bestsellers, the English-language bookstore at no. 11. They stock travel books here, especially on Eastern Europe. Returning now to the Danube, you'll find yourself emerging into:

10. Roosevelt tér, at the head of the famous Chain Bridge. Built in the revolutionary year 1848–49, the bridge was the first permanent span across the Danube. Roosevelt Square itself is really too full of traffic to be beautiful, but there are several important and lovely buildings here:

11. The Gresham Palace, built in 1907, is one of Budapest's best known art nouveau buildings. You can pass through its main courtyard through any of three gates, including one on Zrínyi utca. To your right, as you face the river, is the Neo-Renaissance facade of:

12. The Hungarian Academy of Sciences, built in 1864. Like the Chain Bridge, it was the brainchild of the 19th-century Count István Széchenyi (called "the Greatest Hungarian"), whose statue also adorns the square. Guards prevent access beyond the lobby of the Academy, but it is worth a peek inside. A statue of Ferenc Deák, architect of the 1867 Compromise with Austria, is in a shady grove in the southern end of the square by the Atrium Hyatt Hotel. Turn left away from the river onto bustling:

13. József Attila utca, named for the poet whose statue embellishes Kossuth tér. You are now walking along a portion of the Inner Ring (Kiskörút), which separates the Inner City (Belváros) to your right from the Leopold Town (Lipótváros) to your left. At József nádor tér you may want to stop in at the:

14. Herend Shop. Herand china is perhaps Hungary's most famous product, and this museum-like shop is definitely worth a look. Continuing up József Attila utca, you'll pass Erzsébet tér, site of Budapest's main bus station, just before reaching Bajcsy-Zsilinszky út. Endre Bajcsy-Zsilinszky, a heroic leader of Hungary's wartime anti-fascist resistance, was executed by the Arrow Cross (Hungary's Nazis) on Christmas Eve, 1944. Crossing Bajcsy-Zsilinszky út, you'll find yourself at the head of stately:

15. Andrássy út, fin-de-siècle Pest's greatest boulevard. If you're in the mood for a snack, walk one short block to your left on Bajcsy-Zsilinszky to reach the next:

REFUELING STOP **Finom Sütemények Boltja,** Révay utca 2. This bustling little place, whose name means "Shop of Delicious Pastries," has only a small selection, but you'll be hard pressed to find a better *pogácsa* (flaky biscuit) or *rétes* (fruit strudel) anywhere in the city.

Returning now to Andrássy út, look for no. 3, a building with a stunning entryway, which is:

16. **The Post Office Museum;** its main attraction is clearly the opulently appointed apartment in which it's located. This is how the wealthy of Andrássy út used to live! The frescoes in the entryway are by Károly Lotz, whose frescoes also decorate the Opera House and Matthias Church, in the Castle District. Cross to the even-numbered side of Andrássy. Stop to peek into other entryways and courtyards. In the vestibule of:

17. **Andrássy út 8** you'll find more ceiling frescoes; this courtyard is typical of this kind of Pest apartment building. Andrássy út 12, a building belonging to the once-feared Interior Ministry, has a gorgeous entryway and an inner courtyard full of frescoes. A policeman guards the entrance, but welcomes tourists. Continue on Andrássy út until reaching the Neo-Renaissance:

18. **State Opera House.** Designed by Miklós Ybl, it was built in 1884. Almost alone among the great buildings of the city, the Opera House survived the siege of Budapest at the end of World War II nearly unscathed. Its huge cellars provided shelter for thousands during the bombing. Turning left on Hajós utca, walk around the Opera House. English-language tours (daily at 3pm and 4pm, all year) start at the Nappali Pénztár entrance on Hajós utca; the cost is 250 Ft ($2.80) per person, 120 Ft ($1.35) for students).

You'll find the Opera station of the Yellow metro line just in front of the Opera House.

WALKING TOUR 4 — THE JEWISH DISTRICT

Start: Dohány Synagogue.
Finish: Wesselényi utca.
Time: About 2 hours (excluding museum visit).
Best Times: Any day except Saturday, when the museum and most shops are closed.

The Jewish district of Pest has a long and ultimately tragic history. It first grew up in medieval times just beyond the Pest city wall (which stood where today's Inner Ring boulevard stands) as Jews were forbidden to live inside the town. Later Pest expanded beyond the medieval walls and the Jewish district actually became one of the more centrally located neighborhoods in the city. The huge synagogues which you'll see on this tour give some idea of its former vitality. Under the German occupation in World War II the district became a walled ghetto, with 220,000 Jews crowded inside; almost half did not survive the war. Not much has changed physically in the neighborhood in the post-war years; your footsteps still echo through the winding, narrow streets, although most of the buildings are in a state of slow decay. The actual area covered in this tour is quite small, but the evocative neighborhood is filled with wonderful little sights.

Halfway between Astoria (Red metro line) and Deák tér (all metro lines) is the:

1. **Dohány Synagogue,** a striking Byzantine building, Europe's largest and the world's second-largest synagogue. Built in 1859, it is still used by Budapest's *Neolog* (Conservative) Jewish community, although until 1996 the entrance hours are unpredictable due to an ambitious reconstruction project. The small free-standing brick wall inside the courtyard, to the left of the synagogue's entrance, is a piece of the original:

2. **Ghetto Wall** that isolated Budapest's Jews inside this district during World War II. This is not actually where the wall stood: It was situated on Károly körút, the nearby stretch of the Inner Ring boulevard. To the left of the wall, on the spot marked as the birthplace of Theodor Herzl, the founder of modern Zionism, is the:

3. **National Jewish Museum,** where ornaments and art from the long history of Hungarian Jewry are displayed. The last of the four rooms is given over to a moving exhibit on the Holocaust in Hungary. (Note the peculiar open hours: May through October only, Monday and Thursday 2pm to 6pm; Tuesday, Wednesday, Friday, and Sunday 10am to 1pm.) The synagogue courtyard can be entered through the rear of the complex on Wesselényi utca. Inside the courtyard is a newly unveiled:

4. **Holocaust Memorial.** Designed by Imre Varga, the well-known contemporary Hungarian sculptor, it is in the form of a weeping willow tree. The thin metal leaves, purchased by survivors and descendants to honor martyred relatives, are slowly filling the many branches. Now head down Rumbach utca. Near the corner of Rumbach utca and Dob utca is the rather bizarre:

5. **Memorial to Charles Lutz,** the Swiss consul who aided Swedish diplomat Raoul Wallenberg's heroic attempts to save Budapest's Jews from the Nazi death camps. The inscription from the Talmud reads: "Saving one soul is the same as saving the whole world." A lonely memorial to the far better-known Wallenberg stands irrelevantly on Szilágyi Erzsébet fasor, in Buda. Half a block further on Rumbach utca is the:

6. **Rumbach Synagogue,** a handsome yellow-and-rust–colored

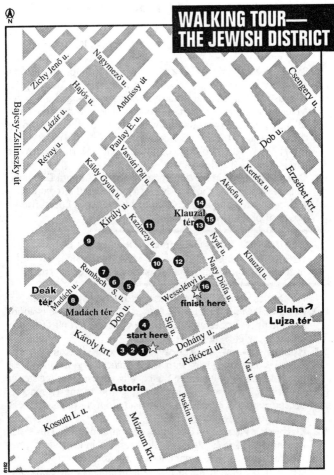

WALKING TOUR—
THE JEWISH DISTRICT

① Dohány Synagogue
② Ghetto Wall
③ National Jewish Museum
④ Holocaust Memorial
⑤ Memorial to Charles Lutz
⑥ Rumbach Synagogue
⑦ ETK Bookstore
⑧ Madách tér
⑨ Connected Courtyards
⑩ Fonalbolt (Yarn Store)
⑪ Kosher Salami Workshop
⑫ Orthodox Kazinczy Synagogue
⑬ Klauzál tér
⑭ Made In Tel Aviv store
⑮ District Market Hall
⑯ Judaica Art Gallery

building, in its own way as impressive as the Dohány Synagogue. Built in 1872 by the Vienna architect Otto Wagner, the Orthodox synagogue is no longer in use. You can't go inside, but the facade is a sight worth seeing. Next door to the synagogue, on the corner of Madách út, is the:

7. ETK Bookstore, the only place in town where you can buy *Századeleji Házak Budapesten* (see "Recommended Books and Films," in Chapter 1), the marvelous little handbook celebrating turn-of-the-century architecture in Budapest. Take a look at the giant archway of:

8. Madách tér. In the 1930s a plan was drawn up for the creation of a great boulevard similar in form and style to Andrássy út. World War II put an end to the ambitious project, and the grand Madách tér leads only to itself now. Looking through the arch, though, you do get a wonderful view of Gellért Hill, crowned by the Liberation Monument. Take a right onto Király utca, which forms the northern border of the historic Jewish district. At Király utca 13, head through the long series of:

9. Connected Courtyards, emerging finally out onto Dob utca, back in the heart of the Jewish district. This kind of complex— with residential buildings connected by a series of courtyards— is typical of the Jewish district.

REFUELING STOP Fröhlich Cukrászda, Dob u. 22, is the only functioning Kosher *cukrászda* (sweet shop) left in the district. Here you can purchase pastries, rolls, or ice cream.

Knitters should be sure to stop at the nearby:

10. Fonalbolt (Yarn Store), at Dob utca 27. The selection is good, and the prices unbeatable. Half a block to the left off Dob utca on Kazinczy utca, at no. 41, is the:

11. Kosher Salami Workshop (Szalámi és Kolbászáru Üzem). Salami is handmade here with ancient machinery. If you make a purchase, be sure to admire the equally ancient cash register in the corner. The sign outside directing you to the entrance is deceptive; simply enter via the courtyard in front of you. Back at Kazinczy u. 29 is the:

12. Orthodox Kazinczy Synagogue, built in 1913. This synagogue is still active. Although much of it is in great decay, the synagogue has a well-maintained courtyard in its center. There are a number of apartments in which members of the community live. While hundreds of tourists a day visit the Dohány Synagogue, far fewer make the trip here. Exit the synagogue complex, either back onto Kazinczy utca or onto Dob utca. You'll soon emerge into:

13. Klauzál tér, the largest square in the district, and its historic center. A grungy park and playground fill the interior of the square. There are a number of sights on Klauzál tér, including two lunch options (see below). At Klauzál tér 12, you'll find the:

14. Made In Tel Aviv store, unmistakable beneath its giant blue-and-white sign. Here Israeli food products are sold. Next door is the:

15. District Market Hall (Vásárcsarnok), one of the half dozen or so great steel girdered market halls built in Budapest in the 1890s. It now houses a Skála grocery store, but the entrance area is filled with smaller vendors, from whom you can buy fruit or vegetables.

REFUELING STOPS You have three lunch options in Klauzál tér and its immediate vicinity, each with a markedly different character. **Hanna Kosher Restaurant,** back at the Kazinczy Synagogue, the city's only Orthodox Kosher restaurant, is the domain of the elderly Jews who live inside the synagogue complex; **Kádár Étkezde,** at Klauzál tér 9, is a simple, local lunchroom (open only Tuesday through Saturday 11:30am to 3:30pm) serving a regular clientele, ranging from young paint-spattered workers to elderly Jews; and **Shalom Restaurant,** at Klauzál tér 1-3 (tel. 173-2467), a somewhat fancier establishment which does a brisk business with tourists.

Now head back to Wesselényi utca, where you can end the walking tour at:

16. **The Judaica Art Gallery,** at Wesselényi u. 13. Here you can find Jewish-oriented books, both new and second-hand (some are in English). Clothing, ceramics, art, and religious articles are also for sale.

CHAPTER 8

SHOPPING FROM A TO Z

Budapest is not quite Paris, but the shopping scene has improved dramatically since the political changes of 1989. Even under the old regime, the Hungarian capital was one of the brighter spots in the bleak commercial landscape of the East Bloc; vacationing Easterners went home happy, shopping bags bulging out of the trunks of their Trabants and Ladas. Now most of the shopping is done by Westerners.

MAIN SHOPPING STREETS All year long, foreigners and Hungarians alike throng the pedestrian-only stretch of the **Váci utca,** from the roar of Kossuth Lajos utca to the wide, stately Vörösmarty tér, the center of Pest. Váci utca, and the pedestrian streets bisecting it, are lined with fine shops. Fashionable boutiques, not visible from the street, fill the courtyards. The increasing prevalence of Euro-fashion items, mainly Italian and French designer names, is a recent development on the Váci utca. The increased "western-style" prices are also relatively new. Payment by credit card is not always possible, so plan ahead. The **Castle District** in Buda, with its abundance of folk art boutiques and galleries, is another popular area for souvenir hunters.

While Hungarians enjoy window-shopping in these two neighborhoods, they make precious few purchases. Hungarians love to shop though, and you don't have to wander far to see where they do their buying. The most popular street is undoubtedly Pest's **Outer Ring** (Nagykörút); another bustling shopping street is Pest's **Kossuth Lajos utca,** off the Erzsébet Bridge, and its continuation **Rákóczi út,** which extends all the way out to Keleti Station. In Buda, Hungarian crowds visit the shops of the **Margit körút** and the neighborhood of **Móricz Zsigmond körtér,** where the Buda Skála department store is located.

HOURS, TAXES & SHIPPING Most stores are open from 10am to 6pm on weekdays, and from about 9am to about 1pm on Saturday. Some stores stay open an hour or two later on Thursday, while many close for an hour at lunchtime. Almost all shops are closed on Sunday. All prices in Hungary carry a built-in 25% Value-Added Tax (VAT). Individuals making *cumulative* noncommercial purchases exceeding 25,000 Ft ($278) are entitled to a VAT refund on the amount over 25,000 Ft. You must save all store receipts, in addition to your currency-exchange receipts (or credit-card receipts). The refund procedure is rather complicated and is likely to be changed in the near future; your best bet is to inquire about it at Tourinform, where the most up-to-date information is available.

Hungarian Customs regulations do not limit the export of non-commercial quantities of most goods. However, the export of some food staples like coffee and chocolate is strictly regulated (but rarely enforced). There is no limit on wine, but only one liter of spirits and 400 cigarettes may be exported.

At present, very few shops will organize shipping for you. You can ship a box to yourself from any post office, but the rules on packing boxes are as strict as they are arcane. The Hungarian postal authorities prefer you to use one of their official shipping boxes, for sale at all post offices. They are quite flimsy, and have been known to break open in transit.

BEST BUYS Hungarian folk items are the most popular souvenirs among foreigners visiting Budapest. The state-owned Folkart shops (Népművészeti Háziipar) have a great selection of handmade goods at unbeatable prices. Popular items include pillow cases, pottery, porcelain, dolls, dresses, skirts, and vests.

Another source of authentic folk items is the ethnic Hungarian women who come to Budapest with bags full of exquisite handmade items from Transylvania, a region of Romania heavily populated with ethnic Hungarians. A few years ago, they congregated on Váci utca displaying their colorful wares. The police have driven them from that showcase shopping street, and they now wander elsewhere, always a half step ahead of the police. Keep your eyes open for these vendors: They're unmistakable in their characteristic black boots, long skirts, and red or black kerchiefs tied around their heads. Their prices are generally quite reasonable, and bargaining is customary.

Another popular Hungarian item is porcelain, particularly from the country's two best-known producers, Herend and Zsolnay. Although both brands are widely available in the West, here you'll find a better selection and prices about 50% lower.

Typical Hungarian foods also make great gifts. Hungarian salami is world famous. Connoisseurs generally agree that Pick Salami, produced in the southeastern city of Szeged, is the best brand. Herz Salami, produced locally in Budapest, is a slightly lesser product, but much easier to find. Another typical Hungarian food product is chestnut paste (*gesztenye püré*), available in a tube or a tin; it's used primarily as a pastry filling, but can also top desserts and ice cream. Paprika paste is something else you'll scarcely find outside Hungary. It comes most commonly in a tube. Three styles are available; hot (*csípős*), deli style (*csemege*), and sweet (*édes*). All of these items can be purchased in grocery stores (*élelmiszer* or *ABC*) and delicatessens (*csemege*).

If you are a lover of open markets, Budapest is the place for you. There are numerous markets here: flea markets (*használtáru piac*) filled not only with every conceivable kind of junk and the occasional relic of Communism, but also with great quantities of mostly low-quality new items like clothing, cassettes, and shoes; and food markets (*vásárcsarnok, csarnok* or *piac*), with row after row of succulent fruits and vegetables, much of it freshly picked and driven in from the surrounding countryside. By definition, a journey into a market is a journey off the tourist track.

ANTIQUES

When shopping for antiques in Budapest, you should know that Hungary forbids the export of many items designated as "cultural treasures." Some purchases come with a certificate allowing export; with other purchases the responsibility is the buyer's alone to go to the correct office (in the National Museum or National Gallery) and apply for the certificate. Our advice is to buy only from those shops which supply the certificate for you. A journey through Hungarian bureaucracy can be a withering experience.

Although it no longer has a monopoly on the sale of antiques, the still state-owned **BÁV** (Bizományi Kereskedőház és Záloghitel Rt.) continues to control the lion's share of the antique market in Hungary. Here is a partial list of BÁV shops: The BÁV store at I. Hess András tér 1 (tel. 175-0392), in the Castle District, specializes in porcelain and silver; the one at V. Bécsi u. 1-3 (tel. 117-2548), near Deák tér, specializes in antique furniture and chandeliers; the one at V. Ferenciek tere 5 (tel. 118-3773) specializes in carpets; the one at V. Kossuth L. u. 1-3 (tel. 118-6808), just across the street from the Ferenciek tere shop, specializes in antique furniture, chandeliers, and paintings; the one at VI. Andrássy út 27 (tel. 142-5525), near the Opera House, specializes in antique art, porcelain, and silver; the one at nearby VI. Andrássy út 34 (tel. 132-5759) specializes in Eastern relics; the one at VII. Dohány u. 16-18 (tel. 142-7935), in the historic Jewish neighborhood, specializes in furnishings, furniture, and carpets; and the ones at IX. Üllői ut 47 (tel. 114-2088) and IX. Tűzoltó u. 14 (tel. 133-9827) both specialize in furniture.

Qualitatas Antiquitas is a private company with three stores: the store at I. Krisztina körút 73 (tel. 175-0658), behind the Castle District, specializes in paintings and furniture; the one at V. Falk Miksa u. 32 (tel. 131-2292), near Parliament, specializes in china; and the one at VII. Dohány u. 1 (tel. 141-5585), near the Dohány Synagogue, specializes in ecclesiastical and glass objects. **Ecclesia Szövetkezet**, at V. Ferenciek tere 7 (tel. 117-3754), next door to the Franciscan Church, has hand-painted icons from Russia, Bulgaria, and Ukraine, starting at around 30,000 Ft ($333); contemporary hand-painted copies start as low as 2,000 Ft ($22).

ART GALLERIES

Budapest is home to a burgeoning—but still fairly unsettled—art gallery scene. The same export rules outlined above regarding antiques apply to all works of art considered to be Hungarian cultural treasures. Before completing a purchase, confirm that you'll be allowed to take the work out of the country.

Galleries tend to keep either normal store hours (weekdays 10am to 6pm, Saturday 9 or 10am to 1 or 2pm) or museum hours (Tuesday through Sunday, 10am to 6pm). They are concentrated in two areas: the Inner City of Pest and Buda's Castle District. Galleries exhibiting the works of contemporary Hungarian artists include: **Hungart Studio,** V. Kossuth Lajos u. 12 (tel. 117-5978); **Gulácsy Gallery,** V. Károly körút 6 (tel. 118-8933); **Várfok 14 Mŭhely Gallery,** I. Várfok u. 14 (tel. 115-2165); **Vár Gallery,** I. Táncsics Mihály u. 17 (tel. 115-9802); **Eve Art Gallery,** VI. Király u. 98/b (tel. 122-8466); **Luttar Gallery,** XIII. Hegedŭs Gyula u. 24 (tel. 149-5045); and **No. 5 Gallery,** V. Apaczai Csere János u. 5 (tel. 117-0541). Art students exhibit their work in the **Gallery of the Young Artist's Studio,** at V. Bajcsy-Zsilinszky út 52 (tel. 111-9882). The **Hologram Gallery,** in the Párizsi Udvar (Paris Passage), off V. Ferenciek tere (tel. 118-3761), is always filled with people. You can even get hologram business cards there.

BOOKSTORES [NEW & SECONDHAND]

BESTSELLERS, V. Október 6 utca 11. Tel. 112-1295.

Budapest's first (and so far only) English-language bookstore, Bestsellers is a popular meeting spot for English speakers. It's located in the middle of the Inner City, not far from Szabadság tér, site of the American Embassy. The store is most notable for its assortment of travel books on Eastern Europe. Newspapers and magazines are also available, including some, like *Rolling Stone,* not found elsewhere in Budapest. Open: Mon–Sat 9am–6:30pm. Metro: Arany János utca (Blue line).

BIBLIOTEKA ANTIKVÁRIUM, VI. Andrássy út 2. Tel. 131-5132.

At the head of Andrássy út, near Bajcsy-Zsilinszky út, this is one of central Pest's better *antikvaria* (used and rare book shops). They have two shelves of English-language books, maps, and prints. Open: Weekdays 10am–6pm, Sat 9am–1pm. Metro: Arany János utca (Blue line) or Deák tér (all lines).

HONTERUS ANTIKVÁRIUM, V. Múzeum körút 35. Tel. 117-3270.

Located near the Központi Antikvárium, across the street from the Hungarian National Museum (Nemzeti Múzeum), this old and rare bookstore has more prints and maps on display than any other antikvárium in town. There is a shelf of mostly arcane, out-of-date English-language academic books as well as a stack of *National Geographic* magazines. Open: Weekdays 10am–6pm, Sat 10am–2pm. Metro: Astoria (Red line) or Kálvin tér (Blue line).

KÖZPONTI ANTIKVÁRIUM, V. Múzeum körút 13-15. Tel. 117-3514.

"Central Antikvárium" is indeed the largest old and rare bookstore in Budapest. Located since 1885 on 'Antikvárium Row' (our term) across the street from the Hungarian National Museum, this shop has books, prints, maps, and a shelf of assorted knick-knacks. Open: Weekdays 9:30am–5:30pm (closed noon–1pm), Sat 9am–12:30pm. Metro: Astoria (Red line) or Kálvin tér (Blue line).

LIBRI IDEGEN NYELVŰ KÖNYVESBOLT [LIBRI FOREIGN LANGUAGE BOOKSHOP], V. Váci u. 32. Tel. 118-2718.

The foreign-language bookstore of the ubiquitous Libri chain, this shop is located on Váci utca, in downtown Pest. It has a fair selection of Corvina English-language books about Hungary, a section of English-language fiction, and a music section. Open: Weekdays 10am–6pm, Sat 9am–1pm. Metro: Vörösmarty tér (Yellow line) or Deák tér (all lines).

UNIVERSUM, V. Váci u. 31-33. Tel. 118-2724.

This is the best of the Váci utca bookshops for those in search of English-language books (mostly Corvina books) about Budapest or Hungary—coffee-table books, guidebooks, fiction and poetry in translation, and scholarly works are available. There's also a good selection of maps, including the Cartographia trail map of the Buda Hills (*A Budai Hegység*), hard to find in Budapest. Open: Weekdays 10am–7pm, Sat 9am–1pm. Metro: Vörösmarty tér (Yellow line) or Deák tér (all lines).

CLOTHING & SHOES

FANATIQ COLLECTION, V. Váci u. 19-21. Tel. 118-9688.

Casual Euro-fashion for men and women in a spiffy tri-level store, which specializes in women's cotton tops and men's sport coats. Open: Weekdays 10am–7pm, Sat 10am–2pm. Metro: Vörösmarty tér (Yellow line) or Deák tér (all lines).

INSIDE, V. Váci u. 6. Tel. 117-7207.

This is definitely one of the most chic shops on Váci utca. A closet-sized boutique, Inside features the cutting edge of Italian and French women's fashion and accessories—high quality silk, cotton, and leather. Open: Weekdays 10am–6pm, Sat 10am–1:30pm. Metro: Vörösmarty tér (Yellow line) or Deák tér (all lines).

JOKER APPLIED ARTS, VII. Akácfa u. 5/a. Tel. 141-4281.

This innovative design studio is located just off Blaha Lujza tér, next door to the Hotel Emke. In business since the late 1970s (a long time in Budapest), Joker features unique handmade goods by local artisans, as well as Asian import items. Merchandise includes clothing, shoes, and accessories. Friendly proprietor Judit Maior speaks fluent English. Open: Weekdays 10am–6pm, Sat 10am–2pm. Metro: Blaha Lujza tér (Red line).

KALÁKA DESIGN STUDIO, V. Haris köz 2. Tel. 118-3313.

This shop has ultra-hip Italian and Hungarian women's shoes (and clothing): Attamo, Aenmdia, Balaton Marianna, and Bodor Ágnes designs. It's located on Haris köz, a pedestrian street off Váci utca. Open: Weekdays 10am–6pm, Sat 10am–2pm. Metro: Vörösmarty tér (Yellow line) or Deák tér (all lines).

RAJNAI, V. Váci u. 6. Tel. 138-0222.
A tiny boutique in an alleyway, Rajnai is stocked with casual Italian men's wear: pants, shirts, and silk ties. Prices are quite reasonable. The proprietor recommends a good tailor for those needing alterations. Open: Weekdays 10am–6pm, Sat 10am–1pm. Metro: Vörösmarty tér (Yellow line) or Deák tér (all lines).

COINS

NUMIZMATIKAI GALÉRIA, V. Nádor u. 5. Tel. 137-7940.
This small shop, not far from Deák tér in a quiet part of the Inner City, has a variety of coins and antique paper money for sale. Of particular note are the Roman coins. Open: Mon noon–5pm, Tues–Fri 9am–5pm. Metro: Deák tér (all lines).

DEPARTMENT STORES

Sprawling Örs Vezér tere, the eastern terminus of the Red metro line, is home both to Budapest's branch of the internationally known Swedish **Ikea** chain and to the city's only quasi-American style mall, **Sugár.** Ikea (open weekdays 9am to 6pm, Sat 9am to 1pm) has a cafeteria where homesick Scandinavians can go for Swedish meatballs. In Sugár, you can find branches of Fotex, Julius Meinl Csemege (Austrian grocery store), Fonicia (shoe store), and Azur (drugstore), as well as a post office, a Laundromat, and a place called Lombardi Formula, which has decent Italian-style ice cream. All shops have their own hours, but the mall is open weekdays 9am to 8pm, Saturday 9am to 1pm.

Closer to the center, try the ever-crowded **Skála Metro,** at Nyugati tér across from Nyugati Station, or the equally popular **Buda Skála,** on Október 23 utca, near Móricz Zsigmond körtér. Both are open weekdays 10am to 6pm, Saturday 9am to 1pm.

FINE CHINA & CRYSTAL

HEREND SHOP, V. József nádor tér 11. Tel. 118-9200.
Hand-painted Herend porcelain, first produced in 1826 in the town of Herend near Veszprém in western Hungary, is world renowned. This shop has the widest Herend selection in the capital. Unfortunately, they can't arrange shipping. Even if you don't intend to buy, come just to see some gorgeous examples of Hungary's most famous product. The store is located in Pest's Inner City, in quiet

József nádor tér, just a few minutes' walk from Vörösmarty tér. If you plan a trip to Veszprém or Lake Balaton, ask about the Herend Museum (in Herend) at Tourinform. Open: Weekdays 10am–6pm, Sat 9am–1pm. Metro: Vörösmarty tér (Yellow line) or Deák tér (all lines).

ZSOLNAY MÁRKABOLT, V. Kígyó u. 4. Tel. 118-3712.

Delightfully gaudy Zsolnay porcelain from the southern city of Pécs is Hungary's second most celebrated brand of porcelain. This shop has Budapest's widest selection. Like the Herend shop, they don't arrange shipping. Even if you don't intend to buy, come just to see some fabulous examples of Hungary's other internationally known porcelain. The Zsolnay Museum is in Pécs; ask about it at Tourinform. Open: Weekdays 9am–6pm, Sat 9am–1pm. Metro: Vörösmarty tér (Yellow line) or Deák tér (all lines).

FIMCOOP, V. Apáczai Csere János u. 7. Tel. 118-8321 or 118-3912.

Near the Danube, behind the Hotel Duna Intercontinental, the state-run Fimcoop has two separate shops at the same address: the Studio Shop and the Exclusive Shop. In the Studio Shop you can find Herend, Zsolnay, and Hollóháza porcelain, as well as Parád crystal. Next door at the Exclusive Shop, Zsolnay and Zeldmann Weiden porcelain are displayed, along with Ajka crystal and a variety of other decorative objects, including rugs and paintings. Open: Studio Shop, weekdays 10am–6pm; Exclusive Shop, weekdays 9:30am–5:30pm. Metro: Vörösmarty tér (Yellow line) or Deák tér (all lines).

FOLK CRAFTS

Except for a few tiny specialty shops like the ones listed below, the stores of the state-owned **Folkart Háziipar** should be your main source of Hungary's justly famous folk items. Well located throughout the city, the Folkart shops have unbeatable prices. Almost everything is handmade: from tablecloths to miniature dolls, from ceramic dishes to vests. You can shop with the knowledge that all items have been passed by a critical jury. This is represented by the distinctive label (or sticker) you'll find on all Folkart products: a circle with a bird in the center, surrounded by the words FOLKART/ NÉPMŰVÉSZETI HUNGARY. The private folk-art shops lining Váci utca and the streets of the Castle District tend to be much more expensive; and their products, unlike Folkart's, often tend toward the kitschy (with some notable exceptions). The main store, **Folkart Centrum,** is at V. Váci u. 14. (tel. 118-5840). It's open weekdays 9:30am to 6pm (Thursday until 7pm), Saturday 9:30am to 5pm, and Sunday 9:30am to 2pm.

You'll find eight other Folkart stores in Budapest with similar offerings at similar prices; unlike Folkart Centrum, they are closed on Sunday.

One outstanding private shop on Váci utca is **Vali Folklor,** in the courtyard of Váci u. 23 (tel. 118-6495). It's a tiny, cluttered shop run by a soft-spoken man named Vali who travels the villages of Hungary and neighboring countries buying up authentic folk items. He is extremely knowledgeable about the products he sells, and enjoys speaking with customers (in German or English). The most appealing items here are the traditional women's clothing. Prices are fair. Hours are weekdays 10am to 6pm, and Saturday 10am to 2pm.

For a wide selection of handmade wicker baskets, try **Andi és Bandi,** at VII. Dob u. 3 (tel. 122-7344), a tiny family-run workshop near the Dohány Synagogue on the edge of Pest's old Jewish district. Prices are low, with baskets going for as little as 400 Ft ($4.45). The most interesting items here are the wicker cat boxes, which come in several sizes. Homemade brushes of all types—from paint brushes to shaving brushes to brooms—are available too. The store is open weekdays 9am to 5pm.

For doll collectors no visit to Budapest would be complete without meeting Mrs. Berényi, the gregarious older woman who runs the **Baba Klinika,** at V. Múzeum körút 5 (tel. 129-9742), near Astoria. She makes and repairs dolls and doll clothing in her doll clinic. Watch her at work on her antique sewing machine. Mrs. Berényi loves to talk and doesn't mind if you understand no Hungarian. The shop is open weekdays 9:30am to 5:30pm, and Saturday 9:30am to 1:30pm.

MARKETS

Most markets tend to be very crowded, so you need to be wary of pickpockets. Carry your valuables in a money belt rather than a wallet.

OPEN MARKETS [PIAC]

JÓZSEFVÁROSI PIAC, VIII. Kőbányai út.

The market closest to the center of the city, the Józsefvárosi piac is situated on the side of a railroad yard, near the Józsefváros Station. It's a bit smaller than the Kondorosi úti piac (see below), but basically the same kinds of goods are offered. Open: Daily 7am–6pm. Tram: 28 from Blaha Lujza tér or 36 from Baross tér (Keleti Station).

KONDOROSI ÚTI PIAC, XI. Kondorosi út.

Located in a factory yard in Kelenföld, a blighted, industrial part of southern Buda, the Kondorosi út market is not really a flea market since most of the goods are not second-hand. But with vendors from every corner of Eastern Europe, the former Soviet Union, and, increasingly, Asia, there are bargains aplenty. The Chinese offer silk shirts; the Russians display caviar, vodka, and toy tanks; the Romanians sell socks, slippers, and bad chocolate. All prices are negotiable. Hard currency is welcomed, but you'll attract far less attention by using Forints. Dozens of languages are spoken in the tightly packed, crowded lanes of this outdoor market; the sign at the parking lot is in Hungarian, Russian, Polish, and Romanian. Get off the tram at the

Hotel Ventura; the market is a 10-minute walk east on Kondorosi út (follow the crowds). Open: Weekdays 6am–6pm. Tram: 47 from Deák tér to Kondorosi út.

FRUIT AND VEGETABLE MARKETS
[CSARNOK OR *PIAC*]

There are five vintage market halls (*vásárcsarnok*) in Budapest. Vast cavernous spaces, wonders of steel and glass, all were built in the 1890s in the ambitious grandiose style of the time. Three are still in use as markets and provide a measure of local color you certainly won't find in the grocery store. A visit to any of the markets is well worth the time. Hungarian produce is sensational, and you'll seldom go wrong with a kilo of strawberries, a cup of raspberries, or a couple of peaches. There is no admission charge to any of the markets.

The **Központi Vásárcsarnok** (Central Market Hall), at IX. Vámház körút, is the largest and most spectacular of the market halls. Located on the Inner Ring (Kiskörút), on the Pest side of the Szabadság Bridge, it's presently closed for reconstruction. While the reconstruction is under way the market is temporarily set up behind the market hall, between Közraktár utca and the Danube, in a series of old warehouses. Open: Mon 6am–4pm, Tues–Fri 6am–6pm, Sat 6am–2pm. Metro: Kálvin tér (Blue line).

The **Belvárosi Vásárcsarnok** (Inner City Market Hall), at V. Hold utca, is located in central Pest in the heart of the Lipótváros (Leopold Town), behind Szabadság tér. Open: Mon 6:30am–3pm, Tues–Fri 6:30am–6pm, Sat 7am–2pm. Metro: Kossuth tér (Red line) or Arany János (Blue line).

The **Józsefváros Vásárcsarnok,** at VIII. Rákóczi tér, badly damaged by fire in 1988, was restored to its original splendor and reopened in 1991. There's only a small area of private vendors; the rest of the hall is filled with retail booths. Open: Mon 6am–4pm, Tues–Fri 6am–6pm, Sat 6am–1pm. Metro: Blaha Lujza tér (Red line) or tram 4 or 6 directly to Rákóczi tér.

Budapest has dozens of produce markets in addition to those in the classic market halls. Here are two centrally located ones:

The **Fehérvári úti Vásárcsarnok,** is at XI. Fehérvári út, in front of the Buda Skála department store, just a block from the Móricz Zsigmond korter transportation hub. Open: Mon–Thurs 6am–6pm, Fri 6am–7pm, Sat 6am–2pm. Tram: 47 from Deák tér to Fehérvári út, or any tram or bus to Móricz Zsigmond körtér.

The **Fény utca Piac,** at II. Fény utca, is just off Moszkva tér, Buda's main transportation hub. The street in front of the market-place is packed with vendors as well. Open: Mon 6am–5pm, Tues–Fri 6am–6pm, Sat 6am–1pm. Metro: Moszkva tér (Red line).

WHOLESALE MARKET
REAL UDVAR, VIII. Baross tér.

Next door to the Hotel Park on Pest's bustling Baross tér (site of Keleti Station), the Real Udvar is a Hungarian-style wholesale market.

It's open to the public, with no admission charge. Vendors here sell mainly clothing and food. The street vendors whom you've no doubt seen everywhere in the city can be observed making their bulk purchases. All languages of the Carpathian Basin are spoken here, with varying degrees of fluency. Perhaps you've noticed the outrageous "American" sports T-shirts worn by Eastern Europeans ("Chicago Rambs," "What is Ragazzi? Baseball!," and "Dancing Baby Jogging Duo"): many are available here, at cut-rate prices. They make great gifts for the sports-fan-with-a-sense-of-humor back home. Open: Monday–Saturday 7am–6pm. Metro: Keleti pu (Red line).

MUSIC

HUNGAROTON HANGLEMEZSZALON, V. Vörösmarty tér 1. Tel. 138-2810.

The largest record store in Budapest, the Hungaroton Hanglemezszalon is the outlet for the former state recording company Hungaroton. Located on Vörösmarty tér, near Gerbeaud's coffeehouse, it has the best selection of Hungarian folk music in the city. Hungaroton recently filed for bankruptcy. There's no telling what effect it's imminent privatization will have on this store. Open: Weekdays 10am–6pm, Sat 10am–2pm. Metro: Vörösmarty tér (Yellow line) or Deák tér (all lines).

LISZT FERENC ZENEMŰBOLTJA (FERENC LISZT MUSIC SHOP), VI. Andrássy út 45. Tel. 122-4091.

Located near both the State Opera House and the Ferenc Liszt Academy of Music, this shop is much frequented by Budapest's musical crowd. Sheet music, scores, records, tapes, CDs, and books are available. Open: Weekdays 10am–6pm, Sat 10am–1pm. Metro: Oktogon (Yellow line).

WAVE, VI. Bajcsy-Zsilinszky út 15/d. Tel. 111-1824.

On Révay köz, a small side street off Bajcsy-Zsilinszky út directly across the street from the rear of St. Stephen's Basilica, Wave is a popular spot among young Hungarians looking for rock, punk, and rap recordings. Used records are for sale and concert information is available. Open: Weekdays 10am–6pm (until 10pm in summer), Sat 10am–2pm. Metro: Arany János (Blue line).

SOUVENIRS

ROKILAND, VII. Erzsébet körút 4. No tel.

This tiny upstairs shop, just off Blaha Lujza tér, has all sorts of hand-crafted pipe-cleaner animals. At about 50–200 Ft (55¢–$2.25) apiece, they make great gifts for the little ones back home. Several display windows on the street give you an idea of what's available. The best animals here are clearly the monkeys, of which one enthusiastic 31-year-old American collector we met purchased (to the palpable dismay of his wife) no less than 50—all for himself! Open: Weekdays 10am–6pm. Metro: Blaha Lujza tér (Red line).

VÁR-BAZÁR, I. Ostrom u. 10. No tel.

This closet-sized subterranean thrift shop, located in the steep, twisting neighborhood between Buda's Moszkva tér and the Castle District, has a distinctly Hungarian flavor. You can find all sorts of inexpensive knick-knacks, including old postcards, some nice plates, and even the occasional piece of Herend china. Márta and Kati, the two charming women who run the shop, speak no English, but seem able to converse with English speakers anyway. Open: Weekdays 10am–6pm. Metro: Moszkva tér (Red line).

CHAPTER 9

BUDAPEST NIGHTS

1. THE PERFORMING ARTS

2. THE CLUB & MUSIC SCENE

3. THE BAR SCENE

4. MORE ENTERTAINMENT

Budapest is blessed with a rich and varied cultural life. The director of Tourinform boasted that in February 1993 the city was the site of no less than 840 noteworthy performances! What is more, in Budapest you can still go to the Opera House, one of Europe's finest, for less than $1 (the most expensive tickets in the house, in the fabulously ornate royal box once used by the Habsburgs, go for less than $20). Almost all of the city's theaters and halls, with the possible exception of those hosting internationally touring rock groups, offer tickets for as low as one or two dollars. It makes sense here to select a performance based as much on the venue as on the program. If, for example, the Great Hall of the Academy of Music is the venue, you should seriously consider a program you wouldn't ordinarily be interested in.

The opera, ballet, and theater seasons run from September through May or June, but most theaters and halls also host performances during the summer festivals. A number of lovely churches and stunning halls offer concerts exclusively in the summer. While classical culture has a long and proud tradition in Budapest, jazz, blues, rock, and disco have exploded since the recent political changes. New clubs and bars have opened up everywhere; the parties start late and last until morning. So put on your dancing shoes or slip your opera glasses into your pocket; whatever your entertainment preference, Budapest nights offer plenty to choose from.

PROGRAM LISTINGS The most complete schedule of mainstream performing arts is found in the free bimonthly *Koncert Kalendárium,* available at the Central Philharmonic Ticket Office in Vörösmarty tér. *Budapest Week* and *Budapest Sun,* the two English-language weeklies, have comprehensive events calendars; they also list lesser publicized events like modern dance and folk music performances. *Programme in Hungary* and *Budapest Panorama,* the two free monthly tourist booklets, have only partial entertainment listings, featuring what their editors consider the monthly highlights.

TICKET OFFICES For opera, ballet, theater, and concert tickets, you are better off going to one of the commission-free state-run ticket offices than to the individual box offices. There are always schedules

MAJOR CONCERT & PERFORMANCE HALLS

Budapest Convention Center, XII. Jagelló út 1-3 (tel. 161-2869).

Erkel Theater, VIII. Köztársaság tér 30 (tel. 133-0540).

Hungarian State Opera House, VI. Andrássy út 22 (tel. 153-0170).

Ferenc Liszt Academy of Music, VI. Liszt F. tér 8 (tel. 141-4788).

Madách Theater, VII. Erzsébet körút 29-33 (tel. 122-0677).

Municipal Operetta Theater, VI. Nagymező u. 17 (tel. 132-0535).

Pesti Vigadó, V. Vigadó tér 1 (tel. 118-9903).

Petőfi Csarnok, XIV. Zichy M. u. 14 (tel. 142-4327).

posted, and you will have a variety of choices. If none of the cashiers speak English, find a helpful customer who can translate for you. On the day of the performance, though, you might have better luck at the box office. For **classical performances:** Central Philharmonic Ticket Office (Filharmónia Központi Jegyiroda), V. Vörösmarty tér 1 (tel. 117-6222). Hours are weekdays 10am to 6pm (closed 1:30 to 2pm), Saturday 10am to 2pm. For **theater** and **operetta:** Central Theater Ticket Office (Színházak Központi Jegyiroda), VI. Andrássy út 18 (tel. 112-0000). Hours are Monday through Thursday 9am to 6pm, Friday 9am to 5pm (closed 1 to 1:45pm); a second branch is at II. Moszkva tér 3 (tel. 135-9136), with the same open hours. For **opera** and **ballet:** Hungarian State Opera Ticket Office (Magyar Állami Opera Jegyiroda), VI. Andrássy út 20 (tel. 132-7914 or 131-2550). Hours: Weekdays 10am to 6pm. For events in the **Spring Festival:** Spring Festival Box Office (Tavaszi Fesztival Jegyiroda), V. Vigadó tér 2 (tel. 117-5067). Hours: Immediately before and during the festival, weekdays 9am to 5pm and Saturday 10am to 2pm. For **rock concert** tickets: Music Mix, V. Váci u. 33 (tel. 138-2237 or 117-7736). This private agency charges a small commission. Hours: Weekdays 10am to 8pm, Saturday 10am to 2pm.

MAJOR ENSEMBLES The major symphony orchestras in Budapest are the Philharmonic Society Orchestra, the Hungarian State Symphony Orchestra, the Budapest Symphony Orchestra, and the Hungarian Railway Workers' (MÁV) Symphony Orchestra. The major chamber orchestras include the Hungarian Chamber Orchestra, the Ferenc Liszt Chamber Orchestra, and the Budapest String Players. Major choirs include the Budapest Chorus, the Hungarian State Choir, the Hungarian Radio and Television Choir, the Budapest Madrigal Choir, and the University Choir.

Budapest is now on the touring route of dozens of major

European ensembles and virtuosos. Keep your eyes open for the performances of well-known visitors.

---

1. THE PERFORMING ARTS

OPERA, OPERETTA & BALLET

HUNGARIAN STATE OPERA HOUSE [MAGYAR ÁLLAMI OPERAHÁZ], VI. Andrássy út 22. Tel. 153-0170.

Completed in 1884, the Opera House is the crowning achievement of the famous Hungarian architect Miklós Ybl's career. It is easily Budapest's most famous performance hall, and a tourist attraction in its own right. The lobby is adorned with Bertalan Székely's frescoes; the ceiling frescoes in the hall itself are by Károly Lotz. The splendid Opera House, home to both the State Opera and the State Ballet, possesses a rich history. A political scandal marked the first opening performance in 1884: Ferenc Liszt had written a piece to be performed especially for the event, but when it was discovered he had incorporated elements of the "Rákóczi March," a patriotic Hungarian (and anti-Habsburg) melody, he was prevented from playing it. Gustav Mahler and Ferenc Erkel rank as the most famous directors of the Opera House. Hungarians adore opera, and a large percentage of seats are sold on a subscription basis; buy your tickets a few days ahead of time if you have the chance. The season runs from mid-September to mid-June. Summer visitors, however, can take in the approximately 10 performances (both opera and ballet) of the Summer Festival, in July or August. Seating capacity is 1,260.

Tours: Guided tours of the Opera House daily at 3pm and 4pm; the cost is 250 Ft ($2.75), 120 Ft ($1.35) for students.

Tickets: 60–1,200 Ft (65¢–$13.35).

Open: Box office open Tues–Sat 10am–7pm (closed 1:45–2:30pm), Sun 10am–1pm and 4–7pm. Performances usually start at 7pm, but some longer shows start as early as 5pm. Occasional weekend matinees. **Metro:** Opera (Yellow line).

ERKEL THEATER [ERKEL SZÍNHÁZ], VIII. Köztársaság tér 30. Tel. 133-0540.

The Erkel Theater is the second home of the State Opera and Ballet. The largest theater in Hungary, it seats as many as 2,400 people. Though it was built in art nouveau style in 1911, little of its original character shows through the various renovations it has undergone. If you have a choice, go to the Opera House instead (their seasons—mid-September to mid-June—are the same). Chamber orchestra concerts are also performed here.

Tickets: 60–600 Ft (65¢–$6.65).

Open: Same as State Opera House, above. **Metro:** Keleti pu. (Red line).

MUNICIPAL OPERETTA THEATER [FŐVÁROSI OPE-RETTSZÍNHÁZ], VI. Nagymező u. 17. Tel. 132-0535 or 153-2172.

In the heart of Budapest's theater district, the Municipal Operetta Theater is the site not just of operetta, but also of rock opera and musicals. Recent hits have included *The Sound of Music* and *Jesus Christ Superstar*. The off-season is from mid-July to mid-August.

Tickets: 150–500 Ft ($1.65–$5.55).

Open: Box office open daily 1–6pm. Ticket office next door open weekdays 9am–6pm. **Metro:** Opera or Oktogon (Yellow line).

CLASSICAL MUSIC

BÉLA BARTÓK MEMORIAL HOUSE [BARTÓK BÉLA EMLÉKHÁZ], II. Csalán út 29. Tel. 116-4123.

This charming little hall is in Béla Bartók's last Budapest residence, which is also the site of a Bartók museum. A regular Friday concert series is given by the Bartók String Quartet, a prolific group founded in 1957 (they play a lot more than just Bartók). Concerts are given occasionally on other days as well. For schedule information check Budapest's free bimonthly *Koncert Kalendárium*.

Tickets: 200–300 Ft ($2.20–$3.35).

Open: Performances on Fridays at 6pm, and occasionally other days. **Bus:** 5 from Március 15 tér or Moszkva tér to Pasaréti tér (last stop).

BUDAPEST CONVENTION CENTER [BUDAPESTI KON-GRESSZUSI KÖZPONT], XII. Jagelló út 1-3. Tel. 161-2869.

A large modern hall which is the site of conventions as well as concerts, the Convention Center has established itself in recent years as one of the more important halls in the city. The hall is spacious and comfortable, but lacks the character of the older venues. It's part of the Novotel complex in central Buda.

Tickets: 150–800 Ft ($1.65–$8.90).

Open: Schedule varies. **Tram:** 61 from Moszkva tér or Móricz Zsigmond körtér.

FERENC LISZT ACADEMY OF MUSIC [ZENEAKADÉMIA], VI. Liszt Ferenc tér 8. Tel. 141-4788 or 142-0179.

The Great Hall (Nagyterem) of the Academy of Music, with a seating capacity of 1,200, is Budapest's premier music hall. Hungary's leading center of musical education, the Academy was built in the early years of the 20th century. The interior of the building is decorated in an art nouveau style. The acoustics in the Great Hall are said to be the best of any hall in the city. If you go to only one performance in Budapest it should be to the Opera House or here. Unfortunately, the Great Hall is not used in the summer months; the smaller Kisterem, also a fine hall, is used then. In addition to major

Hungarian and international performances, you can also attend student recitals (sometimes for free). A weekly schedule is posted outside the Király utca entrance to the Academy.

Tickets: 100–700 Ft ($1.10–$7.80).

Open: Performances almost daily; box office open 10am–showtime on performance days, otherwise weekdays 10am–6pm, Sat 10am–1pm. **Metro:** Oktogon or Opera (Yellow line).

PEST CONCERT HALL [PESTI VIGADÓ], V. Vigadó tér 1. Tel. 118-9903.

Right in the middle of the famed Danube Promenade (Dunakorzó), the Vigadó is one of the city's oldest music halls, dating to 1864. All sorts of classical performances are held here. Although it is one of the city's best-known halls, Hungarian music lovers rate it's acoustics and atmosphere second place to the Academy of Music.

Tickets: 150–500 Ft ($1.65–$5.55).

Open: Concert schedule varies; box office always open during the day before a performance. **Metro:** Vörösmarty tér (Yellow line) or Deák tér (all lines).

SUMMER CLASSICAL-MUSIC VENUES

DOMINICAN COURTYARD OF THE HILTON HOTEL, I. Hess András tér 1-3. Tel. 175-0000.

The historic outdoor Dominican Courtyard, incorporated into the award-winning design of the Castle District's Hilton Hotel, is the venue of a series of classical recitals during the Budapest Summer Program. The schedule varies each year; in 1993 there were 18 recitals between early July and early August.

Tickets: 200–400 Ft ($2.20–$4.45).

Open: Tickets for this and all other summer program venues available at the Central Philharmonic Ticket Office, V. Vörösmarty tér 1 (tel. 117-6222). Hours: Weekdays 10am–6pm (closed 1:30–2pm), Sat 10am–2pm. **Bus:** Várbusz from Moszkva tér, bus 16 from Deák tér, or bus 116 from Március 15 tér.

MATTHIAS CHURCH [MÁTYÁS TEMPLOM], I. Szentháromság tér 2.

The Castle District's beautiful Matthias Church is the venue for a regular Friday-night series of organ concerts (7:30pm) from June through September.

Tickets: 100–320 Ft ($1.10–$3.55).

Open: You can buy tickets at the Central Philharmonic Ticket Office, during the day in the church (9am–7pm), or just before the performance. **Bus:** Várbusz from Moszkva tér, bus 16 from Deák tér, or bus 116 from Március 15 tér.

ST. STEPHEN'S CHURCH [BASILICA], V. Szent István tér 33. Tel. 117-2859.

The Basilica, Hungary's largest church, is the site of a series of organ concerts on Monday evenings (7pm) in July and August.

Tickets: 200 Ft ($2.20).

Open: You can buy tickets at the Central Philharmonic Ticket Office, during the day in the church (6am–7pm), or just before the performance. **Metro:** Arany János utca (Blue line) or Bajcsy-Zsilinszky út (Yellow line).

MUSICAL THEATERS

Although Budapest has an extremely lively theater season from September through June, there are no theaters at which musicals are performed exclusively. Many of the city's theaters, however, do stage musical productions as well as dramatic productions.

MADÁCH THEATER, VII. Erzsébet körút 29-33. Tel. 122-0677 or 122-2015.

The Madách Theater was built in 1961 on the site of the famous Royal Orpheum Theater. It has carried on the tradition of musical entertainment established by the latter. Recent hits have included *Cats, Nunsense,* and *Cabaret.* The Madách Theater is also the venue for non-musical productions. The season runs from September through June.

Tickets: 80–500 Ft (90¢–$5.55).

Open: Box office open daily 1–7pm; performances usually 7pm. **Tram:** 4 or 6 to Wesselényi utca.

VIGSZÍNHÁZ (MERRY THEATER), XIII. Szent István körút 14. Tel. 111-0430.

The delightfully gaudy neo-baroque Vigszínház is currently undergoing restoration, although it may have reopened by the time you arrive in Budapest. A variety of musical performances are staged here.

Metro: Nyugati pu. (Blue line).

ENGLISH-LANGUAGE THEATER

MERLIN THEATER, V. Gerlóczy u. 4. Tel. 117-9338.

The Merlin Theater, located on a quiet street in the heart of the Inner City, marked its third season of English- and German-language dramatic productions in 1993. It is the only primarily foreign-language theater in Budapest, and Hungarian and foreign actors are featured. There is also a jazz club (see "The Club and Music Scene," below) on the premises.

Tickets: 200 Ft ($2.20).

Open: Box office hours vary. **Metro:** Astoria (Red line) or Deák tér (all lines).

FOLK PERFORMANCES

BUDA CONCERT HALL (BUDAI VIGADÓ), I. Corvin tér 8. Tel. 201-5928 or 201-3766.

The Budai Vigadó is the home stage of the Hungarian State Folk Ensemble (Állami Népi Együttes Székháza). The ensemble includes 40 dancers, a 20-member Gypsy orchestra, and a folk orchestra. The *New York Times* calls it "a mix of high art and popular tradition. . . . Every dance crackled with high speed." Under the direction of award-winning choreographer Sándor Timár, the ensemble performs folk dances from all regions of historic Hungary.

Tickets: 600 Ft ($6.70).

Open: Performances Mar–Oct, usually starting at 7pm, on Tues, Wed, and Thurs. Tickets can be reserved by telephone. **Metro:** Batthyány tér (Red line).

SZAKSZERVEZETEK FŐVÁROSI MŰVELŐDÉSI HÁZA (FMH CULTURAL HOUSE), XI. Fehérvári út 47. Tel. 181-1360.

Another popular folk program venue, the "Folklór Centrum," as some advertisements refer to this theater, features the Budapest Dance Ensemble, the Talentum Dance Ensemble, the Törekvés Dance Ensemble, and the Rajko Band. The Rajko Band, originally established in the 1950s, is a leading group of young Gypsy musicians (none is older than 25). A 10-minute film on Budapest precedes the performance. The FMH Cultural House is also the site of a number of other events, including some participatory folk dance houses (*táncház*) (see below).

Tickets: 600 Ft ($6.70).

Open: Performances Apr–Oct, usually starting at 8:45pm, on Mon, Thurs, Fri, and Sat. Tickets can be reserved by telephone. **Tram:** 47 from Deák tér.

---

2. THE CLUB & MUSIC SCENE

MUSIC CLUBS

The club scene in Budapest has found fertile ground since the political changes of 1989, so much so, in fact, that clubs come in and out of fashion overnight. A few, however, like Tilos az Á and Hold, have shown a solid staying power over the past 3 or 4 years. There are few specifically jazz or blues clubs in town; most clubs prefer to be recognized for their decidedly eclectic offerings. Performances usually start late, after 10pm. All establishments serve beer and wine, and many now offer mixed drinks as well. Clubs listed below are the undisputed hot spots at press time, but you'd be wise to read the "Night Beat" column in the *Budapest Sun* for the latest club information.

FREGATT, V. Molnár u. 26. Tel. 118-9997.

Originally intended as an English-style pub, it is far too crowded and noisy to feel like one. American and other English-speaking expatriates make up the better half of the clientele. Live music: Folk, country, jazz. Open: Daily 3pm–midnight. Metro: Ferenciek tere (Blue line).

Admission/Cover: None.

HOLD, XIII. Hegedűs Gyula u. 7. Tel. 131-8590.

A cement basement space with no decoration except a few strategically placed neon moons (*hold* means moon), Hold is one of the city's most popular and avant-garde clubs. Live music: Eclectic, generally, with harder music on weekends. Open: Wed–Sat 8pm–2am (sometimes later). Metro: Nyugati pu. (Blue line).

Admission/Cover: 50 Ft (55¢).

INK & DRINK, V. Királyi Pál u. 6. Tel. 117-7991.

A cozy, crowded three-level hole-in-the-wall, the Ink & Drink is a tattoo parlor during the day and a bar at night. Live music: Blues. Open: Mon–Tues 6pm–midnight, Wed–Sat 6pm–2am. Metro: Kálvin tér (Blue line).

Admission/Cover: 100 Ft ($1.10).

MADE INN MUSIC CLUB, VI. Andrássy út 112. Tel. 132-2959.

The Made Inn Music Club shares the building of the Young Artist's Club (FMK), another rock-music club, but the two establishments are completely different. The Made Inn is, for some obscure reason, *the* place to go on Thursday nights, when crowds overflow onto the street. It features an outdoor patio and a neon-tinted indoor cellar area where the music is played. Live music: Rock. Open: Daily 8pm–5am. Metro: Bajza utca (Yellow line)

Admission/Cover: 200 Ft ($2.20).

MERLIN JAZZ CLUB, V. Gerlóczy u. 4. Tel. 117-9338.

Located in the same complex which houses the Merlin English-language theater (see "The Performing Arts," above), this is a popular restaurant/jazz club. It is a spacious, well-ventilated place, with a long bar and a real stage for the musicians. Meals are moderately priced—main courses 250–550 Ft ($2.80–$6.10)—but it is permissible to come just for drinks. Open: Restaurant: Daily noon–midnight; live music from 10pm nightly. Reservations recommended. Metro: Astoria (Red line) or Deák tér (all lines).

Admission/Cover: 270 Ft ($3).

PIAF, VI. Nagymező u. 25. Tel. 112-3823.

In the heart of Budapest's theater district, Piaf is an elegant French-style nightclub, with plush chairs and an intimate atmosphere. Upstairs is live piano music, while downstairs is a bar. Drinks are pricey. Open: Daily 10pm–6am. Metro: Oktogon (Yellow line).

Admission/Cover: 60 Ft (65¢).

TILOS AZ Á, VIII. Mikszáth Kálmán tér 2. Tel. 118-0684.

With a cult following from the day it opened, just after the political changes, Tilos has become the standard against which all other Budapest clubs are measured. The name is taken from the Hungarian version of the broken "No Trespassing" sign on Piglet's door in Winnie the Pooh. Originally a small, smoky, counter-culture hangout, it has evolved over the years into a larger, equally smoky, slightly more mainstream place. Live performers (usually rock) play downstairs. Open: Varies; stays open very late. Metro: Kálvin tér (Blue line).

Admission/Cover: Usually 100 Ft ($1.10).

DISCOS

FRANKLIN TROCADERO CLUB, V. Szent István körút 15. Tel. 111-4691.

This bilevel establishment looks like a place out of the movie *Blade Runner*. There is a small dance floor and several bars. There is occasional live Latin music. Open: Daily 6pm–2am (sometimes open later). Metro: Nyugati pu. (Blue line).

Admission/Cover: None.

HULLY GALLY, XII. Apor Vilmos tér 9. Tel. 175-9742.

Hully Gally is a huge bilevel disco with all the most modern equipment, including a laser show. The go-go girls add an element of raciness. Hully Gally is next door to another disco, Randevu (see below). Open: Daily 8pm–5am. Tram: 59 from Moszkva tér or Déli pu. to Apor Vilmos tér.

Admission/Cover: 300 Ft ($3.35).

RANDEVU, XII. Apor Vilmos tér 9. Tel. 156-0211.

This hot spot consists of a restaurant, a bar with live music, and a trendy disco. Randevu (evidently Hungarian for rendezvous) is found in Buda's hopping Apor Vilmos tér (formerly Lekai Janos tér), next door to the Hully Gally disco (see above). Open: 8pm–5am daily. Tram: 59 from Moszkva tér or Déli pu. to Apor Vilmos tér.

Admission: 250 Ft ($2.80).

HUNGARIAN DANCE HOUSES

One of Hungary's best cultural experiences is the *táncház,* or dance house. A táncház is an interactive evening of folk music and folk dancing, held in community centers around town (a few of the best known are listed below). The format usually consists of about an hour of dance-step instruction followed by several hours of dancing accompanied by a live band, which might include some of Hungary's best folk musicians, in an authentic, everyday atmosphere. It is permissible to come just to watch and listen, so you don't need to be nervous about not being able to learn the steps. *Budapest Week* and the *Budapest Sun* are the best sources for táncház schedules; there are at least a few every week.

The leading Hungarian folk band Muzsikás hosts a táncház every Tuesday (September to May only) at 5:30pm (60 Ft/65¢) at the **FMH Cultural House** (Szakszervezetek Fővárosi Művelődési Háza) at XI. Fehérvári út 47 (tel. 181-1360). The FMH Cultural House also has a year-round weekly Balkan táncház, on Wednesday at 7pm (100 Ft/$1.10). Tram 47 from Deák tér gets you there. The **First District**

Cultural Center at I. Bem rakpart 6 (tel. 201-0324) hosts the Téka (another well-known folk band) táncház every Friday at 7pm, September to May (100 Ft/$1.10). The First District Cultural Center is near Clark Ádám tér, which is served by a large number of buses and trams, including bus 16 from Deák tér.

3. THE BAR SCENE

CHICAGO SÖRGYÁR, VII. Erzsébet körút 2. Tel. 269-6753.
An American-style microbrewery on one of Pest's busiest squares, the Chicago Sörgyár—with Bulls, Cubs, and White Sox paraphernalia on the walls—has a diehard expatriate clientele, who come not just for the fairly good home-brewed beer, but for the hamburgers, nachos, and french fries as well. Happy hour weekdays 5 to 9pm, with half-price drinks. Open: Mon–Thurs noon–midnight, Fri–Sat noon–1am, Sun noon–11pm. Metro: Blaha Lujza tér (Red line).

JOHN BULL PUB, VI. Lövölde tér 3. Tel. 268-0617.
An authentic little English pub, the John Bull Pub has comfortable chairs and plush carpeting. The walls are decorated in a sporting motif. It's well ventilated and the service is impeccable. There's occasional live music (Irish, folk, country), but no cover charge. There are a few other John Bull Pubs in Budapest, but this is the most pleasant one. Open: Daily noon–midnight. Metro: Kodály körönd (Yellow line).

GAY BARS As with the fickle club scene, "in" bars become "out," or even close down, at a moment's notice. The gay bar scene is exclusively male-oriented at this point, though this too is liable to change. The *Budapest Sun*'s "Night Beat" column is again your best bet for current information.

Angel (VIII. Rákóczi út 51; Metro-Blaha Lujza tér) is a big cellar establishment, with a bar, restaurant, and great dance floor. **My Darling** (V. Szép u. 1; Metro-Astoria) is a much smaller, more intimate bilevel establishment with a bar downstairs and a free video room upstairs. **Mystery Bar** (V. Nagysándor József u. 3; Metro-Arany János utca) is also a small joint, with a larger foreign clientele than either of the above, and live lounge music.

4. MORE ENTERTAINMENT

CASINOS Budapest has about a dozen casinos, mostly in the luxury hotels. At this point, only hard currency is accepted, but that will change if the Forint becomes convertible. Formal dress is generally required. Following are some of the more popular casinos: **Casino Budapest Hilton,** I. Hess András tér 1-3 (tel. 175-1333);

Las Vegas Casino, Atrium Hyatt Hotel, V. Roosevelt tér 2 (tel. 177-6022); and **Orfeum Casino,** Hotel Béke Radisson, VI. Teréz körút 43 (tel. 132-3300).

LASER SHOWS The **Laser Theater** (Lézer Színház) in the Budapest Planetarium has daily rock shows throughout the year (schedule varies seasonally). Laser shows incorporate the music of Pink Floyd, Queen, Genesis, Dire Straits, U2, Mike Oldfield, and Metal Mania. Tickets cost 330 Ft ($3.65). You can get tickets at Music Mix (see "Ticket Offices," at the beginning of this chapter), as well as at the box office. The planetarium (tel. 113-8280 or 134-1164) is in Népliget (People's Park) in the X district. The Blue metro line stops at Népliget; the planetarium is a 5-minute walk into the park from the metro station.

MOVIES There are always a number of English-language movies playing in Budapest. The best source of listings and addresses is in either *Budapest Week* or the *Budapest Sun* (neither of which bothers to list dubbed films). In addition to this, all cinemas post a monthly city-wide program. Or you can pick up the free weekly schedule, *Pesti Est,* at any theater; it has a special page covering English-language films. Movies labelled *szinkronizált* (dubbed) or *mb.* (*magyarul beszél*) are to be avoided; *feliratos* means subtitled. Usually if there is nothing written after the title on the schedule, the movie will be subtitled. When in doubt, ask the ticket clerk. Tickets cost 100–150 Ft ($1.10–$1.55) and can be bought earlier in the day from the box office.

CHAPTER 10

EASY EXCURSIONS FROM BUDAPEST

1. SZENTENDRE
2. VISEGRÁD
3. ESZTERGOM
4. VÁC

About 25 miles north of Budapest the mighty Danube swings abruptly south. The delightful towns along this "bend" can be easy day trips from the capital as well as longer overnight destinations. Despite its tranquility today, this beautiful and strategically located region has been the source of strife for hundreds of years and the site of human settlements for thousands. Under the Roman Empire, the Danube marked the end of "civilized" lands and the main northern line of defense. A millennium later, Hungarian kings dictated to the rest of the country from this natural east-west gateway. The constellation of nobility that inhabited the towns led the Hungarian Renaissance and built numerous monuments to their power. The subsequent Ottoman Turkish invasion resulted in an era of decline and devastation that lasted for the 150-year-long occupation. But many of the ruins, castles, and churches still remain, and their proximity to Budapest makes the Danube Bend ideal for a brief visit.

GETTING THERE   By Boat and Hydrofoil   From April through September **boats** run between Budapest and the towns of the Danube Bend. In fact, the boat ride through the beautiful countryside of the region is one of the highlights of an excursion. All boats leave Budapest's Vigadó tér boat landing, stopping to pick up passengers 5 minutes later at Buda's Batthyány tér landing, before continuing up the river.

Four boats a day depart mid-May through mid-September, and two boats a day run April through mid-May and mid-September through late September. Schedules and towns served are complicated, so contact **MAHART,** the state shipping company, at the Vigadó tér landing (tel. 118-1223) for information. You can also get information from Tourinform or Ibusz offices.

Approximate travel time from Budapest is 1½ hours to Szentendre, 2½ hours to Vác, 3½ hours to Visegrád, and 4 hours to Esztergom.

MAHART also runs a much faster (and more expensive) **hydrofoil** non-stop between Budapest's Vigadó tér and Esztergom. The hydrofoil runs June through mid-September on Fridays, Saturdays, Sundays, and holidays only. It departs at 9am, arriving in Esztergom at 10:20am; it returns from Esztergom at 4:30pm, arriving in Budapest at 5:40pm.

Round-trip prices are: to Szentendre, 260 Ft ($2.90); to Visegrád, 300 Ft ($3.35); to Vác, 300 Ft ($3.35); to Esztergom, 360 Ft ($4) by boat and 1,000 Ft ($11.10) by hydrofoil. Children under 4 ride free; children between 4 and 14 pay half price.

By Train   To Szentendre: The HÉV suburban railroad connects Budapest's Batthyány tér with Szentendre. Trains leave daily, year-round, every 20 minutes or so from 5am to 11pm. The fare is 64 Ft/70¢ (subtract 25 Ft if you have a valid Budapest public transportation day pass). The trip takes 45 minutes. **To Esztergom:** Eleven daily trains make the run between Budapest's Nyugati Station and Esztergom. The trip takes about 1¼ hours. Tickets cost 231 Ft ($2.55) first class, 154 Ft ($1.70) second class. **To Vác:** Ten trains a day depart Budapest's Nyugati Station for Vác. The trip takes 1½ hours. Tickets cost 144 Ft ($1.60) first class, 96 Ft ($1.05) second class. There is no train service to Visegrád.

By Bus   To Visegrád: There are five daily buses from Budapest's Árpád híd bus station (at the Blue line metro station of the same name). The one-way fare is 136 Ft ($1.50). There are also seven daily (weekdays only) buses from Szentendre to Visegrád; the fare is 76 Ft (85¢). In addition to the above, many (but not all) of the Esztergom buses (see below) stop en route at Visegrád. The bus to Visegrád takes about 1½ hours.

To Esztergom: There are 30 daily buses to Esztergom from Budapest's Árpád híd bus station. Departing from stand 8, the bus costs 180 Ft ($2). The ride is interminable (over two hours) as the bus makes local stops along the way; the train to Esztergom is a much better bet.

By Car   From Budapest, route 11 hugs the west bank of the Danube, taking you to Szentendre, Visegrád, and Esztergom. Alternatively, you could head "overland" to Esztergom by the 10 motorway, switching to route 111 at Dorog. Motorway 2 goes up the east bank of the Danube to Vác.

By Guided Tour   Although the towns of the Danube Bend (and particularly Szentendre) are very accessible on your own, a guided tour may make sense if you are pressed for time and wish to see the major sights of more than one town. **Ibusz** (tel. 118-1139 or 118-1043) in particular has a selection of high-quality bus and boat tours to the region. For a full list of their offerings pick up their "Budapest Sightseeing" catalog, available at all Ibusz offices and at major hotels. See "Organized Tours" in Chapter 6 for more information.

---

1. SZENTENDRE

21 km (13 miles) N of Budapest

ESSENTIALS   The main information office is **Dunatours,** just off Fő tér at Bogdányi u. 1 (tel. 26/311-311). They have maps of Szentendre (and the Danube Bend region), and concert and exhibition schedules. They also rent private rooms, and can provide information on other accommodations. The office is open Tuesday through Sunday 10am to 6pm (closed 12:30pm to 1:30pm).

The center of Szentendre must rank with Váci utca and Buda's Castle District as one of the most touristed spots in Hungary. In the summer it becomes one huge marketplace of handicrafts and souvenirs. Despite the excess commercialism, Szentendre is a desperately gorgeous little town. Originally peopled in medieval times by Serbian settlers fleeing Turkish northward expansion, Szentendre counts half a dozen Serbian churches among its rich collection of historical buildings. The town retains a distinctively Mediterranean flavor, seldom experienced this far north in Europe. Since the turn of the century, Szentendre has been home to an artist's colony. As a result, it has a wealth of museums and galleries, the best of which are listed below. After visiting the sites, hike up the winding cobblestone streets to the churchyard at the top of the hill for a terrific view of the red tile rooftops and the tiny streets below.

WHAT TO SEE & DO

MARGIT KOVÁCS MUSEUM, Vastagh György u. 1. Tel. 26/310-244.

In this expansive museum you can view the works of Hungary's best-known ceramic artist, Margit Kovács, who died in 1977. Chances are her work is unlike anything you've ever seen, and the breadth of her talents is displayed in this museum. We were especially moved by her sculptures of elderly women and by her folk art–influenced friezes of village life. When the museum is full, people are required to wait to enter.

Admission: 60 Ft (65¢).

Open: May–Oct, Tues–Sun 9am–5:30pm; Nov–Apr, 10am–4pm. **Directions:** Walk east from Fő tér on Görög utca.

FERENCZY MUSEUM, Fő tér 6.

Next door to the Serbian church in Main Square (Fő tér), the Ferenczy Museum is dedicated to the art of the prodigious Ferenczy family. Károly Ferenczy, one of Hungary's leading Impressionists, more of whose work you can see in Budapest's National Museum, is the featured artist. Works of his children Noémi (tapestry maker), Valer (painter), and Beni (sculptor and medallion maker) are also on display.

Admission: 30 Ft (35¢).

Open: Tues–Sun 10am–3:30pm.

SERBIAN ORTHODOX MUSEUM, Patriarka u. 5.

The Serbian Orthodox Museum is housed next door to the Serbian Orthodox Church, in one of the buildings of the former episcopate just north of Fő tér. This collection—one of the most extensive of its kind in predominantly Catholic Hungary—features

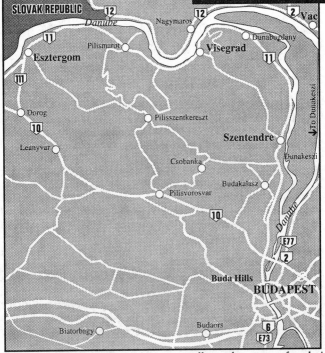

16th- through 19th-century icons, as well as other types of ecclesiastical art.

Admission: 30 Ft (35¢).

Open: Wed–Sun 10am–4pm. **Directions:** Walk north from Fő tér on Alkotmány utca.

THE GALLERY OF THE SZENTENDRE ARTISTS' COLONY, Bogdányi u. 51.

Temporary exhibitions of contemporary colony artists are held in this unmarked building 10 minutes from the town center. Most of the works on display are for sale.

Admission: 30 Ft (35¢); students 15 Ft (15¢).

Open: Wed–Sun 11am–5pm. **Directions:** Walk north from Fő tér on Bogdányi utca.

Outside of Town

OPEN-AIR ETHNOGRAPHICAL MUSEUM (SKANZEN), Szabadság-forrás út. Tel. 26/312-304.

Three kilometers (1.8 miles) northwest of Szentendre is one of Hungary's better *skanzens,* or reproduction peasant villages. This ambitious skanzen represents peasant life from all around the country, not just from the Danube Bend region. There are several reconstructed villages, with thatch-roofed houses, blacksmith and weaving shops, working mills, and churches.

Admission: 60 Ft (65¢); children 30 Ft (35¢).

Open: Apr–Sept, Tues–Sun 9am–5pm; closed Oct–Mar. **Directions:** It's easily reached from platform 8 of Szentendre's bus station, adjacent to the HÉV station (get off at the Szabadság-forrás stop). Bus fare is 18 Ft (20¢).

WHERE TO DINE

ARANYSÁRKÁNY VENDÉGLŐ, Alkotmány u. 1/a. Tel. 26/311-670.

Cuisine: HUNGARIAN. **Reservations:** Recommended. **Directions:** Walk east of Fő tér on Hunyadi utca, which leads into Alkotmány utca.

$ Prices: Soups 60–70 Ft (65¢–80¢); main courses 300–500 Ft ($3.35–$5.55). No credit cards.

Open: Daily noon–10pm.

"The Golden Dragon" is always filled to capacity, and the crowd includes a good percentage of Hungarians, definitely a good sign in a tourist town like Szentendre. Indeed, a former chef brought wide fame to this little restaurant with the publication of a cookbook entitled *Four Seasons at the Golden Dragon Inn*. He's gone now, but the food remains excellent. There are only about 10 main courses listed on the English-language menu. You can choose from among such enticing offerings as alpine lamb, roast leg of goose, and stuffed cabbage. The cold fruit soup is among the best we've encountered in Hungary. Heineken beer is on draft and the restaurant has air conditioning.

RÉGIMODI, Fütő u. 3. Tel. 26/311-105.

Cuisine: HUNGARIAN. **Reservations:** Recommended. **Directions:** Walk directly south from Fő tér, towards the river.

$ Prices: Soups 100 Ft ($1.10); main courses 250–600 Ft ($2.80–$6.65). DC, MC, V.

Open: Daily noon–midnight.

An elegant restaurant in a former private home, Régimodi is furnished with vintage Hungarian carpets and chandeliers. Original artworks decorate the walls. Limited terrace dining is available, though you might not want to miss out on eating amidst the rich interior decor. The English-language menu offers a wide range of Hungarian specialties, with an emphasis on game dishes. The wild-boar stew in red wine is particularly sumptuous, while the less adventurous might opt for the turkey baked with apples. There is an extensive wine list.

2. VISEGRÁD

45 km (28 miles) NW of Budapest

ESSENTIALS There is no official tourist information office in Visegrád, though a few private ones have opened recently. One such agency, located inside a clothing store, is the **Svada Tourist Office,**

at Rév u. 6 (tel. 26/328-160). Erika Schreck, the proprietor, speaks passable English and can supply you with basic information and help you book a private room.

Today, Visegrád (pronounced VEE-sheh-grod) is a sparsely populated, sleepy riverside village, which makes its history all the more fascinating and hard to believe. The Romans built a fort here, which was still extant when Slovak settlers gave the town its present name (meaning "High Castle") in the 9th or 10th century. After the Mongol invasion (1241–42), construction began on both the present ruined hilltop citadel and the former riverside palace. Eventually, Visegrád could boast one of the finest royal palaces ever built in Hungary. Only one king, Charles Robert (1307–1342), actually used it as his primary residence, but monarchs from Béla IV, in the 13th century, through Matthias Corvinus, in the late 15th century, spent time in Visegrád and contributed to its development, the latter expanding the palace into a great Renaissance center known throughout Europe.

WHAT TO SEE & DO The **Royal Palace** covered much of the area where the boat landing and Fő utca (Main Street) are now found. Indeed, the entrance to its ruins, called the **King Matthias Museum,** is at Fő utca 27. The buried ruins of the palace, having achieved a near mythical status, were not discovered until this century. Almost all of what you see is the result of reconstruction. Aside from the general atmosphere of ruined grandeur, the main attractions are the red-marble base of the Hercules Fountain in the Ornamental Courtyard and the reconstructed Gothic arcaded hallway behind it. The museum is open April through October, Tuesday through Sunday 9am to 4:30pm; and November through March, Tuesday through Sunday 8am to 3:30pm. Admission is 30 Ft (35¢); free for students.

The **Citadel** on the hilltop above Visegrád affords one of the finest views you'll find over the Danube. Off to your left, you can see the site of the controversial Nagymaros Dam, an abandoned Hungarian-Czechoslovak hydroelectric project. Although Hungarian environmentalists reviled the whole plan, the Slovaks never wanted the work to stop and indeed it was not halted on their half of the project, a sister dam at Gabčikevo. This unresolved disagreement has exacerbated the historic tensions between Hungary and Slovakia. The citadel is open daily 8am to 6pm. Admission is 30 Ft (35¢); 15 Ft (15¢) for students; and 5 Ft (5¢) for children. Directions: A public bus connects lower Visegrád with the citadel *(vár).* Costing 15 Ft (15¢), it departs from the main highway, across the street from Fekete Holló restaurant, at 9:12am, 10:12am, 11:12am, 1:37pm, 2:37pm, 3:37pm, 4:37pm, and 5:37pm. Alternately, look around town for József Farkas and his red VW van; he cruises the boat landing area looking for passengers (30 Ft/35¢ each).

WHERE TO DINE One of Visegrád's precious few eateries, the

Fekete Holló Vendéglő (Black Crow Restaurant) at Rév u. 12 has indoor and outdoor seating. Reasonably good Hungarian fare—mainly the standard meat dishes—is served in generous portions; main courses are 220–340 Ft ($2.45–$3.80). The *palacsinta* (dessert pancakes) are delicious. To get here from the boat landing, walk 10 minutes west along the waterfront; the entrance is just before Rév utca. It's open Tuesday through Sunday 10am to 10pm.

3. ESZTERGOM

46 km (29 miles) NW of Budapest

ESSENTIALS   Komturist, centrally located at Mártírok útja 6 (tel. 33/312-082), is the one of several sources of information in Esztergom. The office is open May through September, weekdays 8am to 5pm, Saturday 8am to 11:30pm; October through April, weekdays 8am to 4pm, Saturday 8am to 11:30am. You can get city maps, concert information, and book private rooms here.

Formerly a Roman settlement, Esztergom was for 300 years the seat of the Hungarian kingdom. Prince Géza and his son Vajk, who was crowned by the pope in 1000 AD as Hungary's first king, István I (Stephen I), were the first rulers to call Esztergom home. It was István who converted Hungary to Catholicism, and Esztergom became the center of the early church in the country. Though its glory days are far behind it, the quiet town remains today the seat of the archbishopric-primate—the "Hungarian Rome."

From Esztergom west all the way to the Austrian border, the Danube marks the border between Hungary and newly independent Slovakia. There is a ferry crossing at Esztergom, but unfortunately it is not open to third-country nationals. The ruins of a bridge which once connected Esztergom to the Slovak town of Sturovo can be seen by walking down Táncsics Mihály utca until you hit the river.

WHAT TO SEE & DO

ESZTERGOM CATHEDRAL, Szent István tér.
This massive, neoclassical cathedral on Castle Hill, Esztergom's most popular attraction and one of Hungary's most impressive buildings, was built in the last century to replace the cathedral ruined during the Turkish occupation. The intricately carved red-marble Renaissance-style **Bakócz Chapel** inside the cathedral (to the left) dates from the early 16th century. The chapel survived the Turkish destruction of the former cathedral; when the present structure was being built the chapel was dismantled (into 1,600 numbered pieces) to be reincorporated into the new cathedral. The **Cathedral Treasury** (*Kincstár*), contains a stunning array of ecclesiastical jewels and gold works. Since Cardinal Mindszenty's body was moved to the **crypt** in 1991 (he died in exile in 1975), it has been a place of

pilgrimage for Hungarians, who come to see the nationalistic display at the final resting place of the uncompromisingly anti-Communist cleric. The **cupola,** has, as far as church towers go, one of the scarier and more cramped ascents. You are rewarded at the top with unparalleled views of Esztergom and the surrounding Hungarian and Slovak countryside.

Admission: Cathedral (including Bakócz Chapel and crypt) free; treasury 50 Ft (55¢), 10 Ft (10¢) for students; cupola 20 Ft (20¢), 10 Ft (10¢) for students.

Open: Cathedral, daily, in summer 7am–7pm, in winter 7am–5pm; treasury, daily 9am–4pm, but closed in Jan; cupola, daily 9am–5pm. **Directions:** Just look up from anywhere; you can't miss it.

CASTLE MUSEUM, Szent István tér. Tel. 33/334-400.

This museum is next door to the cathedral, in the reconstructed Royal Palace. The palace, vacated by Hungarian royalty in the 13th century, was used thereafter by the archbishop. Though it was one of only two fortresses in Hungary which were able to withstand the Mongol onslaught in 1241–42, it fell into decay under the Turkish occupation. The museum has an extensive collection of weapons, coins, pottery, stove tiles, and fragments of old stone columns; unfortunately, the descriptions are only in Hungarian. Outside the palace, sections of the fortified walls have been reconstructed.

Admission: 30 Ft (35¢); students free.

Open: from May–Oct, Tues–Sun 9am–4:30pm; Nov–Apr, Tues–Sun 10am–3:30pm. **Directions:** Next door to the cathedral.

CHRISTIAN MUSEUM, Berenyi Zsigmond u. 1.

This museum, in the neoclassical former primate's palace, houses Hungary's largest collection of religious art and the largest collection of medieval art outside the National Gallery. The Lord's Coffin of Garamszentbenedek is probably the most famous piece in the museum; an ornately carved, gilded coffin on wheels, it was originally used in Easter celebrations.

Admission: 50 Ft (55¢).

Open: Tues–Sun 10am–5pm. **Directions:** Continue past the Watertown Parish Church on Berenyi Zsigmond utca.

WHERE TO STAY

HOTEL ESZTERGOM, Prímás-sziget, Nagy-Duna sétány, 2500 Esztergom. Tel. 33/312-883. Fax 33/312-853. 34 rms, 2 suites (with shower or bath) TEL **Directions:** Bus nos. 1, 5, or 6 from the train station to the foot of Castle Hill; walk east on Bajcsy-Zsilinszky út; turn left over the small bridge.

$ Rates (including breakfast): DM 66–72 ($41.25–$45) single; DM 92–98 ($57.50–$61.25) double; DM 128 ($80) suite for two people; DM 26 ($16.25) extra bed. AE, DC, MC, V. **Parking:** Free.

Located on Prímás-sziget, an island not far from the center of

Esztergom, this Danubius Hotel boasts tennis courts and a sports center from which you can rent kayaks or canoes. Every room has a balcony more or less overlooking the river. All rooms have refrigerators and most have TVs. There is a restaurant in the hotel.

PLÁTÁN PANZIÓ, Kis-Duna sétány 11, 2500 Esztergom.
  Tel. 33/311-355. 26 rms (some with bath and toilet, some with shower and no toilet, some with only sink). **Directions:** Bus nos. 1, 5, or 6 from the train station to Rákóczi tér; walk west on Mártírok útja to Kis-Duna sétány; turn right.
$ Rates: 424 Ft ($4.70) per person in single, double, triple, or quad without bath; 636 Ft ($7.05) per person in single, double, or triple with shower but no toilet; 1,378 Ft ($15.30) for double with bath and toilet. No credit cards. **Parking:** Free.

The prices in this nondescript pension make this the great budget-travel bargain of Esztergom. The pension is located in a large institutional neo-baroque building, in which it takes up one wing. Rooms are worn and bare, but clean. The public facilities are also clean, and there is a TV room. No breakfast is available. No English is spoken by the pleasant receptionists. The street is quiet and is just minutes from the center of the city.

WHERE TO DINE

ANONIM VENDÉGLŐ, Berenyi Zsigmond u. 4.
  Cuisine: HUNGARIAN. **Directions:** Continue past the Christian Museum on Berenyi Zsigmond utca.
$ Prices: Soups 60–150 Ft (65¢–$1.65); main courses 300–560 Ft ($3.35–$6.20).
  Open: Daily noon–9pm.

In the heart of Esztergom's quiet, tranquil Watertown neighborhood (between Castle Hill and the Danube), this tourist-oriented garden restaurant is named after "Anonymous," the famous 13th-century chronicler of early Magyar history. The food is good but not as good as at Szalma Csárda (see below). The paprika chicken is savory and portions are hearty. The menu is in English.

SZALMA CSÁRDA, Nagy Duna sétány 2.
  Cuisine: HUNGARIAN. **Directions:** Walk 250 yards past the Hotel Esztergom; it's directly across from the boat landing.
$ Prices: Soups 125 Ft ($1.40); main courses 135–300 Ft. ($1.50–$3.35).
  Open: June–Sept, daily 10am–10pm; Oct–May, daily 10am–4pm.

A quiet breezy place directly across from the boat landing, József Szalma's little restaurant is unique in Esztergom (a town filled with tourist-oriented eateries)—it is an authentic *csárda* (inn), which is visited mostly by Hungarians. With its wooden floors, white-washed walls, and smattering of Hungarian folk ornaments, Szalma captures that inimitable csárda atmosphere. The food is absolutely first-rate, with everything made to order and served piping hot (the menu is only in German and Hungarian). The fish soup (*halászlé*), goulash (*gulyásleves*), and bean soup (*babgulyás*) are all large enough to constitute meals in themselves for the less-than-famished. The stuffed chicken leg (*töltött csirkecomb*) is also delicious. Finish off your meal with a cup of chestnut purée (*gesztenyepuré*), a Hungarian specialty prepared here to perfection.

4. VÁC

34 km (21 miles) N of Budapest

ESSENTIALS The best source of information is **Tourinform,** at Dr. Csányi László körút 45 (tel. 27/316-160). They have free city maps as well as a useful little guide book on Vác monuments. Hours are daily 9am to 5pm, all year.

Often overlooked by tourists, who generally neglect the flatter east bank of the Danube Bend, Vác (pronounced *vahts*), halfway between Szentendre and Visegrád, is a quietly charming baroque town. Though King Stephen established a bishopric here when he set up the Hungarian church, Vác's golden age was the late 15th century, when Miklós Báthori, the bishop, oversaw the town's blossoming. Most of the sights in the historic core, however, date from the early 18th century; Vác was destroyed by the late 17th-century battles to recapture it from Turkish occupation and rebuilt in the baroque style of the time. You will be charmed by the town's elegant, well-maintained squares and its sleepy Danube-side parks.

WHAT TO SEE & DO The best thing to do in Vác is to wander around the historic Inner City and its four main squares, admiring the gorgeous baroque architecture. **Március 15 ter** is the town's central square. Here you'll find the Town Hall (Városház), with its intricate wrought iron gate; the Fehérek Church, with its elegant facade dominating the southern end of the square; and a row of baroque houses across from the Town Hall. Nearby **Szentháromság tér** features an elaborate Plague Column and the Piarist Church, whose church bell is the favorite of locals. Large, empty **Konstantin tér** is ringed by lush beds of roses. The square is the domain of boys with trick bicycles, a new rage in Hungary. The Bishop's Cathedral, one of Hungary's earliest examples (1765–77) of neoclassical architecture, dominates Konstantin tér. **Géza király tér,** the center of medieval Vác, was the site of the former fortress and cathedral. Now you can see the baroque Franciscan church here.

There is a pleasant park along the Danube bank. Near the northern end of the Inner City, on Köztársaság tér, you'll find Hungary's only triumphal arch, built to celebrate the 1764 visit of Habsburg empress Maria Theresa. It stands near Vác's infamous prison, where political prisoners were held under both the inter-war Horthy regime and the early Communist regime.

There are a few museums of note in Vác. The **Ignác Tragor Museum,** with exhibits on the town's history, is located at Múzeum u. 4 (tel. 27/315-064), but the building is closed for an ambitious reconstruction; it's not due to open again until 1996. The exhibits have been temporarily set up in the building of the **Gyula Hincz Collection,** at Káptalan u. 16 (tel. 27/313-463). Hours are Tuesday through Sunday 10am to 4pm; admission is 30 Ft (35¢). The **Medieval Cellar Exhibition** (Középkori pince kiállítás), at Széchenyi u. 3-7, features a 15th-century winepress in an excavated cellar. It's open Tuesday through Sunday 10am to 4pm; admission is 20 Ft (20¢).

WHERE TO DINE   Halászkert Étterem (Liszt Ferenc sétány 9, tel. 27/315-985), an outdoor garden restaurant set right on the Danube Promenade at the northern end of the Inner City, is the best choice in Vác for a Hungarian meal. The extensive menu features a number of fish specialties (the restaurant's name means "fish garden"). Main courses are priced 210-550 Ft ($2.35-$6.10). The restaurant is open daily 10am to 10pm.

You can also try **Barlang Pizza and Disco** (Március 15 ter, tel. 27/315-584). The pizza is mediocre at best, but the restaurant, doubling as Vác's hottest disco at night, does have a certain appeal. Located as it is, deep in an original medieval cellar (*barlang* means cave) in the center of Március 15 tér (reached by stairs), the temperature is always cool. If you ignore the tacky decor (strobe lights, speakers, fake palm trees), it's a pleasant place to dine. Stick with the simplest pizza, *Margareta;* use the ketchup freely. Pizzas cost 100-260 Ft ($1.10-$2.90). Hours are Sunday and Monday 7pm to 11pm, Tuesday through Thursday 12:30pm to 11pm, Friday and Saturday 12:30pm to 1am.

APPENDIX

A. VOCABULARY

My transcription of the Hungarian language used here is of necessity approximate. Your best best is to mimic the pronunciation of Hungarians whenever possible.

a	t*au*t	ö	sub*u*rb or French p*eu*r
á	b*ah*	o	sub*u*rb or French p*eu*r (but slightly longer)
e	*e*ver		
é	d*ay*	u	l*oo*k
i	m*i*t	ú	m*oo*n
í	t*ee*n	ü	like the German *u*nd
o	b*o*ne	u	like the German *u*nd (but slightly longer)
ó	b*o*ne (but slightly longer)		

Most Hungarian consonants are pronounced approximately as they are in English, including the following: *b, d, f, h, k, l, m, n, p, t, v,* and *y.* There are some differences, however, particularly in the consonant combinations, as follows:

c	ge*ts*	r	slightly rolled
cs	*ch*ill	s	*sh*eet
g	*g*ill	sz	*s*ix
gy	he*dge*	z	*z*ero
j	*y*outh	zs	a*z*ure, plea*s*ure
ny	as in Russian *ny*et		

Phrases

ENGLISH	HUNGARIAN	PRONOUNCED
Hello	**Jó napot**	*yoh* naw-poht
Good morning	**Jó reggelt**	*yoh* rej-jelt
Good evening	**Jó estét**	*yoh* esh-tayt
My name is . . .	**. . . vagyok**	. . . *vodge*-yoke
How are you?	**Hogy van?**	*hoj* vawn?
Very well	**Nagyon jól**	naw-jon *yohl*
Thank you	**Köszönöm**	*kur*-sur-nurm
You're welcome	**Kérem**	*kay*-rem
Please	**Legyen szíves**	*leh*-jen see-vesh
Yes	**Igen**	*ee*-gen
No	**Nem**	nem
Excuse me.	**Bocsánat.**	*boh*-chah-vawt.
How much does it cost?	**Mennyibe kerül?**	*men*-yee-beh keh-reel?
I don't understand.	**Nem értem.**	*nem* ayr-tem.

ENGLISH	HUNGARIAN	PRONOUNCED
Good-bye	**Viszontlátásra**	*vee*-sont-lah-tahsh-raw
Where is the? . .	**Hol van?** . . .	*hohl* vawn? . .
bus station	**az autóbusz-állomás**	awz *ow*-toh-boos-ah-loh-mahsh
train station	**a vasútállomás**	aw *vah*-shoot-ah-loh-mahsh
airport	**a repülőtér**	aw *reh*-pee-lur-tayr
Where can I find a taxi?	**Hol kaphatok taxit?**	*hohl* kawp-haw-tok *tawk*-seet?
How much is the fare?	**Mennyi a viteldíj?**	*men*-yee aw *vee*-tel-dee
I am going to .	**. . . -ig akarnék menni**	. -eeg aw-kawr-nayk men-ee
One-way ticket	**csak**	choke *oh*-da
Round-trip ticket	**oda-vissza**	oh-daw-*vees*-saw
I'm looking for a hotel.	**Egy szállodát keresek.**	ej *sah*-loh-daht keh-reh-shek.
I'm looking for a pension.	**Egy panziót keresek.**	ej *pen*-zee-oht keh-reh-shek.
I'm looking for a youth hostel.	**Egy ifjúsági szállót keresek.**	ej *eef*-yoo-shah-gee *sah*-loht keh-reh-shek.
I am staying . .	**Néhány . . .**	*nay*-hahn . . .
a few days	**napig leszek itt**	*naw*-peeg leh-sek eet
two weeks	**két hétig leszek itt**	*kayt hayt*-eeg leh-sek eet
I have a reservation.	**Foglaltam már.**	*fohg*-lawl-tawm mahr.
Do you have a room? . .	**Van egy szobája?** . . .	*vawn* ej soh-bah-yaw? . . .
for tonight	**ma éjszakára**	*maw* ay-saw-kah-raw
for a week	**egy hétre**	ej *hayt*-reh
I would like . . .	**Kérek . . .**	*kay*-rek . . .
a single	**egy egyágyas szobát**	ej *ej*-ah-jawsh sho-baht
a double	**egy kétágyas szobát**	ej *kayt*-ah-jawsh soh-baht
with bath	**fürdővel**	*feer*-dur-vel
without bath	**fürdő nélkül**	*feer*-dur *nayl*-keel
with shower	**zuhanyozóval**	*zoo*-hawn-yoh-zoh-vawl
without shower	**zuhanyozó nélkül**	*zoo*-hawn-yoh-zoh *nayl*-keel

ENGLISH	HUNGARIAN	PRONOUNCED
How much is the room?	**Mennyibe kerül a szoba?**	*men*-yee-beh keh-reel aw *soh*-baw?
May I see the room?	**Megnézhetem a szobát?**	*meg*-nayz-hem-tem aw *soh*-baht?
I'm looking for a . . .	**Keresek egy . . .**	*keh*-reh-shek ej . .
I'm looking for the . . .	**Keresem a . . .**	*keh*-reh-shem aw . . .
bank	**bankot**	*bawn*-koht
museum	**múzeumot**	*moo*-zeh-oo-moht
pharmacy	**patikát**	*paw*-tee-kaht
park	**parkot**	*pawr*-koht
theater	**színházat**	*seen*-hah-zawt
tourist office	**turista ügynökséget**	*too*-reesh-taw eej-nurk-shay-get
embassy	**nagykövetséget**	*nawj*-kur-vet-shay-get
Where is the nearest telephone?	**Hol van a legközelebbi telefon?**	*hohl* vawn aw *leg*-jur-zeh-leb-bee *teh*-leh-fohn?
I would like to buy . .	**Kérek . . .**	*kay*-rek . . .
a stamp	**egy bélyeget**	ej *bay*-eh-get
a postcard	**egy levelezólapot**	ej *leh*-veh-leh-zur-law-poht
a map	**egy térképet**	ej *tayr*-kay-pet
Restaurant	**Vendéglő**	*ven*-dayg-lur
Breakfast	**Reggeli**	*reg*-geh-lee
Lunch	**Ebéd**	*eh*-bayd
Dinner	**Vacsora**	*vaw*-choh-raw
A table please.	**Kérek egy asztalot.**	*kay*-rek ej *ah*-stah-lote
Waiter	**Pincér**	*peent*-sayr
Waitress	**Pincérnó**	*peent*-sayr-nur
I would like .	**Kérnék . . .**	*kayr*-nayk . . .
a menu	**egy étlapot**	ej *ayt*-law-poht
a fork	**egy villát**	ej *veel*-laht
a knife	**egy kést**	ej *kaysht*
a spoon	**egy kanalat**	ej *kaw*-naw-lawt
a napkin	**egy szalvétát**	ej *sawl*-vay-taht
a glass (of water)	**egy pohár (vizet)**	ej poh-hahr (*vee*-zet)
the check, please	**fizetek**	*fee*-zeh-tek

ENGLISH	HUNGARIAN	PRONOUNCED
Is the tip included?	**A borravaló szerepel a számlában?**	aw *bohr*-raw-vaw-loh seh-reh-pel aw sahm-lah-bawn?

Signs

Bejárat Entrance
Kijárat Exit
Információ Information
Tilos a dohányzás No Smoking
Érkezések Arrivals

Indulások Departures
Toalettek Toilets
Vigyázat Beware
Veszélyes Danger

Numbers

1 **egy** (*ej*)
2 **kettő** (*ket*-tur)
3 **három** (*hah*-rohm)
4 **négy** (*nayj*)
5 **öt** (*urt*)
6 **hat** (*hawt*)
7 **hét** (*hayt*)
8 **nyolc** (*nyohlts*)
9 **kilenc** (*kee*-lents)
10 **tíz** (*teez*)
11 **tizenegy** (*teez*-en-ej)
12 **tizenkettő** (*teez*-en-ket-tur)
13 **tizenhárom** (*teez*-en-hah-rohm)

14 **tizennégy** (*teez*-en-nayj)
15 **tizenöt** (*teez*-en-urt)
16 **tizenhat** (*teez*-en-hawt)
17 **tizenhét** (*teez*-en-hayt)
18 **tizennyolc** (*teez*-en-nyohlts)
19 **tizenkilenc** (*teez*-en-kee-lents)
20 **húsz** (hoos)
30 **harminc** (*hawr*-meents)

40 **negyven** (*nej*-ven)
50 **ötven** (*urt*-ven)
60 **hatvan** (*hawt*-vawn)
70 **hetven** (*het*-ven)
80 **nyolcvan** (*nyohlts*-vawn)
90 **kilencven** (*kee*-lents-ven)
100 **száz** (*sahz*)
500 **ötszáz** (*urt*-sahz)
1,000 **ezer** (*eh*-zer)

B. MENU SAVVY

General Terms

Levesek soups
Tojás eggs
Saláták salads
Hús meats
Húsételek meat dishes
Halak fish

Főzelék vegetable stew
Tészták desserts
Gyümölcs fruits
Italok beverages
Kenyér bread
Vaj butter

Condiments

Majonéz mayonnaise
Mustár mustard
Só salt

Bors black pepper
Paprika paprika

Cooking Terms

Friss fresh
Fűszerezve spicy
Sós salty
Sútve baked/fried
Párolt steamed
Töltött stuffed
Pirított toasted

Főzött boiled
Félig nyersen rare
Közepesen kisütve medium
Agyonsütve well done
Csípős hot (peppery)
Forró hot (in temperature)
Hideg cold

Soups

Húsleves bouillon
Zöldborsóleves pea soup
Zöldségleves vegetable soup

Paradicsomleves tomato
  soup
Gulyásleves goulash soup
Gombaleves mushroom soup

Eggs

Tükörtojás fried eggs
Rántotta scrambled eggs
Omlett omelet
Lágy tojás soft-boiled eggs

Kemény tojás hard-boiled
  eggs
Szalonnával with bacon
Kolbásszal with sausage
Sonkával with ham

Meats and Meat Dishes

Marha beef
Borjú veal
Sertés pork
Csirke chicken
Kacsa duck
Liba goose
Bárány lamb
Pörkölt stew
Bécsi szelet wienerschnitzel

Tokány ragoût
Gulyas goulash
Nyársonsült shish kebab
Kotlett cutlet
Pecsenye roast
Paprikás csirke chicken
  paprikash
Malacsült roast piglet

Fish

Ponty carp
Csuka pike
Fogas Balaton pike-perch
Pisztráng trout

Tonhal tuna
Halászlé fish stew
Csuka tejfölben pike with
  sour cream

Vegetables and Salads

Burgonya potato
Káposzta cabbage
Rizs rice
Gomba mushrooms
Spenót spinach
Lecsó pickled vegetables
Bab beans

Zöldbab green beans
Paradicsom tomato
Fejes saláta green salad
Paprikasaláta pepper salad
Uborkasaláta cucumber salad
Vegyes saláta mixed salad

Desserts

Almás rétes apple strudel
Cseresznyes retes cherry strudel
Túrós rétes cheese strudel

Csokoládé torta chocolate cake
Lekváros palaccsinta palacsinta with preserves
Fagylalt ice cream

Fruits

Barack apricot
Cseresznye cherries
Dinnye melon

Körte pear
Narancs orange
Szőlő grapes

Beverages

Víz water
Tej milk
Narancslé orange juice
Kávé coffee
Tea tea

Fehér bor white wine
Vörös bor red wine
Koktél cocktail
Sör beer
Barna sör dark beer

C. THE METRIC SYSTEM

LENGTH

1 millimeter (mm)	=	.04 inches (*or* less than ¹⁄₁₆ in.)
1 centimeter (cm)	=	.39 inches (*or* just under ½ in.)
1 meter (m)	=	39 inches (*or* about 1.1 yards)
1 kilometer (km)	=	.62 miles (*or* about ⅔ mile)

To convert kilometers to miles, multiply the number of kilometers by .62. Also use to convert kilometers per hour (kmph) to miles per hour (m.p.h.)

To convert miles to kilometers, multiply the number of miles by 1.61. Also use to convert speeds from m.p.h. to kmph.

CAPACITY

1 liter (l)	=	33.92 fluid ounces	=	2.1 pints
	=	1.06 quarts	=	.26 U.S. gallons
1 Imperial gallon	=	1.2 U.S. gallons		

To convert liters to U.S. gallons, multiply the number of liters by .26.

To convert U.S. gallons to liters, multiply the number of gallons by 3.79.

To convert Imperial gallons to U.S. gallons, multiply the number of Imperial gallons by 1.2.

To convert U.S. gallons to Imperial gallons, multiply the number of U.S. gallons by .83.

WEIGHT

1 gram (g)	=	.035 ounces (*or* about a paperclip's weight)
1 kilogram (kg)	=	35.2 ounces
	=	2.2 pounds
1 metric ton	=	2,205 pounds = 1.1 short ton

To convert kilograms to pounds, multiply the number of kilograms by 2.2.

To convert pounds to kilograms, multiply the pounds by .45.

TEMPERATURE

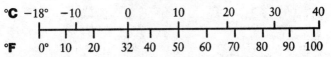

To convert degrees Celsius to degrees Fahrenheit, multiply °C by 9, divide by 5, and add 32 (example: 20°C × 9/5 + 32 = 68°F).

To convert degrees Fahrenheit to degrees Celsius, subtract 32 from °F, multiply by 5, then divide by 9 (example: 85°F − 32 × 5/9 = 29.4°C).

INDEX

GENERAL INFORMATION

SIGHTS & ATTRACTIONS

BUDAPEST

Note: * Asterisk indicates author's favorite.

EXCURSION AREAS

ACCOMMODATIONS

BUDAPEST

ESZTERGOM

Key to abbreviations: * = Author's favorite; $ = Super-value choice; *VE* = Very
Expensive; *E* = Expensive; *M* = Moderate; *I* = Inexpensive; *P* = Pension.

RESTAURANTS

BY CUISINE

EXCURSION AREAS

Key to abbreviations: * = Author's favorite; $ = Super-value choice; VE = Very Expensive; E = Expensive; M = Moderate; I = Inexpensive.

Please Send Me the Books Checked Below:

FROMMER'S COMPREHENSIVE GUIDES
(Guides listing facilities from budget to deluxe,
with emphasis on the medium-priced)

	Retail Price	Code		Retail Price	Code
☐ Acapulco/Ixtapa/Taxco 1993–94	$15.00	C120	☐ Morocco 1992–93	$18.00	C021
☐ Alaska 1994–95	$17.00	C131	☐ Nepal 1994–95	$18.00	C126
☐ Arizona 1993–94	$18.00	C101	☐ New England 1994 (Avail. 1/94)	$16.00	C137
☐ Australia 1992–93	$18.00	C002	☐ New Mexico 1993–94	$15.00	C117
☐ Austria 1993–94	$19.00	C119	☐ New York State 1994–95	$19.00	C133
☐ Bahamas 1994–95	$17.00	C121	☐ Northwest 1994–95 (Avail. 2/94)	$17.00	C140
☐ Belgium/Holland/ Luxembourg 1993–94	$18.00	C106	☐ Portugal 1994–95 (Avail. 2/94)	$17.00	C141
☐ Bermuda 1994–95	$15.00	C122	☐ Puerto Rico 1993–94	$15.00	C103
☐ Brazil 1993–94	$20.00	C111	☐ Puerto Vallarta/ Manzanillo/Guadalajara 1994–95 (Avail. 1/94)	$14.00	C028
☐ California 1994	$15.00	C134	☐ Scandinavia 1993–94	$19.00	C135
☐ Canada 1994–95 (Avail. 4/94)	$19.00	C145	☐ Scotland 1994–95 (Avail. 4/94)	$17.00	C146
☐ Caribbean 1994	$18.00	C123	☐ South Pacific 1994–95 (Avail. 1/94)	$20.00	C138
☐ Carolinas/Georgia 1994–95	$17.00	C128	☐ Spain 1993–94	$19.00	C115
☐ Colorado 1994–95 (Avail. 3/94)	$16.00	C143	☐ Switzerland/ Liechtenstein 1994–95 (Avail. 1/94)	$19.00	C139
☐ Cruises 1993–94	$19.00	C107	☐ Thailand 1992–93	$20.00	C033
☐ Delaware/Maryland 1994–95 (Avail. 1/94)	$15.00	C136	☐ U.S.A. 1993–94	$19.00	C116
☐ England 1994	$18.00	C129	☐ Virgin Islands 1994–95	$13.00	C127
☐ Florida 1994	$18.00	C124	☐ Virginia 1994–95 (Avail. 2/94)	$14.00	C142
☐ France 1994–95	$20.00	C132	☐ Yucatán 1993–94	$18.00	C110
☐ Germany 1994	$19.00	C125			
☐ Italy 1994	$19.00	C130			
☐ Jamaica/Barbados 1993–94	$15.00	C105			
☐ Japan 1994–95 (Avail. 3/94)	$19.00	C144			

FROMMER'S $-A-DAY GUIDES
(Guides to low-cost tourist accommodations and facilities)

	Retail Price	Code		Retail Price	Code
☐ Australia on $45 1993–94	$18.00	D102	☐ Israel on $45 1993–94	$18.00	D101
☐ Costa Rica/Guatemala/ Belize on $35 1993–94	$17.00	D108	☐ Mexico on $45 1994	$19.00	D116
☐ Eastern Europe on $30 1993–94	$18.00	D110	☐ New York on $70 1994–95	$16.00	D120
☐ England on $60 1994	$18.00	D112	☐ New Zealand on $45 1993–94	$18.00	D103
☐ Europe on $50 1994	$19.00	D115	☐ Scotland/Wales on $50 1992–93	$18.00	D019
☐ Greece on $45 1993–94	$19.00	D100	☐ South America on $40 1993–94	$19.00	D109
☐ Hawaii on $75 1994	$19.00	D113	☐ Turkey on $40 1992–93	$22.00	D023
☐ India on $40 1992–93	$20.00	D010	☐ Washington, D.C. on $40 1994–95 (Avail. 2/94)	$17.00	D119
☐ Ireland on $45 1994–95 (Avail. 1/94)	$17.00	D117			

FROMMER'S CITY $-A-DAY GUIDES
(Pocket-size guides to low-cost tourist accommodations and facilities)

	Retail Price	Code		Retail Price	Code
☐ Berlin on $40 1994–95	$12.00	D111	☐ Madrid on $50 1994–95 (Avail. 1/94)	$13.00	D118
☐ Copenhagen on $50 1992–93	$12.00	D003	☐ Paris on $50 1994–95	$12.00	D117
☐ London on $45 1994–95	$12.00	D114	☐ Stockholm on $50 1992–93	$13.00	D022

FROMMER'S WALKING TOURS
(With routes and detailed maps, these companion guides point out the places and pleasures that make a city unique)

	Retail Price	Code		Retail Price	Code
☐ Berlin	$12.00	W100	☐ Paris	$12.00	W103
☐ London	$12.00	W101	☐ San Francisco	$12.00	W104
☐ New York	$12.00	W102	☐ Washington, D.C.	$12.00	W105

FROMMER'S TOURING GUIDES
(Color-illustrated guides that include walking tours, cultural and historic sights, and practical information)

	Retail Price	Code		Retail Price	Code
☐ Amsterdam	$11.00	T001	☐ New York	$11.00	T008
☐ Barcelona	$14.00	T015	☐ Rome	$11.00	T010
☐ Brazil	$11.00	T003	☐ Scotland	$10.00	T011
☐ Florence	$ 9.00	T005	☐ Sicily	$15.00	T017
☐ Hong Kong/Singapore/ Macau	$11.00	T006	☐ Tokyo	$15.00	T016
			☐ Turkey	$11.00	T013
☐ Kenya	$14.00	T018	☐ Venice	$ 9.00	T014
☐ London	$13.00	T007			

FROMMER'S FAMILY GUIDES

	Retail Price	Code		Retail Price	Code
☐ California with Kids	$18.00	F100	☐ San Francisco with Kids (Avail. 4/94)	$17.00	F104
☐ Los Angeles with Kids (Avail. 4/94)	$17.00	F103	☐ Washington, D.C. with Kids (Avail. 2/94)	$17.00	F102
☐ New York City with Kids (Avail. 2/94)	$18.00	F101			

FROMMER'S CITY GUIDES
(Pocket-size guides to sightseeing and tourist accommodations and facilities in all price ranges)

	Retail Price	Code		Retail Price	Code
☐ Amsterdam 1993–94	$13.00	S110	☐ Montréal/Québec City 1993–94	$13.00	S125
☐ Athens 1993–94	$13.00	S114	☐ Nashville/Memphis 1994–95 (Avail. 4/94)	$13.00	S141
☐ Atlanta 1993–94	$13.00	S112	☐ New Orleans 1993–94	$13.00	S103
☐ Atlantic City/Cape May 1993–94	$13.00	S130	☐ New York 1994 (Avail. 1/94)	$13.00	S138
☐ Bangkok 1992–93	$13.00	S005	☐ Orlando 1994	$13.00	S135
☐ Barcelona/Majorca/ Minorca/Ibiza 1993–94	$13.00	S115	☐ Paris 1993–94	$13.00	S109
☐ Berlin 1993–94	$13.00	S116	☐ Philadelphia 1993–94	$13.00	S113
☐ Boston 1993–94	$13.00	S117	☐ San Diego 1993–94	$13.00	S107
☐ Budapest 1994–95 (Avail. 2/94)	$13.00	S139	☐ San Francisco 1994	$13.00	S133
☐ Chicago 1993–94	$13.00	S122	☐ Santa Fe/Taos/ Albuquerque 1993–94	$13.00	S108
☐ Denver/Boulder/ Colorado Springs 1993–94	$13.00	S131	☐ Seattle/Portland 1994–95	$13.00	S137
☐ Dublin 1993–94	$13.00	S128	☐ St. Louis/Kansas City 1993–94	$13.00	S127
☐ Hong Kong 1994–95 (Avail. 4/94)	$13.00	S140	☐ Sydney 1993–94	$13.00	S129
☐ Honolulu/Oahu 1994	$13.00	S134	☐ Tampa/St. Petersburg 1993–94	$13.00	S105
☐ Las Vegas 1993–94	$13.00	S121	☐ Tokyo 1992–93	$13.00	S039
☐ London 1994	$13.00	S132	☐ Toronto 1993–94	$13.00	S126
☐ Los Angeles 1993–94	$13.00	S123	☐ Vancouver/Victoria 1994–95 (Avail. 1/94)	$13.00	S142
☐ Madrid/Costa del Sol 1993–94	$13.00	S124	☐ Washington, D.C. 1994 (Avail. 1/94)	$13.00	S136
☐ Miami 1993–94	$13.00	S118			
☐ Minneapolis/St. Paul 1993–94	$13.00	S119			

SPECIAL EDITIONS

	Retail Price	Code		Retail Price	Code
☐ Bed & Breakfast Southwest	$16.00	P100	☐ Caribbean Hideaways	$16.00	P103
☐ Bed & Breakfast Great American Cities (Avail. 1/94	$16.00	P104	☐ National Park Guide 1994 (Avail. 3/94)	$16.00	P105
			☐ Where to Stay U.S.A.	$15.00	P102

Please note: if the availability of a book is several months away, we may have back issues of guides to that particular destination. Call customer service at (815) 734-1104.